MAKING STRATEGIC I
WORK IN PRACT

THE BEST OF LONG RANGE PLANNING

The aim of this series is to bring together in each volume the best articles on a particular topic previously published in *Long Range Planning* so that readers wishing to study a specific aspect of planning can find an authoritative and comprehensive view of the subject, conveniently in one volume.
Whereas each issue of *Long Range Planning* normally contains a 'horizontal slice' of Long Range Planning at a particular time, in different fields and in various kinds of organizations across the world, each volume in the new series will take a 'vertical slice' through more than a hundred issues, pulling out the outstanding articles on a given subject.

Titles in the *Best of Long Range Planning* Series:
Strategic Planning — The Chief Executive and the Board (Number 1)
Edited by Bernard Taylor

Entrepreneurship — Creating and Managing New Ventures (Number 2)
Edited by Bruce Lloyd

Making Strategic Planning Work in Practice (Number 3)
Edited by Basil Denning

Planning for Information as a Corporate Resource (Number 4)
Edited by Alfred Collins (forthcoming)

Later volumes will deal with other topical themes, such as:

- Strategic Management in Major Multinational Companies.
- Developing Strategies for Competitive Advantage.
- Strategic Planning for Human Resources, and
- Implementing Corporate Strategy: Turning Strategy into Action.

Each volume will contain 10–12 articles, and about 120 pages. In due course they will provide a comprehensive and authoritative reference library, covering all important aspects of Strategic Planning.

The titles in this series are available individually, or can be obtained on annual subscription at an advantageous rate. Further details can be obtained from Brian Cox, Journal Sales Director, Pergamon Press plc, Headington Hill Hall, Oxford OX3 0BW, UK.

A Related Journal
LONG RANGE PLANNING*

The Journal of the Strategic Planning Society and of the European Planning Federation.

Editor: Professor Bernard Taylor, Henley — The Management College, Greenlands, Henley-on-Thames, Oxon RG9 3AU, UK.

The leading international journal in the field of long-range planning, which aims to focus the attention of senior managers, administrators, and academics on the concepts and techniques involved in the development and implementation of strategy and plans.

*Free sample copy gladly sent on request to the Publisher.

MAKING STRATEGIC PLANNING WORK IN PRACTICE

Edited by

BASIL DENNING
Strategic Planning Society

PERGAMON PRESS
OXFORD · NEW YORK · BEIJING · FRANKFURT
SÃO PAULO · SYDNEY · TOKYO · TORONTO

U.K.	Pergamon Press plc, Headington Hill Hall, Oxford OX3 0BW, England
U.S.A.	Pergamon Press, Inc., Maxwell House, Fairview Park, Elmsford, New York 10523, U.S.A.
PEOPLE'S REPUBLIC OF CHINA	Pergamon Press, Room 4037, Qianmen Hotel, Beijing, People's Republic of China
FEDERAL REPUBLIC OF GERMANY	Pergamon Press GmbH, Hammerweg 6, D-6242 Kronberg, Federal Republic of Germany
BRAZIL	Pergamon Editora Ltda, Rua Eça de Queiros, 346, CEP 04011, Paraiso, São Paulo, Brazil
AUSTRALIA	Pergamon Press Australia Pty Ltd., P.O. Box 544, Potts Point, N.S.W. 2011, Australia
JAPAN	Pergamon Press, 5th Floor, Matsuoka Central Building, 1-7-1 Nishishinjuku, Shinjuku-ku, Tokyo 160, Japan
CANADA	Pergamon Press Canada Ltd., Suite No. 271, 253 College Street, Toronto, Ontario, Canada M5T 1R5

First edition 1989

Library of Congress Cataloging in Publication Data

Making strategic planning work in practice/edited by Basil Denning.—1st ed.
p. cm.—(Best of long range planning; no. 3)
1. Strategic planning. I. Denning, Basil W. II. Series.
HD30.28.M326 1989 658.4'012—dc20 89–8826

British Library Cataloguing in Publication Data

Making strategic planning work in practice.
1. Companies. Management. Planning. Implementation.
I. Denning, Basil II. Series
658.4'012

ISBN 0–08–037121–3 Hardcover
ISBN 0–08–037408–5 Flexicover

Printed in Great Britain by BPCC Wheatons Ltd, Exeter

Contents

Making Strategic Planning Work in Practice

Basil Denning, Strategic Planning Society

Over the last twenty-five years as companies have experimented with long-range planning, strategic planning and corporate planning, the record of success is still mixed. There has been a clear evolution in practice over time through stages of extended budgeting over 3, 5 or 10 years to esoteric model building. Companies have introduced more formal approaches, abandoned them, and then reintroduced them with different people and different ideas. Today there is a diminishing number of large companies who do not include planning as one of their key management systems.

The last ten years in particular have seen a plethora of techniques, varying in reliability and relevance, developed to assist in resolving the strategic problems of the firms. As with most techniques the results have varied enormously, depending on the skill with which they have been used.

Long Range Planning journal has charted the changing fashions and enthusiasms in the field and the selection of only twelve articles to offer useful guidance 'on making strategic planning work in practice' requires sharp focusing on a small number of key aspects with the exclusion of much relevant material of quality. In making choices I have interpreted the title as meaning:

(1) Developing effective strategy.

(2) Basing strategy formulations on a systematic management.

(3) Executing the strategy and the changes which follow in ways that achieve the strategic aims.

Developing effective strategies requires a high order of judgement, use of the appropriate techniques of analysis and appraisal based on the best available data, and good leadership at many levels. Few articles contribute much to developing good judgement; articles from the journal on techniques of planning are separately collated and the first volume in the *Best of Long Range Planning* series concerned the role of leadership.

The focus of this volume is much more on the organisational process which a company uses to help managers to develop effective strategy. The topic is less well covered in the literature and remains a relatively neglected area of study. Yet the evidence from my own consulting experience, and wide discussion with others in the field is that the nature of the process is a major determinant both of the quality of the planning and of successful implementation.

A simple analogy can be drawn from the engineering world. If a company has a poor manufacturing process, with inadequate machines, work in process inventory piled up in the corridors, erratic supply of components, poor working conditions and inadequate maintenance, would you really expect to produce a high quality product which fully meets all the required specifications including prompt delivery? The answer is a simple NO. Furthermore, applying intensive analysis and improvement at just one point of the process such as doubling the speed of just one key machine does little to improve the whole. The analogy is close, yet the managers of many companies and even more 'not for profit organisations' still seem to believe that high quality strategic thinking, planning and action can be achieved with a creaking and inadequate process.

Organising an effective process raises a set of issues with which most executives are familiar as they introduce other processes such as budgeting, management appraisal, or production control. The key requirements are to organise:

by responsibility — who will do what?

by time — in what sequence, to what time schedule, and with what discipline will tasks be done?

by information — is appropriate information available to those charged with tasks at the right time for the tasks to be done?

There are few imperatives or absolutes about creating an effective process because of the enormous variety of organisations. One absolute imperative, however, is worth stating.

Responsibility for strategy and plans rests firmly with line management. The role of any planner is to help line management to do a thorough and effective job of strategy making, developing the subsequent plans and implementing them. There are many ways in which this help can be given but the moment line management at any level believes that planners have taken responsibility for strategy and plans, the planners should be sacked—as of course many have been.

Within this absolute there is and should be an extraordinary variety of processes. An unfortunate jargon has developed which focuses attention on two slogans, 'top down' or 'bottom up'. While we certainly see organisations who represent caricatures of these two positions, virtually all actual processes offer some combination of the two modes. Good planning processes reflect a coherent and relevant combination at the right points in time.

The variety of processes arises from many points of variation between organisations. In companies the most important single determinants are the key business characteristics in terms of profit and risk. For example, if you are at the top of a business which stakes its whole future every few years on a new model or a new generation of products and which requires massive research and fixed investment to produce a limited number of products and services from capital intensive facilities, you delegate very little of the strategic task. If on the other hand you supply a very wide diversity of products and services in a large number of very different markets you will delegate large amounts of strategic initiative to divisions or operating units, and the nature of the strategic task at the top becomes quite different.

In addition to this fundamental business characteristic, organisations vary enormously in their structure and in their culture, their current situations can be very different and there will be different types of leaders with different aspirations. An effective planning process for any organisation must reflect the fundamentals and take into account these other aspects.

Key Considerations in Designing a Planning Process

The first four articles in this volume are addressed to these key questions. George Steiner and Hans Schöllhammer have examined a large number of organisations and identified a wide variety of common pitfalls. Some nations appear more prone to certain pitfalls than others and this certainly matches my own experiences. The list of pitfalls provides a valuable tool for auditing a strategic planning process. Most companies can readily identify which particular pit they have fallen into. The pitfalls are evident in all companies, not just the multi-nationals, and equally appropriate to non-profit and governmental organisations.

Within this general pattern of pitfalls there are different patterns or styles of planning. The article by Michael Goold and Andrew Campbell articulates three distinctive styles based on the degree to which the centre of the company exercises planning control and financial control. While there are many variations within each type, the broad classifications are useful in terms of identifying where responsibility for certain types of work will rest. There are some dangers in adopting any simple classification, but even more in adopting the wrong fundamental style. Again the key to choosing a basic style should centre on the fundamental business characteristics, not the whim of the Chief Executive.

Of considerable significance in creating an effective process will be the choice of the individual to lead the work under the Chief Executive. Again the choice should reflect a variety of considerations; the nature of the style and the process which matches it, the present situation of the company, the stage of development of planning and the future aspirations of management. Relevant considerations on these matters are thoughtfully argued by Milton Leontiades in his article, 'What Kind of Corporate Planner Do You Need?'.

The last general consideration of importance, one of the pitfalls identified by Steiner, is the extent to which planning becomes integrated into the other management processes of the company. Where planning becomes an extraneous activity performed during the 'planning silly season' and then forgotten while executives get on with the 'real work', it is unlikely to have a significant impact or to be effective in terms of action. The article by Thomas Naylor identifies important differences between strategic planning, project planning and operation planning with guidance on how to integrate these different activities into a coherent process within the other managerial systems.

Specific Aspects and Relationships

Strategic planning is concerned with creating an appropriate relationship between the company as a whole and the outside world which will give some continuing and satisfactory balance of profit and risk. A key requirement of any effective process must include relevant scanning of the outside world. This is a complicated task and one which is often not approached in a sufficiently systematic way. One important aspect of successful strategic planning must be the building of an appropriate, cost-effective information system and data-base about the company's external environment. The article by John Diffenbach on Corporate Environmental Analysis raises important lessons from US experience on different approaches in practice and the implications for management.

It has already been argued that strategic planning processes must not exist in a vacuum. Crucial to its success will be the relationships that planners and their processes create with other groups. Building productive relationships with other functions at the centre or in decentralised groups is critical but often difficult. Different perspectives about strategic planning and its role will often exist, and in certain areas strategic planning may seem a threat to the existing power and influence of a functional team.

Two main considerations should guide the strategic planner in building these relationships. It is vital that functional inputs and data are freely available, and that a feeling of active involvement with strategy-making is created. Secondly, and sometimes more difficult, the strategic planner must bring to the issues raised by a function a framework for debate and discussion relevant to the whole company, not merely a second opinion on the merits of some functionally-backed initiative.

Five articles have been selected which offer help to the strategic planner in building this type of positive relationship with the groups responsible for marketing, technology, manufacturing and information systems. The final article focuses on an issue of considerable complexity, namely the relationship with the capital-budgeting system.

A significant proportion of strategic decisions involve major capital investments. In most companies, a thorough capital evaluation process and approval system is a major mechanism of control. The system has a momentum and power of its own. For example in ICI for many years, corporate planning was seen as a useful adjunct to the capital budgeting system. Analysis over a period of five years in one division showed clearly that the actual allocation of capital followed the criteria of the financially-driven capital-budgeting process. Brave words in the strategic plan about priority and emphasis for different types of investments had had little impact on the decisions.

The strategic planner's job in this area is to develop a usable framework for testing capital projects against strategic criteria in addition to the existing tests based on financial criteria. This is a complex subject but the article by J A Piper on 'Classifying Capital Projects for Top Management Decision-Making' offers useful thoughts on some usable frameworks and the limitations of a number of those in current use.

Executing Strategic Plans

Brilliant strategic thinking and magnificently prepared pieces of paper called 'Strategic Plans' have little value unless implementation follows. Again companies and other types of organisation use widely different processes to ensure that their plans are implemented. To a great extent implementation in an organisation will be a function of how power is used and the nature of the political system. One has only to look at the well established archetypes of corporate culture, power, role, task and person to be certain that there is no one path to salvation.

Strategy and strategic change are of immense significance in the power game within organisations. A great deal is at stake for the organisation and for key individuals. The role of value judgements is central, and there will be winners and losers with any new strategy. Some companies, often in their earlier days or while still creatures of their founders, will be swift and effective at implementing once the leader has decided. Power and authority will force the decision through.

Most organisations, however, have a less autocratic pattern and have influential groups with varying patterns of influence and power. It is in these organisations that it is vital to create a process which enables thorough and relevant examination, initiation and discussion to take place. While a good process does not eliminate political problems and difficulties, it goes a long way to assist in gaining the necessary consensus from key groups and individuals. Obtaining that necessary degree of consensus is critical to successful implementation. In most successful organisations it is achieved through a mixture of relevant processes and political activity.

Even with the necessary degree of consensus, however, there are wellknown barriers to implementation and a useful summary of the most frequently found difficulties in implementation is provided by Larry Alexander in his researched article 'Successfully Implementing Strategic Decisions'. His examples draw attention to the need for an effective system to monitor strategic progress, a very different monitoring from that achieved through conventional budgetary control.

And finally, and integrally linked with implementation, is that good strategy making is about adaptation and change. An effective strategic planning process can be a major means for identifying needed change and thinking through its implications. However, without an understanding of how to manage the changes, successful execution of plans is unlikely. Colin Carnall in his article 'Managing Strategic Change' pulls many threads together into an integrated approach to this exceedingly difficult subject.

In summary, 'Making Strategic Planning Work in Practice' is a complex affair. Routes to success lie in the creation of an appropriate and relevant process, in the choice of style, the integration of planning into the whole managerial pattern, the creation of appropriate key relationships and actively working at the issues of implementation and change as part of planning. The articles selected offer a little guidance along a difficult path, in the hope that some of the well-known pitfalls may be avoided.

PART ONE

Key Considerations in Designing a Planning Process

Pitfalls in Multi-National Long-Range Planning

George A. Steiner and Hans Schöllhammer

Graduate School of Management, University of California

The authors of this article argue that too many companies are not getting the benefits which should be produced by their long-range planning systems. Of the many possible explanations for this, the authors concentrate on the major pitfalls which should be avoided in order to ensure good results. The article is based upon the results of a survey of planning pitfalls among corporations in six industrialized countries.

CORPORATE LONG RANGE PLANNING IS INCREASingly practised throughout the world. It is our belief, however, that too many companies are not getting the benefits which should be produced by their long range planning systems.

There are many explanations for this. First, the planning system may not be designed correctly for the company. Second, what a long range planning system can do for a company may be misunderstood and, therefore, expectations of results may be unrealistic. Third, the planning system may be blamed for what actually is poor management. Fourth, unexpected environmental changes may adversely affect company operations and the planning system may get the blame for it. Finally, a company may fall into one or more of the major pitfalls which should be avoided if good results are to be achieved from its planning system.

This paper deals with the last factor. We present here the results of a survey of planning pitfalls among corporations in six industrialized countries.

THE PITFALLS SURVEY

Over a period of years one of the authors accumulated a list of 50 pitfalls considered to be most important to avoid in starting, understanding, and doing long range planning, and in using the results. This list is shown in Appendix A and was the basis for a questionnaire sent to companies in six countries. As noted above, a complete list of pitfalls would include traps to be avoided in the entire process of management. Also, many pitfalls in doing planning are not included in the list. For instance, it is obviously a mistake to forecast sales on the basis of a simple extrapolation of current trends. Nevertheless, tests of the list lead us to conclude that it covers the major traps to be avoided.[1]

Respondents were asked to indicate whether their company had fallen into a specific pitfall completely, partly, or not at all. In addition, each was asked to specify the extent to which a pitfall that his company did not avoid had affected its planning effectiveness. Respondents were asked to rank order the most important, and the least important, pitfalls to be avoided. The questionnaire requested further information about the company's organizational structure, the degree of formality of the planning system, the degree of documentation in the planning system, and how satisfied or dissatisfied each company was with its planning system.

There are biases in this survey which should be recognized. To begin with, the questionnaire contained few definitions of terms so the responses reflected definitions of the respondents. The data, therefore, are not precisely comparable. Also, the mix of respondents among executives and staffs varied from country to country. In addition, the proportion of responses to the total number of questionnaires sent and to the total received varies among countries. Depsite these biases we believe the data reveal accurately certain selected and important aspects of the state-of-the art of corporate planning around the world.

Table 1 shows the distribution among six countries of the 460 usable questionnaires which were returned to us.

The differences in the size of the sample by country are obvious. However, an analysis of thirty randomly selected responses from among the U.S. and the Japanese replies revealed that the results are essentially the same on the basis of the limited sample as on the much larger number of actual responses from these two countries. For this reason, we feel confident that the responses from

Table 1. Number of Responses by Country

Country	Number of Responses	
U.S.A.	215	47%
Japan	118	26%
Canada	42	9%
England	32	7%
Italy	31	6%
Australia	22	4%
Total	460	100%

Canadian, English, Italian and Australian companies are reasonably representative and reflect an accurate cross-section of the planning situation in the countries surveyed.

Table 2 shows the responses distributed by sales volume. Since about 40 per cent of all respondents in each of the surveyed countries had annual sales between $100 and $500m., there is less disparity than might appear at first glance.

The responding firms were also asked to provide information about their organizational characteristics. Table 3 shows how firms were distributed in terms of centralized or decentralized, and divisionalized or nondivisionalized. Among the U.S., Canadian and Australian respondents centralized and decentralized firms are represented in about equal proportions. As far as the Japanese and Italian firms are concerned, centralized organizational structures are much more prevalent than decentralized organizations. In the case of the English firms the situation is reversed. Table 3 also shows that with the exception of the Japanese firms most responding firms are divisionalized. These differences in organizational characteristics are well in line with other empirical research studies[2] and are an indication of the samples' representativeness.

THE MOST IMPORTANT PITFALLS TO AVOID

Respondents were asked to identify, in rank order, the most important pitfalls which they felt should be avoided. The results are shown in Table 4. The pitfall which led the list is 'Top management's assumption that it can delegate the planning function to a planner'. Canadian, English and Italian executives ranked this pitfall as being the most important. U.S. executives ranked it second, for Japanese respondents this factor was fourth in importance and only Australians considered seven other pitfalls as being more aggravating. This result suggests that a very large percentage of firms

Table 2. Distribution of Respondents by Volume of Sales (in per cent of total respondents per country)

Sales Volume (Mill. $)	U.S.A.* (*N* = 202)	Canada† (*N* = 39)	England‡ (*N* = 28)	Italy (*N* = 31)	Australia§ (*N* = 20)	Japan¶ (*N* = 109)
Under $50	7·4	12·8	7·1	38·7	35·0	17·4
$50–$99	5·0	7·7	25·0	22·6	30·0	15·6
$100–$250	20·3	28·2	29·3	19·3	25·0	28·5
$251–$500	21·3	20·5	10·7	12·9	10·0	18·3
$501–$750	8·9	12·9	14·3	—	—	5·5
$751–$999	3·9	5·1	3·6	6·5	—	5·5
Over $1,000	33·2	12·8	—	—	—	9·2

*13 firms did not show sales volume.
†3 firms did not show sales volume.
‡4 firms did not show sales volume.
§2 firms did not show sales volume.
¶9 firms did not show sales volume.

Table 3. Organizational Characteristics of Responding Firms (in per cent of total number of responses per country)

Organization Forms	U.S.A.		Canada		England		Italy		Australia		Japan	
	N	%	*N*	%	*N*	%	*N*	%	*N*	%	*N*	%
Centralized	87	53	15	45	11	41	13	62	10	48	68	62
Decentralized	78	47	18	55	16	59	8	38	11	52	42	38
	165	100	33	100	27	100	21	100	21	100	110	100
Not reporting	50		9		5		10		1		8	
Total sample	215		42		32		31		22		118	
Divisionalized	173	92	38	97	27	93	20	74	21	95	45	41
Not divisionalized	15	8	1	3	2	7	7	26	1	5	65	59
	188		39	100	29	100	27	100	22	100	110	100
Not reporting	27		3		3		4		0		8	
Total sample	215		42		32		31		22		118	

Table 4. The Ten Most Important Pitfalls to be Avoided as Ranked by Respondents

Pitfall Number (See Appendix A)	Description of Pitfall	Total Sample	U.S.A.	Canada	England	Italy	Australia	Japan
1	Top managements assumption that it can delegate the planning function to a planner.	1	2	1	1	1	8	4
24	Top management becomes so engrossed in current problems that it spends insufficient time on long-range planning, and the process becomes discredited among other managers and staff.	2	1	2	8	2	1	1
28	Failure to develop company goals suitable as a basis for formulating long-range plans.	3	3	3	2	6	3	3
11	Failure to create a climate in the company which is congenial and not resistant to planning.	4	4		3	5	9	7
42	Failure of top management to review with departmental and divisional heads the long-range plans which they have developed.	5	8				2	2
26	Failure to assure the necessary involvement in the planning process of major line personnel.	6	5	10	9	10	7	9
15	Assuming that corporate comprehensive planning is something separate from the entire management process	7	6	4	10	4		
16	Failure to make sure that top management and major line officers really understand the nature of long-range planning and what it will accomplish for them and the company.	8	10	5			6	10
12	Failing to locate the corporate planner at a high enough level in the managerial hierachy.	9	9		6	7		
47	Failure to use plans as standards for measuring managerial performance.	10	7					
27	Too much centralization of long-range planning in the central headquarters so that divisions feel little responsibility for developing effective plans.			6	4			
43	Forgetting that the fundamental purpose of planning is to make better current decisions.			7				5
13	Failure to make sure that the planning staff has the necessary qualities of leadership, technical expertise, and personality to discharge properly its responsibilities in making the planning system effective.			8			5	
14	Forgetting that planning is a political, a social, and an organizational, as well as a rational process.			9				
10	Failure to develop a clear understanding of the long-range planning procedure before the process is actually undertaken.				5			8
18	Assuming that plans can be made by staff planners for line managers to implement.				7			
31	Failure to make realistic plans (e.g., due to overoptimism and/or overcautiousness).							
45	Top management's consistently rejecting the formal planning mechanism by making intuitive decisions which conflict with the formal plans.					3		
8	Assuming that a formal system can be introduced into a company without a careful and perhaps "agonizing appraisal" of current managerial practices and decision-making processes.					8	4	
37	Doing long-range planning periodically and forgetting it in-between cycles.					9	10	
39	Failure of top management, and/or the planning staff, to give departments and divisions sufficient information and guidance (e.g., top management interests, environmental projections, etc.)							6

in various industrial countries have not yet learned to do justice to a major planning principle which states that: 'There can and will be no effective comprehensive corporate planning in any organization where the chief executive does not give it firm support and make sure that others in the organization understand his depth of commitment.[3] Without top management's support and active involvement in the development of company plans, the planning effort is largely unproductive and may be discredited without valid reason. It seems to be difficult to make many top executives really planning-conscious.

The second most important pitfall—on the basis of the total responses—is a direct consequence of the first one: 'Top management becomes so engrossed in current problems that it spends insufficient time on long range planning, and the process becomes discredited among other managers and staff'. For a majority of the U.S., Japanese and Australian respondents this pitfall is the most important one. Only English executives gave this pitfall a relatively low eighth rank. In England, other planning pitfalls are even more serious. The relative lack of planning consciousness among English top managers has been widely documented. David Granick, for example, characterized the typical English enterprise as 'the home of the amateur' and concluded his chapter on this issue by pointing out that 'a common theme runs through all these examples: rejection of professionalism in management and of the enormous attention to planning and control which has accompanied professionalization in the United States. British executives are far more concerned with a straightforward "getting on with the job". Theirs are the advantages and disadvantages of simplicity'.[4]

'Failure to develop company goals suitable as a basis for formulating long range plans' was ranked as the third most important pitfall. With the exception of the Italian respondents, the majority of all others ranked this condition among the top three pitfalls. For Italian managers the third most important planning pitfall to avoid is No. 45, 'Top management consistently rejecting the formal planning mechanism by making intuitive decisions which conflict with formal plans.'

These three pitfalls seem to be universally the most important since a majority of all the respondents of the various countries ranked them among the top 10 pitfalls. These three pitfalls must thus be considered as inherent planning weaknesses with which managers and staff planners everywhere are faced, in which they get very frequently entrapped, and which are very difficult to overcome.

Space does not permit detailed comments on other top pitfalls[5] but a few highlights of Table 4 may be noted. A number of the pitfalls in the top 10 reveal a lack of understanding of the way in which long range planning is related to management. For instance the ranking of Nos. 11, 42, 26, and 15 seem to say that too many managers do not realize that planning is inextricably interrelated in the entire process of management. To get best results there must be a climate congenial to doing planning; managers up and down the line, especially top managers, must become involved; and top managers must review plans of lower-level managers.

It is noteworthy that generally speaking the top 10 important pitfalls are identified by most managers in the countries surveyed. To be sure, there are exceptions as Table 4 shows since a total of 21 pitfalls were identified as being in the top 10. It seems clear that in Italian companies entrepreneural decisions very frequently override the planning system. In Japanese companies top management does not give much guidance to lower-level line and staff in doing planning. But, fundamentally Table 4 shows that there are remarkable similarities to those planning pitfalls considered to be highly important among managers in different countries of the world.

THE MOST IMPORTANT PLANNING PITFALLS CLASSIFIED BY ORGANIZATIONAL SIZE

This study also attempted to find out which pitfalls are the most common and important in firms of different size (as measured by their volume of sales). Table 5 shows the findings. This table shows a somewhat surprising finding: regardless of their size, firms identify as being most important to avoid the same planning pitfalls. For instance, on the basis of all reponsess, pitfall No. 1 ('Top management's assumption that it can delegate the planning function to a planner') has been consistently ranked among the five most important pitfalls, regardless of the size of the responding firm. The same result was found with regard to pitfall No. 24 ('Top management becomes so engrossed in current problems that it spends insufficient time on long range planning'.) Pitfall No. 28 ('Failure to develop company goals suitable as a basis for formulating long range plans') was also ranked among the five most important planning problems by the responding companies in each of the three size categories. In addition, pitfall No. 11 ('Failure to create a planning climate in the company which is congenial to planning') was ranked among the five most important weaknesses by firms with annual sales under \$100m. as well as those with a sales volume over \$1 billion.

Among the five most important pitfalls there is thus only one which was ranked exclusively in one size category. For the large firms with sales over a billion dollars it is pitfall No. 9 ('Ignoring the power structure of a company in organizing the planning process'). For the small firms it is pitfall No. 42 ('Failure of top management to review with departmental or divisional heads the plans which they have developed'). For the medium size firms the unique pitfall is No. 41 ('Failure to secure that minimum of system and information to make the planning process and its results creditable and useful').

Table 5. Ranking of Most Important Pitfalls to Avoid by Size of Firm (Dollar Sales) Total Samples (Responses of Six Countries)

Rank Order	Under $100 Million		$100 Million to $1 Billion		Over $1 Billion	
	Responses	Pitfall	Responses	Pitfall	Responses	Pitfall
1st	37	24	82	24	28	1
2nd	36	28	70	1	22	28
3rd	34	1	66	28	19	11
4th	24	11	48	41	16	24
5th	22	42	45	14	15	9
U.S.A.						
1st	15	24	34	1	22	1
2nd	13	28	33	28	28	18
3rd	10	44	24	46	17	11
4th	9	1	25	15	14	26
5th	7	16	23	26	12	24
Canada						
1st	3	15	11	1	4	1
2nd	3	26	11	24	2	11
3rd	2	7	8	28	2	15
4th	2	27	6	16	2	28
5th	2	37	5	15	2	43
England						
1st	7	1	8	1		
2nd	5	26	6	27		
3rd	4	10	5	10		
4th	4	28	5	11		
5th	4	42	5	25		
Italy						
1st	5	1	6	45		
2nd	4	11	4	1		
3rd	4	15	4	24		
4th	4	28	3	11		
5th	3	24	3	12		
Australia						
1st	5	8	4	29		
2nd	5	24	4	26		
3rd	4	10	3	42		
4th	4	28	2	12		
5th	4	42	2	28		
Japan						
1st	10	24	19	24	4	42
2nd	10	25	18	42	3	9
3rd	10	39	15	28	3	23
4th	9	1	14	1	3	30
5th	8	26	11	43	3	37

A country-by-country analysis of the ranking of the most important pitfalls according to the size of the firm yields essentially the same results. Firms of different size come essentially to the same assessment about their difficulties in avoiding common planning pitfalls. There are, as Table 5 shows, variations in the ranking of the significance of individual pitfalls; however, the similarities tend to outweight the differences.

THE LEAST IMPORTANT PLANNING PITFALLS

The rational for a special focus on the least important pitfalls is two-fold: (a) they indicate potential planning difficulties which companies find relatively easy to avoid, and (b) their negative impact on planning effectiveness is rather limited. Table 6 gives the results of this part of the analysis. It shows that the pitfalls least likely to create problems are: No. 21 ('Assuming that planning is hard'), No. 20 ('Assuming that planning is easy'), and No. 35 ('Assuming that new quantitative techniques are not as useful as advertised). Besides these three least important pitfalls the ranking of others which are considered low in significance does not reflect marked differences from one country to the other. However, the responses from English executives show a somewhat greater variation in this regard. For example, pitfall No. 9 ('Ignoring the power structure of the company in organizing the planning process') and No. 49 ('Failing to encourage managers to do good long range planning by basing reward solely on short range performance measures') were ranked among the three least important pitfalls. Indeed, the frequently

Table 6. The Ten Least Important Pitfalls in Planning as Ranked by Respondents (Ranks 1–10)

Pitfall No.	Total Sample	U.S.A.	Canada	England	Italy	Australia	Japan
1							
2							
3							
4	4	5	7			8	4
5							
6							3
7	10	7			8		7
8			10				
9				3			
10							
11							
12							
13							
14				9		9	
15							
16							
17			9				
18							
19				7	9		
20	2	2	3	2	2	5	1
21	1	1	1	4	1	1	2
22	6	8		5		7	8
23							
24							
25	5	6	4	8	4		9
26							
27							
28							
29	9	9	5		6	2	
30							
31							
32							
33		10			10		
34	7					6	6
35	8	3	6		5	10	
36	3	4	2	6	3	4	5
37							
38							
39							
40			10	10		3	
41							
42							
43							
44							
45							
46							
47							
48				1	7		
49							10
50							

The Least Important Pitfalls

1 : 21—Assuming that planning is hard.
2 : 20—Assuming that planning is easy.
3 : 36—Assuming that new quantitative techniques are not as useful as advertised.
4 : 25—Long-range planning becomes unpopular because top management spends so much time on long-range problems that it ignores short-range problems.
5 : 29—Assuming that equal weight should be given to all elements of planning (i.e., that the same emphasis should be placed on strategic as on tactical planning, or that the same emphasis should be accorded to major function plans).
6 : 35—Assuming that older methods to choose from among alternatives should be discarded in favour of newer techniques.
7 : 4—Assuming that the present body of knowledge about planning is insufficient to guide fruitful comprehensive planning.
8 : 22—Assuming that long-range planning can get a company out of a current crisis.
9 : 7—Thinking that a successful corporate plan can be moved from one company to another without change and with equal success.
10 : 40—Attempting to do too much in too short a time.

observed emphasis on the use of personal criteria for evaluating executives in English firms[6] makes it unlikely that they would get entrapped by such pitfalls as Nos. 9 and 49.

In general, the results of Table 6 show less disparity than the results on the most important pitfalls. This means that there is an even greater unanimity among the respondents concerning the less significant pitfalls as compared with the assessment of the most important pitfalls to be avoided.

THE IMPACT OF SPECIFIC PITFALLS ON PLANNING EFFECTIVENESS

Every planning situation creates its own pitfalls in which companies get entrapped. Not every pitfall has the same negative impact on planning effectiveness, however, even though it may be considered an important one to avoid. Table 8 shows how the respondents ranked the five most important pitfalls to be avoided and the degree to which these pitfalls reduced effectiveness.

The interesting result of this part of the survey is that pitfall No. 24 ('Top management becomes so engrossed in current problems that it spends insufficient time on long range planning, and the process becomes discredited among other managers and staff') is shown as having the greatest negative impact on planning effectiveness. This is followed by pitfall No. 28 ('Failure to develop company goals suitable as a basis for formulating long range plans'). Pitfall No. 11 ('Failure to create a climate in the company that is congenial to planning') was ranked third in its negative impact on planning effectiveness.

In contrast, pitfall No. 1 ('Top managements assumption that it can delegate the planning function to a planner') has been pointed out as the most common planning error, yet its negative effect on planning effectiveness is reported to be less severe than pitfalls Nos. 24, 28 and 11. Pitfall No. 42 ('Failure of top management to review with subordinates the long range plans they have developed') was viewed as the fifth most common planning error and the assessment of its negative impact on planning effectiveness corresponds precisely with this rank.

The essential lesson to be learned from the results presented in Table 7 is that the greater is top management's awareness of the importance of planning, and the more attention it pays to a clear delineation of organizational objectives, the higher will be the effectiveness of the company's planning effort. A company's planning effectiveness can be reduced more significantly by falling into these two traps than by any other planning pitfalls.

THE DEGREE OF SATISFACTION WITH PLANNING SYSTEMS

A quick glance at Table 8 shows there is somewhat more satisfaction than dissatisfaction with planning systems in all the nations surveyed except Japan. In Japan not one correspondent felt highly satisfied with his company's planning system. This is probably due to the fact that most of the respondents were managers who did not get what they considered to be sufficient association with and feedback from top management.

The results of Table 8 do not support the asserted widespread dissatisfaction which some observers

Table 7. Incidence of Entrapment and Affect on Planning System of Five Pitfalls Ranked 'Most Important to Avoid' (Total Responses from Six Countries)

Pitfall Number		Entrapment Has Your Company at this Time Fallen into this Pitfall?			Affect If You have fallen into the Pitfall, has it Affected the Effectiveness of Your Long-range Planning System?		
	Rank order	(1) No	(2) Partly	(3) Completely	(1) Not at all	(2) Some	(3) Much
1	1	247	175	31	10	128	68
24	2	106	251	88	12	189	138
28	3	179	193	76	9	153	107
11	4	189	215	43	8	179	71
42	5	235	143	52	4	108	83

Incident of Entrapment of 'Most Important Planning Pitfalls to Avoid'

Rank Order	U.S.A. Pitfall No.	Canada Pitfall No.	England Pitfall No.	Italy Pitfall No.	Australia Pitfall No.	Japan Pitfall No.
1	24	1	1	1	24	24
2	1	24	28	11	42	42
3	28	28	11	15	28	8
4	11	15	27	24	1	28
5	26	16	10	45	39	13

Table 8. Degree of Satisfaction with the Reported Planning System (In Percentage of Total Number of Responses per Country)

Degree of Satisfaction	U.S.A. (N = 211*)	Canada (N = 41*)	England (N = 30*)	Italy (N = 27*)	Australia (N = 21*)	Japan (N = 116*)
1. Highly satisfied	10·0	19·5	6·7	11·1	4·8	0
2. Above average satisfaction	34·1	34·1	26·7	22·2	38·1	10·3
3. Average satisfaction	32·2	22·0	50·0	40·7	33·3	38·8
4. Some dissatisfaction	15·2	17·1	13·3	18·5	19·0	44·0
5. Highly dissatisfied	8·5	7·3	3·3	7·4	4·8	6·9

*Remaining firms (see total sample size) did not answer this question.

have seen.[7] On the other hand, the dissatisfaction shown is significant. The level of dissatisfaction is not at all surprising, however, in light of the numerous violations of standard planning principles which this survey has revealed.

In the U.S. survey cited earlier, degrees of dissatisfaction were related to whether or not a company had fallen into one of the major pitfalls. It was concluded that: 'Without exception, those companies which said they had fallen completely into one of the top 10 most important pitfalls to avoid were more dissatisfied than satisfied with their planning programs.'[8] It is our guess that when similar comparisons are made for the data in the worldwide survey that much the same results will appear.

The conclusion to be drawn from these results is that corporate planning is still too often poorly done and misunderstood. At too many companies one does not yet find the attitudes and clear insights that would be conducive to an avoidance of the most important planning pitfalls. As a consequence, satisfactions with current planning systems are not as high as they ought to be.

Table 9. Satisfaction—With Planning System Versus Organization Structure—Total Sample (Six Countries)

Structural Characteristics	Degree of Satisfaction (in % of total sample) Very High to High	Average	Low to Very Low	Total Sample
Centralized	28·5	34·0	37·5	200
Decentralized	38·1	32·4	29·5	170
Divisonalized	40·4	32·8	69·8	317
Non-Divisionalized	8·9	44·4	46·7	90
U.S.A.				
Centralized	39·2	28·7	32·1	87
Decentralized	47·5	34·6	17·9	78
Divisionalized	45·0	31·0	24·0	171
Non-Divisionalized	13·3	60·0	26·7	15
Canada				
Centralized	60·0	13·3	26·7	15
Decentralized	58·8	11·8	29·4	17
Divisionalized	54·0	21·6	24·3	37
Non-Divisionalized	100·0	—	—	1
England				
Centralized	20·0	60·0	20·0	10
Decentralized	37·6	43·7	18·7	16
Divisionalized	34·6	50·0	15·4	26
Non-Divisionalized	0	50·0	50·0	2
Italy				
Centralized	38·9	44·4	16·7	18
Decentralized	0	42·9	57·1	7
Divisionalized	38·9	44·4	16·7	18
Non-Divisionalized	0	42·9	57·1	7
Australia				
Centralized	40·0	50·0	10·0	10
Decentralized	50·0	20·0	30·0	10
Divisionalized	45·0	30·0	25·0	20
Non-Divisionalized	0	100·0	0	1
Japan				
Centralized	6·0	40·2	53·8	67
Decentralized	16·6	31·0	52·4	42
Divisionalized	13·3	35·6	51·1	45
Non-Divisionalized	7·8	40·6	51·6	64

PLANNING SATISFACTION RELATED TO ORGANIZATION STRUCTURE

Table 9 shows that companies with a decentralized organizational structure tend to be somewhat more satisfied with their current planning systems than those that are centralized. A country-by-country analysis, however, does not confirm the universality of this conclusion. In the case of Canadian and Italian firms, for example, the centralized ones expressed greater satisfaction than others. Divisionalized firms expressed consistently a higher degree of satisfaction than nondivisionalized ones.

DATES THAT PRESENT PLANNING SYSTEMS WERE CREATED

Table 10 shows that the planning system of most of the responding companies in the various countries is of very recent origin. For a majority of the firms, comprehensive and systematic long range planning is still in an evolutionary phase. In more than half of the responding Australian firms, for example, the currently used planning system originated only in 1970 or later and approximately one third of the responding companies from Canada, England and Italy fall into the same category. Only about one fourth of the U.S., and Japanese firms have a relatively mature planning system with more than 10 years of experience with it.

DEGREE OF FORMALITY AMONG PLANNING SYSTEMS

Table 11 reveals that there is a rather uniform distribution of degrees of formality in planning systems. The highest incidence of formal systems is found in the United States and the least is in Japan. The most informal are found in Italy and the least in England.

DEGREES OF DOCUMENTATION AMONG PLANNING SYSTEMS

The degrees of documentation among planning systems are shown in Table 12. The heaviest documentation appears to be in planning systems in Australia, Cana, U.S. and England. Systems having the least documentation appear to be in Italy.

Table 10. Distribution of Respondents by Origination of Planning System (in Percentage of Total Respondents per Country)

Origination of Planning System	U.S.A.* (*N* = 190)	Canada† (*N* = 38)	England‡ (*N* = 28)	Italy§ (*N* = 29)	Australia¶ (*N* = 21)	Japan‖ (*N* = 109)
Before 1950	1·6	—	—	—	—	3·7
1950–1954	2·6	—	—	—	—	1·8
1955–1959	5·3	5·3	3·4	6·9	4·8	7·3
1960–1964	23·7	15·8	10·4	17·2	23·8	31·2
1965–1969	48·8	39·4	45·2	44·9	19·0	37·7
1970 to date	17·0	39·5	31·0	31·0	52·4	18·3

Number of companies that did not answer the question about the year the planning system was introduced: *—25; †—4; ‡—4; §—2; ¶—1; ‖—9.

Table 11. Degrees of Formality Reported in Planning System (in Percentage of Total Number of Responses per Country)

Degree of Formality	U.S.A. (*N* = 210*)	Canada (*N* = 42)	England (*N* = 31*)	Italy (*N* = 29*)	Australia (*N* = 22)	Japan (*N* = 117*)
1. Highly formal	16·7	11·9	16·1	10·3	13·4	6·8
2. Formal	31·9	31·0	25·8	13·8	36·4	15·4
3. Medium	25·2	31·0	38·7	34·5	27·3	41·9
4. Somewhat informal	16·2	16·6	9·7	27·6	18·2	21·4
5. Very loose and flexible	10·0	9·5	9·7	13·8	4·5	14·5

*Remaining firms (see total sample size) did not provide an answer to this question.

Table 12. Extent of Documentation in Planning (in Percentage of Total Number of Responses per Country)

Extent of Documentation	U.S.A. (*N* = 210*)	Canada (*N* = 42)	England (*N* = 31*)	Italy (*N* = 29*)	Australia (*N* = 21*)	Japan (*N* = 116*)
1. Substantial written documentation	33·8	35·7	25·8	10·3	28·6	5·2
2. Above average documentation	25·7	26·2	32·3	13·8	38·0	22·4
3. Average documentation	26·2	16·7	35·5	34·5	28·6	45·7
4. Below average documentation	8·6	14·3	3·2	27·6	4·8	19·0
5. Short, rough notations	5·7	7·1	3·2	13·8	0	7·8

*Remaining firms (see total sample size) did not answer this question.

POSITIVE CORRELATIONS BETWEEN SATISFACTIONS, FORMALITY, DOCUMENTATION AND BIRTHDATE OF PLANNING SYSTEMS

Correlations were computed, but not presented here, which showed that there is a high and significant relationship between the degree of satisfaction of planning systems and the degree of formality of the systems. About the same level of correlation exists between satisfaction and the extent of written documentation in plans. There was a lower level of correlation but a positive one between the date the planning system was begun and satisfaction. The earlier the year started the higher the satisfaction. This probably supports the thesis that experience with planning really does improve the system and the product.

MAJOR CONCLUSIONS

This survey identified the pitfalls which companies around the world feel are the most important ones to avoid if the best results are to be achieved from their planning system. The study also showed that satisfactions with planning systems are higher than dissatisfactions. Those companies having higher formality and greater documentation are also more satisfied with their planning systems. Divisionalized companies are generally more satisfied with their planning systems than nondivisionalized ones. Finally, companies having the most experience with planning, as indicated by the birthday of their planning system, tend to be the most satisfied. ■

APPENDIX A

A. Pitfalls in getting started:

1. Top management's assumption that it can delegate the planning function to a planner.
2. Rejecting planning because there has been success without it.
3. Rejecting formal planning because the system failed in the past to foresee a critical problem and/or did not result in substantive decisions that satisfied top management.
4. Assuming that the present body of knowledge about planning is insufficient to guide fruitful comprehensive planning.
5. Assuming that a company cannot develop effective long-range planning in a way appropriate to its resources and needs.
6. Assuming that comprehensive corporate planning can be introduced into a company and overnight miraculous results will appear.
7. Thinking that a successful corporate plan can be moved from one company to another without change and with equal success.
8. Assuming that a formal system can be introduced into a company without careful and perhaps "agonizing reappraisal" of current managerial practices and decision-making processes.
9. Ignoring the power structure of a company in organizing the planning process.
10. Failure to develop a clear understanding of the long-range planning procedure before the process is actually undertaken.
11. Failure to create a climate in the company which is congenial and not resistant to planning.
12. Failing to locate the corporate planner at a high enough level in the managerial hierarchy.
13. Failure to make sure that the planning staff has the necessary qualities of leadership, technical expertise, and personality to discharge properly its responsibilities in making the planning system effective.

B. Pitfalls Related to a Misunderstanding of the Nature of Long-Range Planning:

14. Forgetting that planning is a political, a social, and an organizational, as well as a rational process.
15. Assuming that corporate comprehensive planning is something separate from the entire management process.
16. Failure to make sure that top management and major line officers really understand the nature of long-range planning and what it will accomplish for them and the company.
17. Failing to understand that systematic formal planning and intuitive (opportunistic, or entrepreneurial) planning are complementary.
18. Assuming that plans can be made by staff planners for line managers to implement.
19. Ignoring the fact that planning is and should be a learning process.
20. Assuming that planning is easy.
21. Assuming that planning is hard.
22. Assuming that long-range planning can get a company out of a current crisis.
23. Assuming that long-range planning is only strategic planning, or just planning for a major product, or simply looking ahead at likely development of present product. (In other words, failing to see that comprehensive planning is an integrated managerial system.)

C. Pitfalls in Doing Long-Range Planning:

I. Managerial Involvement

24. Top management becomes so engrossed in current problems that it spends insufficient time on long-range planning, and the process becomes discredited among other managers and staff.
25. Long-range planning becomes unpopular because top management spends so much time on long-range problems that it ignores short-range problems.
26. Failure to assume the necessary involvement in the planning process of major line personnel.
27. Too much centralization of long-range planning in the central headquarters so that divisions feel little responsibility for developing effective plans.

II. The Process of Planning

28. Failure to develop company goals suitable as a basis for formulating long-range plans.
29. Assuming that equal weight should be given to all elements of planning (i.e., that the same emphasis should be placed on strategic as on tactical planning, or that the same emphasis should be accorded to major functional plans).
30. Injecting so much formality into the system that it lacks flexibility, looseness, and simplicity, and restrains creativity.
31. Failure to make realistic plans (e.g., due to over-optimism and/or overcautiousness.)
32. Extrapolating rather than rethinking the entire process in each cycle (i.e., if plans are made for 1971 through 1975, adding 1976 in the 1972 cycle rather than redoing all plans from 1972 to 1975).
33. Developing such a reverence for numbers that irreverence for intuition and value judgments predominates the thinking going into planning.
34. Seeking precision of numbers throughout the planning horizon.

35. Assuming that older methods to choose from among alternatives should be discarded in favor of newer techniques.
36. Assuming that new quantitative techniques are not as useful as advertised.
37. Doing long-range planning periodically and forgetting it in between cycles.

III. Creditability of Results

38. Failure to develop planning capabilities in major operating units.
39. Failure of top management, and/or the planning staff, to give departments and divisions sufficient information and guidance (e.g., top management interests, environmental projections, etc.).
40. Attempting to do too much in too short a time.
41. Failure to secure that minimum of system and information to make the process and its results creditable and useful.

D. Pitfalls in Using Long-Range Plans

42. Failure of top management to review with departmental and divisional heads the long-range plans which they have developed.
43. Forgetting that the fundamental purpose of the exercise is to make better current decisions.
44. Assuming that plans once made are in the nature of blueprints and should be followed rigorously until changed in the next planning cycle.
45. Top management's consistently rejecting the formal planning mechanism by making intuitive decisions which conflict with the formal plans.
46. Assuming that, because plans must result in current decisions, it is the short-run that counts and planning efforts as well as evaluations of results concentrate on the short-run.
47. Failing to use plans as standards for measuring managerial performance.
48. Forgetting to apply a cost-benefit analysis to the system to make sure advantages are greater than costs.
49. Failing to encourage managers to do good long-range planning by basing reward solely on short-range performance measures.
50. Failing to exploit the fact that formal planning is a managerial process which can be used to improve managerial capabilities throughout a company.

REFERENCES

(1) Very few of the U.S. respondents and practically none of the foreign respondents listed additional pitfalls. Those that were suggested, such as 'developing a planning cycle which is much too long,' or 'failure to develop an adequate system to monitor those long-range plans,' were invariably modifications of one or more of those pitfalls already listed in the questionnaire.

(2) See, e.g. Serge Grosset, *Management: European and American Styles.* Wadsworth, Belmont (1970); Michael Y. Yoshino, *The Japanese Managerial System,* MIT Press, Cambridge (1940); Paul J. Gordon, Organizational Strategies—The Case of Foreign Operations by Non-U.S. Companies. *Journal of Comparative Administration* (May 1970); Hans Schöllhammer, Organization Structures of Multi-national Corporations. *Academy of Management Journal* (September 1971).

(3) George A. Steiner, *Top Management Planning.* Macmillan, New York (1968), p. 88.

(4) David Granick, *The European Executive.* Doubleday & Company, New York (1964), p. 250; see also Robert Dubin, Management in Britain—Impressions of a Visiting Professor. *Journal of Management Studies,* **7** (2), (May 1970) p. 183 ff.

(5) Fuller descriptions are contained in George A. Steiner, *Pitfalls in Comprehensive Long Range Planning,* The Planning Executives Institute, Oxford, Ohio, U.S.A. (1972).

(6) *Op. cit.,* Dubin, p. 195 f.

(7) Patrick H. Irwin, 'Why Aren't Companies Doing a Better Job of Planning?' *Management Review* (November 1971, pp. 11–16); Merritt L. Kastens, 'Who Does the Planning?' *Managerial Planning* (January/February 1972), pp. 1–3; Malcolm W. Pennington, "Why has Planning Failed?' *Long Range Planning* (March 1972), pp. 2–9; Kjell A. Ringbakk, 'Why Planning Fails,' *European Business* (Spring 1971), pp. 15–27.

(8) *Op. cit.,* Steiner, p. 25.

Managing Diversity: Strategy and Control in Diversified British Companies

Michael Goold and Andrew Campbell

Many large companies today operate in a range of different businesses. These companies need to fine tune their management styles to the specific requirements of each business in their portfolio. But they also wish to avoid unmanageable organizational complexity, and, as far as possible, to operate with a single, consistent, widely understood corporate culture throughout the company. Managing diversity therefore causes particular problems and conflicts. This article puts forward three alternative philosophies for managing diversity that the authors have encountered in extensive research on this topic with 16 large U.K. companies. It brings out the advantages and disadvantages of each philosophy and discusses the results that companies following each approach achieve.

> We are in a range of different businesses. We regard this diversity as a source of strength. It spreads our risks and gives us the opportunity to switch resources from low growth, low return areas to fund expansion in opportunity areas. But we do pay a penalty in the complexity of the management task this creates. Whether our degree of diversity is manageable, I'm not sure.

This concern, voiced by the planning director of a major U.K. company, must strike an echo in the board rooms of many multibusiness companies.

For senior managers at the corporate headquarters of most large companies, diversity is a fact of life. The portfolios of these companies frequently include businesses from several industries, at different stages of maturity, with different growth options and different financial performance. Understanding and controlling each of the businesses in a portfolio of this sort is a severe test of corporate management.

During the last 3 years we have undertaken research with a cross-section of 16 large U.K. companies to examine how different companies cope with this problem of managing diversity.[1] We began by examining the ways in which the corporate centre relates to its subsidiaries. This led us to distinguish three main different central management 'styles': Strategic Planning, Strategic Control and Financial Control. (A fuller description of these styles is provided at the end of this article, in a separate section, which describes the nature of the research which we undertook.) We believe that each style is more or less appropriate in different business circumstances. For example a stable and mature business such as London Brick (part of Hanson Trust's porfolio) may respond well to a centre that stresses control of financial results—the Financial Control style. But in the oil exploration business, or in information technology, a combination of long lead times, large investments and technological complexity requires a central style with more stress on prior planning of strategy—the Strategic Planning style.

It follows that different businesses in a diverse portfolio may respond best to different styles, and hence that the centre may need to adjust or fine tune its relationship with each subsidiary or group of subsidiaries. Furthermore, as businesses change —encountering new competitors, breaking into new markets, employing new technologies—the centre's style may need to change with the changing environment.

Courtaulds, for example, includes within its portfolio small, national clothing businesses, with short lead times, fragmented competitors and a need for

---

Michael Goold and Andrew Campbell are Senior Research Fellows at the London Business School Centre for Business Strategy. They were previously strategy consultants working in Europe and the United States. Michael Goold was Vice-President and Director with the Boston Consulting Group's London Office. Andrew Campbell was a consultant with McKinsey in London and Los Angeles. Together they are setting up an Institute for Strategic Management to focus on research into the management of diversified companies. Their book *Strategies and Styles: The Role of the Centre in Managing Diversified Corporations* will be published by Basil Blackwell (Oxford) in the autumn 1987.

careful financial control; and also an international marine paint business that requires global co-ordination across markets, state-of-the-art research into new coatings and a willingness to invest for long-term competitive advantage. These businesses each require rather different handling by the centre.

As another example, STC grew up as a subsidiary of ITT, with most of its business in the supply of telecommunications equipment to the British Government. This was a stable and comparatively protected competitive situation. ITT's emphasis on meeting budget was appropriate. In the early 1980s ITT reduced its shareholding to a minority interest, British Telecom was privatized, liberalizing its purchasing to include overseas suppliers, and the technologies and markets of telecommunications, data processing and computing began to converge rapidly. STC found itself in a different business environment. It began to create a new management style with greater emphasis on long-term planning to cope more effectively with the dramatic changes in the nature of its business circumstances.

Ideally, therefore, corporate management need to be flexible in the styles they adopt for different parts of the portfolio, and to fine tune those styles as businesses change.[2] But, given a large and diverse portfolio, is this a feasible requirement?

In our research we found that companies tend to employ a uniform style across most of their businesses, and that changes in style occur seldom. When they do come, they normally involve the trauma of extensive senior management (and chief executive) turnover. We found few examples of the central team adopting a radically different style with different parts of the portfolio.

We believe that this is no coincidence. It reflects the importance of simplicity and consistency in organizational structures and systems.[3] With a single style across all businesses it is easier for the centre to communicate its priorities and intentions to subsidiary management. It can also ensure that information systems, organization charts, incentive and career development systems are supportive of the underlying style. Whereas with flexible or changing styles, clarity of communication is harder, and subsidiary management can more easily be confused about the signals they are receiving. We all now appreciate the power of a shared corporate culture;[4] flexible or multiple styles are at odds with any such unifying values.

Even more fundamentally, we noted in our research that companies' styles almost always reflect the personality and views of their chief executives. The style is an embodiment of the beliefs and attitudes of the CEO. As such, flexibility in style calls for a degree of schizophrenia that is rare amongst the strong individuals who are typically found at the top of large organizations.

Diverse businesses that require different styles are therefore hard to reconcile with the need to maintain simple organization structures and systems within a unified corporate culture. This means that building and managing a successful corporate portfolio encounters some intractable problems:

☆ how to handle a diversity of business types without running into unmanageable organizational complexity

☆ how to maintain organizational simplicity without encountering major problems of style mismatch

☆ how far, and in what circumstances, diversification should be sought or avoided.

In our research we have encountered three main philosophies for building and managing a diverse portfolio. These broadly correspond to the three most popular strategic management styles.

They are:

- Core Businesses (Strategic Planning style)
- Diverse Businesses (Strategic Control style)
- Manageable Businesses (Financial Control style).

Core Businesses

In its 1984 Annual Report, Cadbury Schweppes stated its Group objectives in these terms:

> The Group will concentrate on its principal business areas. . . . Our objective is to maximize the use of existing assets rather than to diversify into unrelated areas.
>
> In confectionery we at present hold a 5 per cent share of the world chocolate market and are ranked as the fifth largest company in it. We intend to increase that share and to climb the league of international chocolate companies.
>
> In soft drinks, we are currently number three in the market outside the U.S.A., but fifth in the world overall. Our aim is to become the world's leading non-cola carbonated soft drinks company.

During the year following this statement, Cadbury's divested itself of two major divisions, Beverages and Foods and Health and Hygiene, to concentrate more exclusively on the core areas of confectionery and soft drinks.

This is classic 'Core Businesses' thinking. The company commits itself to a few industries (usually two or three), and sets out to win big in those industries. Growth is through organic development of the businesses in these industries, and through related acquisitions that help to strengthen and extend the core businesses. A push into international markets is often a feature. More peripheral (non-core) businesses are starved of funds or divested. The organization structure of the typical Core Businesses portfolio is shown in Figure 1. The CEO has strong central functional support, and the businesses oper-

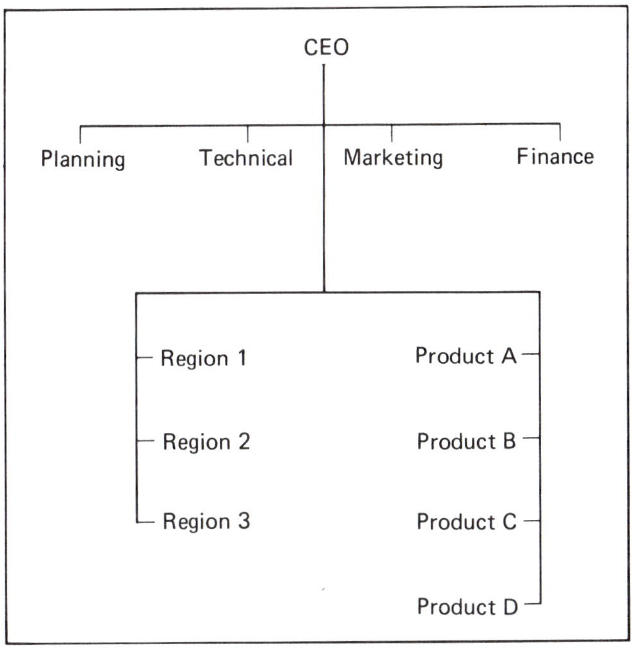

Figure 1. Core businesses' organization structure

ate in some form of product–geographic matrix, to ensure global co-ordination of strategy. Examples of companies from our research adopting the Core Businesses philosophy were Cadburys, BOC, Lex and STC (see Table 1).

In a Core Businesses portfolio, the Strategic Planning style works best. Limited diversity means that the centre can be knowledgeable about each of the core businesses, and can make constructive suggestions about their strategies. Furthermore they can provide co-ordination between businesses where this is needed. At STC we were told: 'For our approach to succeed, the centre must understand the businesses well to be able to challenge the management companies on the quality of their proposals. Our limited size and diversity allows us to do this.'

The core businesses are selected, in part, because they offer opportunities for major growth, and hence strategies for the core businesses often involve big, bet-your-company decisions. To reach agreement on these decisions close corporate involvement and sponsorship is needed. The pay-off to these decisions is sought in the long term, and it is accepted that there may be hiccoughs along the route to building up the core businesses. Lex would probably not have plunged so heavily into the wholly new business of electronic component distribution without strong corporate sponsorship for the move; nor would they have weathered the storms in the business during the last 2 years without continuing corporate support.

A Strategic Planning style—close central involvement in strategy development and flexible strategic controls—is therefore generally appropriate to the portfolio and to the ambitions associated with this philosophy. If applied consistently across the whole portfolio, it causes few serious problems of mismatch.

The strengths of the philosophy are, therefore, that it gives industry focus, making it easier for the centre to add value; it provides growth opportunities within the core businesses; and it can be managed with a single style, thereby permitting shared values and organization simplicity.

There are, however, weaknesses in the philosophy.

☆ Lack of diversity across industries provides less spread of risks. The downturn in the electronics industry left both STC and Lex exposed. Moreover reliance on the core industries for growth creates problems when those industries go ex-growth, as companies in the tobacco and oil businesses have found.

Table 1. Companies adopting core business philosophy

Company	Core business	Recent investments, acquisitions (1980–1985)	Recent disposals, closures (1980–1985)
BOC	Gases Healthcare Carbon products	Japanese and S. American gases acquisitions Healthcare acquisitions Major investment in carbon graphite electrode business	Computer services division Welding interests Variety of smaller businesses
Cadbury's	Confectionery Soft drinks	Joint company with Coca-Cola for U.K. soft drinks Various soft drinks acquisitions in U.S. and Europe Investments to increase share of U.S. and European confectionery	Beverages and food division Health and hygiene division
Lex	Vehicle distribution Electronic component distribution	Nine electronic component distribution companies in U.K., U.S. and Europe	Transportation interests Hotel division
STC	Information technology	IAL ICL (computers) Major component investments	(Several since 1985)

☆ Changes in the business environment can make the Strategic Planning style less generally appropriate, leading eventually to the need for a difficult change in style. In the mid-1970s, Courtaulds began to feel that the linkages between their textile businesses were less important than flexibility and responsiveness. But it took a further 7 to 8 years before a move to a Strategic Control style was fully established.

☆ Non-core businesses that remain within the portfolio tend to feel unloved and constrained in their strategies. These problems were brought out forcibly by the managing director of a non-core business in one of the Strategic Planning companies.

> They were not particularly interested in the strategy of the division. What knowledge at the centre there was of the business tended to be based on past personal experience of people who had worked in the area, often several years earlier at a time when circumstances were quite different. The central contribution to strategy has been mainly negative as a result of all this. One never knew from day to day when someone was going to come in and want to try to sell part of the business.

This is no atmosphere in which to plan and execute strategy.

Manageable Businesses
Like Cadbury Schweppes, Hanson Trust spells out its objectives and philosophy. In 1984, Lord Hanson, the Chairman, stated his objectives ('determined 21 years ago') as:

> To invest in good quality basic businesses providing essential goods and services for the consumer and industry and to obtain an improving return for shareholders by maximizing earnings per share and dividend growth . . . . Those in the operating companies have clear responsibility for running their businesses.

The notable points about this statement are that it is consistent with diversification into a wide range of industries, and that goals are essentially financial in nature. This is in sharp contrast to Cadbury Schweppes's objectives.

In the period since this statement of objectives, Hanson has entered a range of new industries through the acquisitions of SCM in the United States and Imperial Group in the United Kingdom. These acquisitions have taken Hanson from 55th place in the Times 1000 largest British companies in 1983 into the top 10 in 1987.

But underlying the aggressive, acquisitive growth of Hanson, there is a strong sense of the types of industries ('basic businesses providing essential goods and services') that will respond best to Hanson's management style. Acquisitions in high tech, rapidly changing or capital intensive businesses are avoided, and any subsidiary which began to show these characteristics is liable to be divested. We were told about a Hanson business that made turbochargers which had come up with an investment plan, indicating several years of negative cash flow to get established in a new and developing field of technology. 'This worried us a lot. We sold the business shortly afterwards.' The emphasis is therefore on selecting businesses for the portfolio which can be effectively managed using short-term financial controls. Hanson Trust is in this way a typical example of the 'Manageable Businesses' philosophy.[6] Other examples of the Manageable Businesses philosophy from our research are BTR and Tarmac (see Table 2).

The qualities that make businesses in different industries 'manageable' have been articulated by Hanson and BTR managers:

Table 2. Manageable Businesses philosophy

Company	Style	Business
BTR	Financial Control	Construction, engineering, electrical distribution, valves, pipes, control systems, transportation, healthcare, sporting goods, ceramics, materials, laminates, agricultural equipment, cleaning devices, conveyor belting, polymeric fabrications, power transmission, automotive carpets, automotive components, radiators, reinforced plastics, safely equipment, paper machine clothing, publishing, dental supplies, hospital equipment, rehabilitation products, hosiery, furniture and insurance
Hanson Trust	Financial Control	Department stores, batteries, bricks, electrical and automotive, yarns and threads, engineering, machine tools, control systems, construction equipment services, fabrics, textile finishing machinery, soft furnishings, apparel, footwear, housewares, artificial flowers, meat processing, office and home furniture and furnishings, kitchen cabinets, vanities, fasteners, garden and industrial hand tools, wood mouldings, windows, building materials, lumber, energy equipment, engineering products and services, lighting fixtures and fittings, tobacco, brewing, restaurants, retailing, hotels, catering, snacks, frozen foods, sauces
Tarmac	Financial Control	Stone, sand, gravel, concrete, asphalt, bricks, tiles, installation of building materials, construction, design and management for building work, civil engineering, gas and oil engineering, house building, development of commercial and industrial property, oil and gas exploration, bitumen refining

☆ 'We avoid areas of very high technology. We do not want to be involved in businesses which are highly capital intensive and where decision making has to be centralized.' Lord Hanson, Hanson Trust.

☆ 'We are a fairly low risk organization. We avoid businesses that require major, risky outlays with long payback periods.' Clive Stearnes, Group Chief Executive, BTR.

☆ 'We don't like mass production. We like niche situations that involve customer problem solving.' Lionel Stammers, Joint Chief Executive, European Region, BTR.

There may be extensive diversity in terms of industries, but there is homogeneity in the nature of the businesses and, hence, in the required style of management—the Financial Control style. In practice, this means that the businesses should have few linkages with each other, should be in relatively stable competitive environments, and should not involve large or long-term investment decisions.

Growth is achieved mainly through acquisitions that add new, manageable businesses to the portfolio. Financial Control is less suitable for fast growth, unstable environments and does not encourage aggressive initiatives to achieve organic growth.

Figure 2 is an organization chart for a typical Manageable Businesses company. The headquarters is slim, supported only by a strong finance function. Underneath, there are layers of general management, but prime profit responsibility is pushed right down to the lowest level. It is the high degree of decentralization of strategy and responsibility that allows the extensive diversity to be manageable.

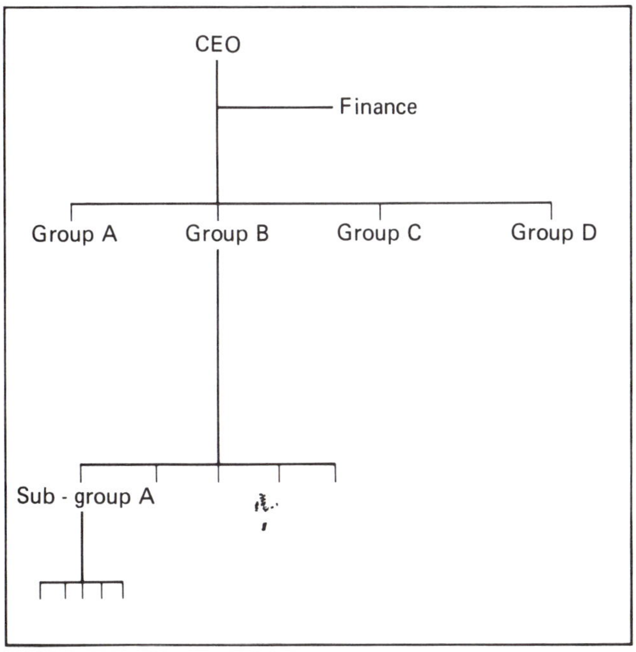

Figure 2. Manageable businesses organization structure

This philosophy therefore achieves a strong culture based on the pursuit of short-term financial objectives despite a high degree of diversity across industries. It avoids mismatches between this style and its businesses by selecting and rationalizing the portfolio with 'fit' in mind. At Tarmac, we were told that they had disinvested from their North Sea oil holding with some relief, since the size and timescale of exploration activities had been uncomfortable for them. And, at BTR, one central manager argued that one of the best decisions they made was to get out of tyres in the 1960s. 'To continue in tyre manufacture we needed to make a large capital investment. However, the business wasn't producing the sort of return we expected and we couldn't see the picture changing.' Portfolio selection and rationalization of this type greatly simplifies the management of diversity. As such, the philosophy has considerable strengths.

However, there are also weaknesses. The philosophy does not lead to much organic growth, and is liable to result in piling up excess cash from a whole range of profitable, mature, cash cows. Fresh acquisitions both create growth and use up the cash. But, when a company reaches the size of a Hanson or a BTR, finding new acquisition targets big enough to maintain the momentum of growth becomes difficult.

The Financial Control style is also vulnerable to aggressive competitors. When the going gets tough, management will typically retrench or divest. Selective tactical withdrawals may be fine, but a general willingness to retreat can be exploited by a well-resourced and ambitious opponent.

Lastly, the philosophy creates small, more specialist, 'niche' businesses rather than global players in big international businesses. From a corporate perspective, this may be no bad thing given the intensity of competition on the major international battlefields. But from a national perspective there is a need for at least some companies who can compete successfully in international industries such as information technology, oil, automobiles and pharmaceuticals.

Diverse Businesses
In the Diverse Businesses philosophy, the emphasis is on diversity rather than focus. The centre seeks to build a portfolio that spreads risk across industries and geographic areas, as well as ensuring the portfolio is balanced in terms of growth, profitability and cash flow. Resources are allocated to grow (or acquire positions in) competitively strong businesses in attractive industries; and there is a willingness—even a desire—to extend the portfolio into a range of different markets, technologies and competitive situations.

Although confident and aggressive diversification of this kind was in vogue during the 1960s and early

1970s, the more recent fashion for sticking to the knitting has meant that few, if any, of the companies in our research sample now wholeheartedly embrace the Diverse Businesses philosophy. The obvious problems in understanding and managing wide diversity have greatly reduced corporate enthusiasm for 'new legs' for the portfolio.

Nevertheless, there were a number of highly diverse companies in our sample, who did seem to be moving towards a distinctive philosophy for managing their portfolios. This philosophy entails creating groups of more homogeneous businesses, and delegating much of the strategy responsibility to those groups. Each group can then adopt its own, perhaps different, style for dealing with its businesses. Figure 3 is a schematic representation of how such a company might be structured.

This sort of structure, with strong and largely independent groups or divisions, allows a portfolio with real diversity to be 'chunked' into more manageable pieces. The divisions can grow organically at their own rates—and new divisions can be added, by acquisition or subdivision, as appropriate.

Companies that appear to be adopting a philosophy of this sort include ICI, where each division has extensive freedom to manage itself as it sees fit, and Courtaulds, which has recently split the company into two groupings, Textiles and Chemical & Industrial, in the belief that each grouping needs a different type of management.

The central style in these companies tends to be Strategic Control. Only Strategic Control is likely to be flexible enough to accommmodate different divisions, each with its own style. The old adage that its hard to have a longer time horizon than your boss

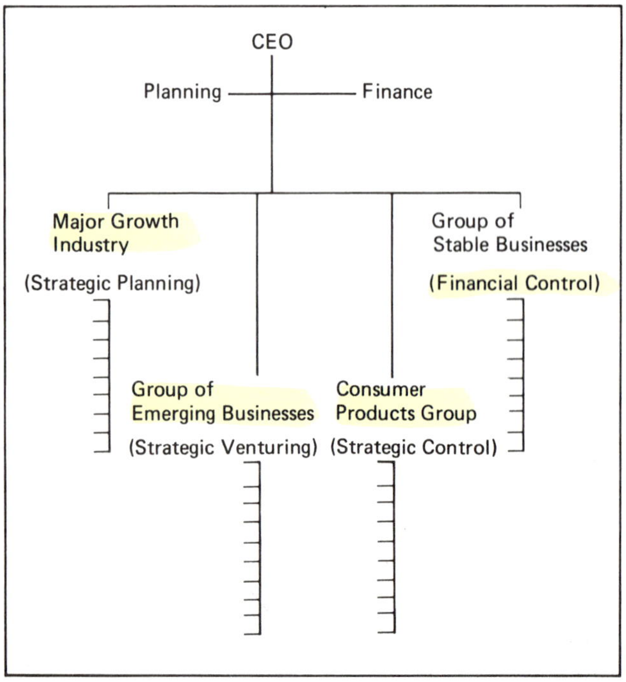

Figure 3. Diverse businesses organization structure

suggests that a corporate style of Financial Control will preclude Strategic Planning or Strategic Control at the divisional level; while a corporate desire to adopt a Strategic Planning style forces divisional line managers to do likewise in order to satisfy headquarters planning requirements.

With Strategic Control, the centre is, in Chris Hogg of Courtauld's words, simply 'a sympathetic and knowledgeable 100 per cent shareholder', allowing the divisions to go their own way in terms of style. By structuring the divisions right, the centre can create homogeneous groupings of businesses, where few mismatches occur, and can adjust the composition of divisions over time, as businesses change.

The Diverse Businesses philosophy, then, appears to be a way of managing diversity with a single central style, and without creating mismatches between business circumstances and central style. But there is a price to be paid. The centre must be willing (and able) to play a chameleon role, adopting a low profile relative to divisional management. This is not likely to be comfortable for a strong CEO, and also raises questions concerning the value-added by the centre. If the centre is so low key, and the divisions have so much autonomy, why would the divisions not be better as independent companies without the corporate overhead?

But an even more difficult issue arises from the cultural complexity implied by different styles in each division. Is it really possible for different styles to flourish side by side, or will certain divisions become second-class citizens? One company that purports to adopt the Diverse Businesses philosophy told us:

> We adapt our style to the different companies in our portfolio. We use Strategic Planning where we are building businesses with a 5–10 year payback. Strategic Control is our normal style and an active strategic dialogue takes place between the Group and the operating companies. And we use Financial Control for our 'dog' companies, when we are sorting out and preparing for disposal operations which do not fit our long term requirements.

It is evident that the Financial Control divisions in these circumstances are a sort of 'sin bin' and face a very different situation to their counterparts in Hanson Trust or BTR.

Cultural complexity is also liable to create succession problems when the existing CEO retires. Candidates from the different divisions may have radically different approaches to management, and each may well find the low-key central role incompatible with their styles. Moreover, if a new more positive central style emerges, it will be hard to preserve the divisional autonomy of style that characterizes the Diverse Businesses philosophy.

Results

Each of these management philosophies represents a

viable managerial alternative. But none is ideal; they all have both strengths and weaknesses. This is illustrated by considering the results that companies pursuing each philosophy have achieved.

In terms of underlying profitability, all the companies that we have mentioned have achieved relatively high levels of return on capital through the period 1981–1985 (see Figure 4). The companies classified as following the Diverse Businesses philosophy (Courtaulds and ICI) have seen a lower average level of profitability but have enjoyed particularly rapid improvements in returns in recent years. (Figure 5).

The differences between companies are more marked when we turn to eps (earnings per share) and share price growth (Figure 6). Here the acquisitions and portfolio rationalizations carried out by the companies following the Manageable Businesses philosophy have yielded dramatic growth in eps and, especially, share price. By contrast, the companies following the Core Businesses philosophy have underperformed on these measures. This reflects problems and set-backs that companies such as STC, Cadbury Schweppes and Lex have encountered in their aggressive strategies to build up their core businesses.

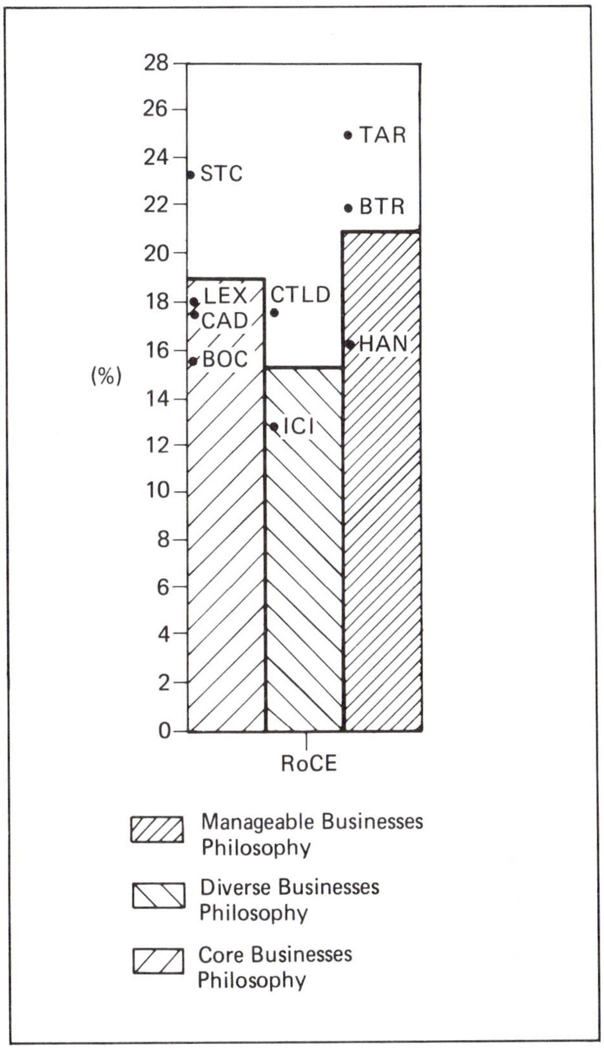

Figure 4. Four-year profitability averages, 1981–1985

In terms of portfolio growth, the Manageable Businesses group appears to have delivered spectacular rates of sales increase (Figure 7), while the Diverse Businesses group has shown little real growth. This overall picture is, however, somewhat misleading, since it combines organic and acquisition growth. In Figure 8[7] we break out growth in fixed assets between these two sources, and find that the vast bulk of the growth in the Manageable Businesses category is attributable to acquisitions. BTR and Hanson Trust have actually shown negative rates of real, organic growth through this period. For organic growth, it is companies such as STC, Cadbury Schweppes and BOC, who follow the Core Businesses philosophy, that have performed best.

The number of companies in our sample is clearly too small to provide the basis for any firm generalizations in terms of performance. However, it would appear that the Manageable Businesses companies have shown the highest rates of profitability and acquisition-based growth; that the Core Businesses have grown fastest organically, though with some setbacks to profitability; and that the Diverse Businesses companies have achieved rapid improvements in profitability, but with little real growth in sales. It is possible to see these differences in results as a consequence of the different emphases in each management philosophy.

Review

Ideally, a company's approach to managing its portfolio will achieve:

☆ enough diversity across industries and geographic areas to spread the risks of sudden changes;

☆ enough balance in types of businesses to ensure an even profit and cash flow profile;

☆ a close match between the nature of the businesses in the portfolio and the strategic management style;

☆ organization and cultural simplicity;

☆ a means of generating growth and regeneration for future portfolio development.

Table 3 summarizes the ways in which each philosophy copes with the problems of managing and growing a diverse portfolio. Each represents an internally consistent, but different, approach to the task. Our research suggests that there are successful companies pursuing each approach, although the Diverse Businesses philosophy has few committed adherents. But we have also found that each philosophy has certain drawbacks. These drawbacks do not represent fatal flaws, but are best seen as contingent liabilities. They are problems which may

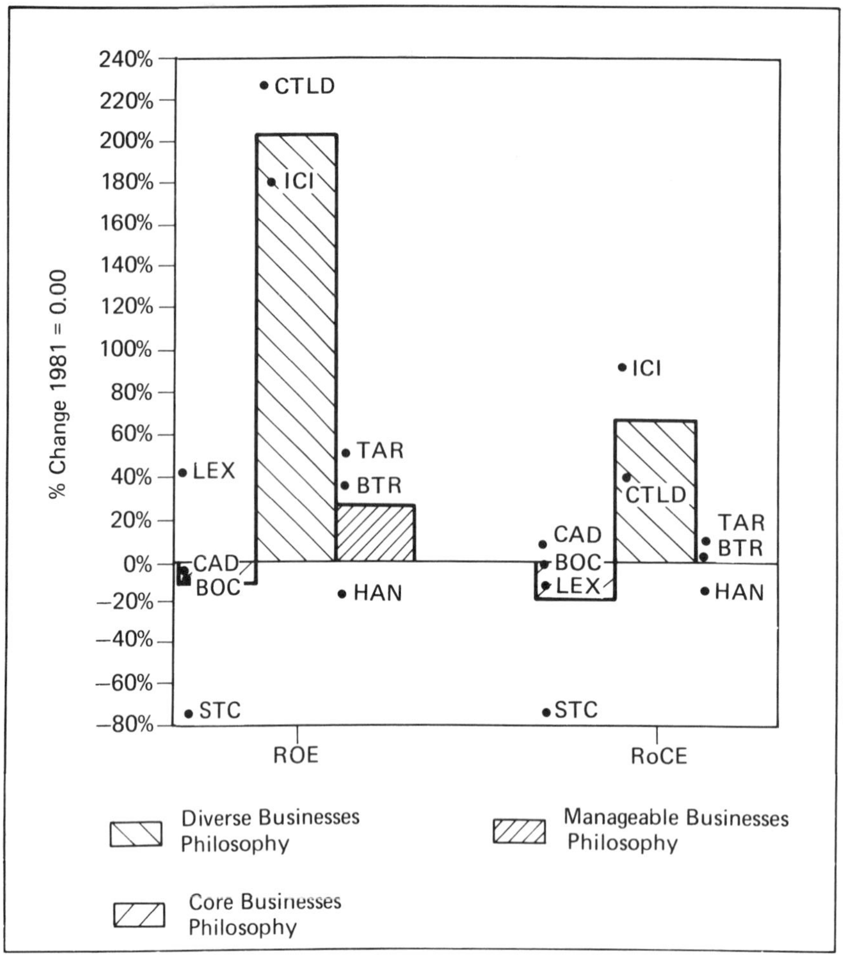

Figure 5. Change in profitability ratios, 1981–1985

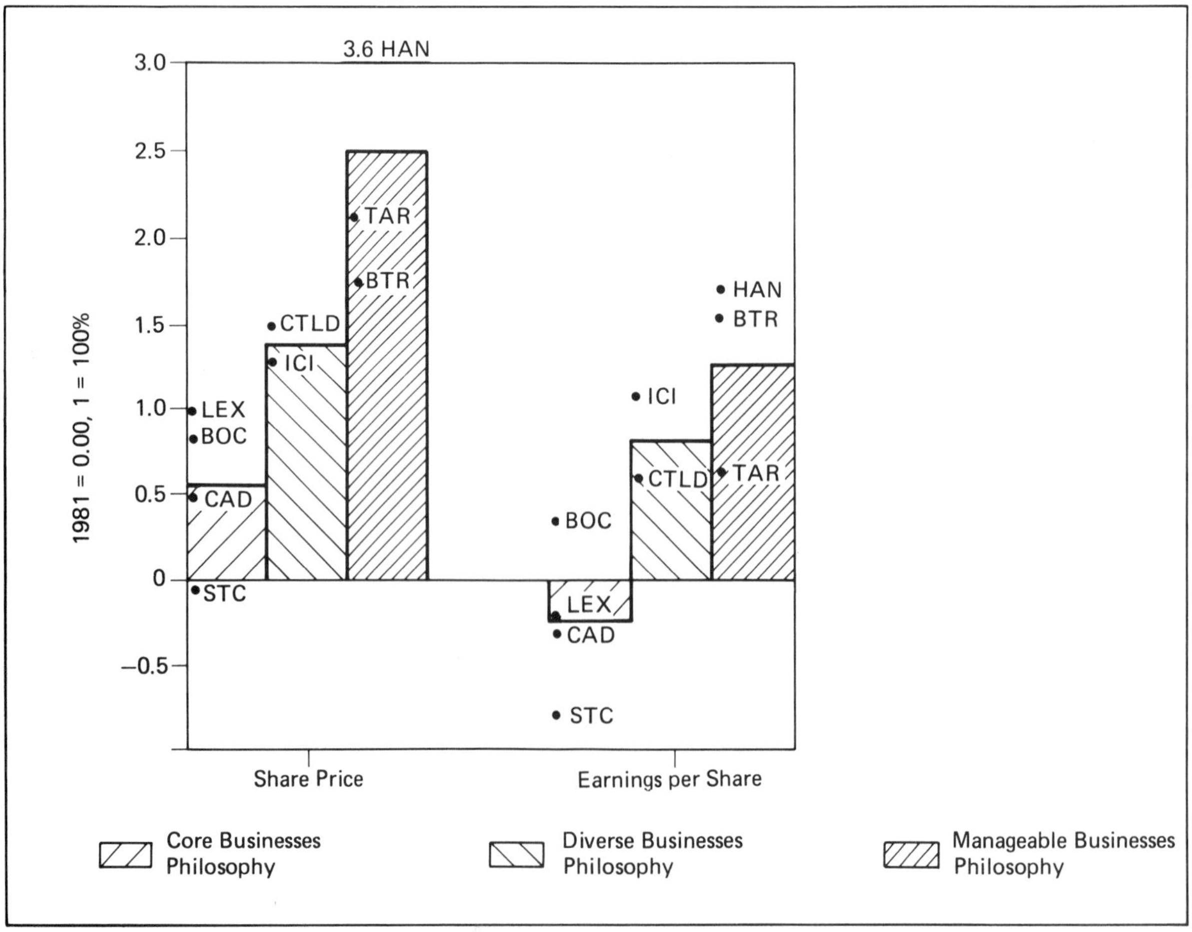

Figure 6. Four-year growth indices, 1981–1985 (real values)

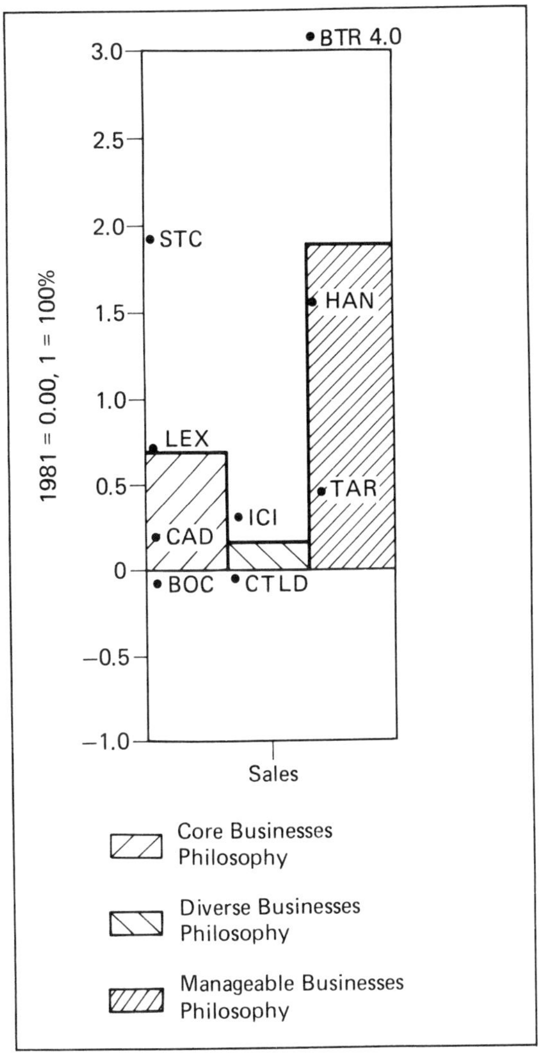

Figure 7. Four-year growth indices, 1981–1985 (real values)

be avoided for long periods of time, but which can come home to roost under certain circumstances. In terms of the results they achieve, each philosophy achieves success on certain measures of performance, but is weaker on other dimensions.

Perhaps most surprisingly, we have found that in most companies the philosophy for managing diversity remains implicit. There may be an approach which approximates one of our philosophies, but it is not normally explicitly articulated and examined. In consequence, the ways in which the philosophy can be reinforced and strengthened are less clearly perceived, and the risks and drawbacks of the approach may not be adequately recognized. We are confident that improvements in performance can be achieved by companies that create a clearer focus on these issues, and make a more conscious choice of their portfolio-building philosophy.

The Research

Our research has involved detailed work with a cross-section of leading British firms. We carried out open-ended interviews with corporate, divisional and business management to determine the range of current practices, to identify major issues as perceived by different levels within the firms, and to relate the strategic decision-making processes of those firms to the results they achieved. In this way we hoped to have some empirical basis for conclusions about what corporate strategic management is, and how the corporate level adds value.

In the event we received co-operation from the 16 companies listed in Table 4. These companies are all publicly quoted, with headquarters in the United Kingdom. They cover a range of manufacturing and service sectors, although we have excluded financial services and retailing. Their main common characteristics are size, diversity and success.

In these companies we conducted interviews with anything from five to 20 senior managers, including in almost all cases the chief executive. In addition we have gathered data from within the company,

Table 3. Management of a diverse portfolio

	Philosophies		
	Core businesses	Manageable businesses	Diverse businesses
Diversity across industries	Low	Very high	High
Diversity across types of businesses	Fairly low	Low	High
Style at centre	Strategic Planning	Financial Control	Strategic control
How mismatches avoided	Core businesses mainly responsive to Strategic Planning	Portfolio selection and retention of 'manageable' businesses	Structure into homogeneous groups
Growth	Mainly organic	Mainly acquisition	Organic and acquisition
Drawbacks	—Limited industry diversity —Maturation of core businesses —Non-core businesses	—Limits to acquisition-based growth —Vulnerable to aggressive competition —Does not build	—Low key centre —Limited central added value —Cultural complexity

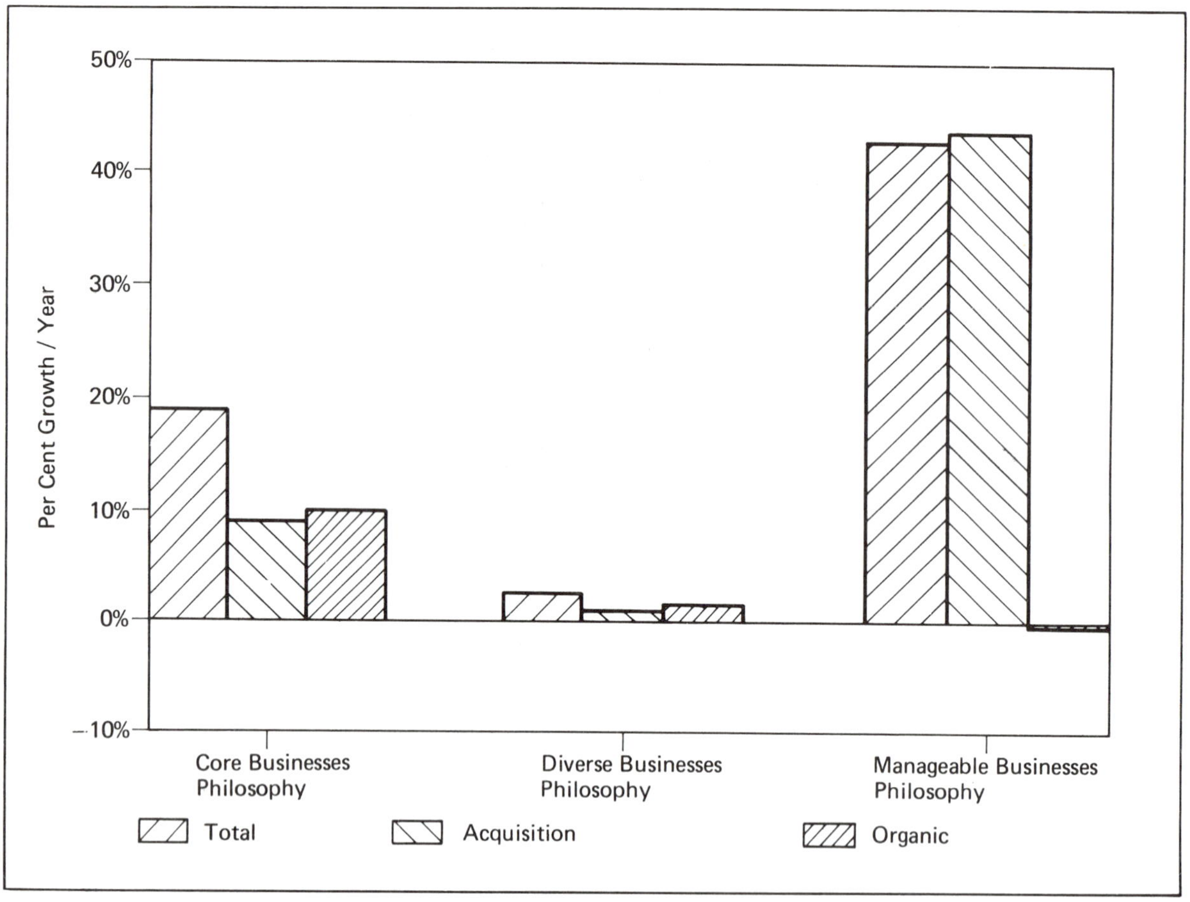

Figure 8. Average yearly fixed asset growth, 1981–1985

usually via the head of planning, concerning formal aspects of the company's strategic decision-making process, and have assembled published information on company results. Our conclusions are based on what we have learned about the advantages and shortcomings, the successes and failures of strategic decision-making in these 16 organizations.

Table 4. Participant companies

Company	Main activity	Sales (£m) 1985	Rank in Times 1000
BP	Oil	47,156	1
ICI	Chemicals	10,725	4
GEC	Electricals	5222	14
Imperial	Tobacco, food, drinks	4919	15
BTR	Diversified	3881	18
Hanson Trust	Diversified	2675	33
Courtaulds	Textiles and chemicals	2173	45
STC	Electronics	1997	48
BOC	Gases and healthcare	1901	54
Cadbury	Confectionery, Soft drinks	1874	56
UB	Foods	1806	60
Tarmac	Construction	1536	72
Plessey	Electronics	1461	76
Lex	Distribution	1041	110
Vickers	Engineering	611	159
Ferranti	Electronics	568	169

Source: The Times 1000, 1986–1987, Times Books Limited, London (1986).

In the research we identified three main styles of corporate strategic management: Strategic Planning, Strategic Control and Financial Control.

Corporate management in *Strategic Planning* companies believe that the centre should participate in and influence the development of business unit strategies. Their influence takes two forms: establishing a planning process and contributing to strategic thinking. In general, they place rather less emphasis on financial controls. Performance targets are set flexibly, and are reviewed within the context of long-term progress. Participant companies who showed these characteristics were BOC, BP, Cadbury Schweppes, Lex Service, STC and UB.

The centre of *Strategic Control* companies is concerned with the plans of its business units. But it believes in autonomy for business unit managers. Plans are reviewed in a formal planning process. The objective is to upgrade the quality of the thinking. But the centre does not want to advocate strategies or interfere with the major decisions. Control is maintained by the use of financial targets and strategic objectives. These are agreed with the centre, and business unit managers are expected to meet the standards. Companies with these characteristics are Courtaulds, ICI, Imperial Group, Plessey and Vickers.

Financial Control companies focus on annual profit targets. There are no long-term planning systems and no strategy documents. The centre limits its role to approving investments and budgets, and monitoring performance. Targets are expected to be stretching and once they are agreed they become part of a contract between the business unit and the centre. Failure to deliver the promised figures can lead to management changes. The Financial Control companies from our sample are BTR, Ferranti, GEC, Hanson Trust and Tarmac.

These styles, the results they achieve and the value that they add, are more extensively described in Michael Goold and Andrew Campbell *Strategies and Styles: The Role of the Centre in Managing Diversified Corporations*, Basil Blackwell (1987).

References

(1) For a full description of the work, see Michael Goold and Andrew Campbell, *Strategies and Styles: The Role of the Centre in Managing Diversified Corporations,* Basil Blackwell, Oxford (1987).

(2) This point is well made in Jay W. Lorsch and Stephen A. Allen III, *Managing Diversity and Interdependence,* Harvard University Graduate School of Business Administration Division of Research (1973).

(3) See, for example, Thomas J. Peters and Robert H. Waterman, Jr, *In Search of Excellence,* Harper & Row, London (1982).

(4) See Terence E. Deal and Alan A. Kennedy, *Corporate Cultures,* Addison-Wesley, Reading, MA (1982).

(5) See, for example, Robert H. Miles, *Coffin Nails and Corporate Strategies,* Prentice-Hall, Englewood Cliffs, NJ (1982), which gives an account of how the U.S. tobacco companies have tried to cope with maturity and decline in their core business area.

(6) The idea that top management groups put together their portfolio around businesses that they feel comfortable managing has also been proposed by C. K. Prahalad and R. A. Bettis: The dominant logic: a new linkage between diversity and performance, *Strategic Management Journal* (November–December 1986).

(7) Breaking out acquisition and organic growth from published information is hard. We have used information on fixed asset growth in published accounts as a proxy for overall growth, supplemented by our own estimates where this information was not available. Fuller details of the methodology are available from the author.

What Kind of Corporate Planner Do You Need?

*Milton Leontiades**

The planning literature ignores distinctions among types of plans and types of planners. Consequently, a systematic pairing of planners and a company's level of planning need is not well understood or implemented in practice. This paper provides two missing links in order to bridge this shortfall between theory and practice. One is a planning matrix which establishes six possible planning modes for a company based on its stage of development and management style. The second is a distinction between three types of planners who would be appropriate to each planning mode. The matrix plus the three categories of planners provides a new tool for management in its responsibility for planning the job of the corporate planner. In doing so, it also surfaces some underlying causes of organizational strain and stress associated with the corporate planner's position.

The Organizational Dilemma of the Corporate Planner

Among the proliferating articles on corporate planning it is difficult to find any discussion of the role of the corporate planner. It is as if planning could exist without regard to who was doing the planning. This oversight is explained to a large extent by the fact that the literature also fails to distinguish among types of plans. Consequently, a need for different planning skills has not been apparent. The implication is left that planners are alike and interchangeable; that is, a planner is a planner is a planner. This is as naive as maintaining a plan is a plan is a plan. Relying on only common sense and observation, it is clear that planning needs of U.S. Steel differ from those of U.S. Industries, and that A & P is essentially different from Beatrice Foods as is Digital Equipment different from Sperry Rand.

Taking a historical perspective, we can observe that companies evolve organizationally and strategically. Alfred Chandler in *Strategy and Structure: Chapters in History of the American Industrial Enterprise*[1] was the first to develop in depth the relationship between strategy and structure. Numerous followers have elaborated and built on Chandler's landmark work. Collectively they have demonstrated that companies evolve through various stages of growth requiring different types of organizational structure and associated with different corporate strategies. It is only logical that planning needs would change with changes in corporate structure and strategy.

Moreover, we can be fairly specific in identifying three broad stages of growth and a normative evolution of organizational structure and strategy to conform with each stage, as illustrated below.

Table 1.

	Stage 1	Stage 2	Stage 3
Structure	Functional	Product	Divisional
Strategy	Single Product Line	Related Product Lines	Unrelated Product Lines

We know, for example, that companies progress from function to product and ultimately to a multi-product or multi-divisional organizational structure. Similarly, in terms of strategy, companies evolve from a typically small business with a single product orientation to large diversified or conglomerate organizations doing business in a number of unrelated fields. These trends, suggested in Table 1, are factually supported by research on organizational and strategic growth as reflected in Figure 1. While these trends are not necessarily representative for any individual company, the data show unmistakably the tendency for companies as a group to mature as Chandler had originally supposed.

However, while the progression of growth from small, simply organized firms into large, complex and multi-divisional organizations has been amply documented, the concept has not been transferred to, and integrated as part of, the literature on planning. This has left the organizational role of the corporate planner elusively

*The author is Associate Professor of Management at Rutgers University, Camden, New Jersey, U.S.A.

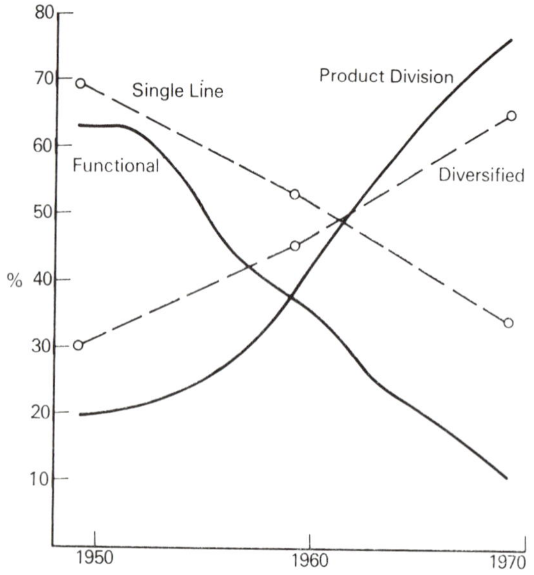

Figure 1. Estimated percentage of firms by organizational structure (——) and strategic category (- - - -). Adapted from Rumelt, *Strategy, Structure and Economic Performance*[2].

vague. Without connecting the planner's function to the different stages of a company's development, there has been no basis for dealing with change in the staff requirements for planning nor difference in skills among corporate planners. It is as if the same planning techniques which serve Falstaff Brewing Corporation, a one product firm, can also serve Philip Morris, a diversified company which happens to be a major brewer through its Miller Brewing Company subsidiary.

What this article suggests is that there are different types of planning skills, and planners, needed at different stages of a company's growth. Commonplace as this sounds, it has escaped systematic attention. At present, the theoretical prescription for planning which exists is at best applicable to a minority of primarily large companies. At worst, it is misleading and frustrating for corporate planners who do not fit into this generalized model.

A Matrix for Identifying Different Corporate Needs

Before we can define the different types of corporate planners, we must devise a system which distinguishes among different types of companies. No single system will catch all variations. Nevertheless it is possible to generalize using stages of growth and management style as our criteria. This proposed approach is adopted from an earlier article which dealt specifically with the classification problem.[3] Basically, it relies on Chandler's original research and applies it with modifications to the field of planning. The criteria for differentiating among companies are:

(1) Stages of growth: 1, 2, and 3;
(2) Management style: broad (B) or narrow (N) scope.

That is, a company may be in one of the three stages of

	Planning Scope	
Stage of Development	Broad (B)	Narrow (N)
Diversified (Stage 3)		
Related Products (Stage 2)	2 (B)	2 (N)
Single Product (Stage 1)		

Figure 2. A means for classifying plans according to a company's stage of development and with broad or narrow planning scope.

growth indicated in Figure 2. Also, management of the company may be oriented to opportunities outside of the present mix of businesses (broad scope) or satisfied to remain basically in those businesses it happens to be in (narrow scope).

A company in square 2(B) would indicate a company with more than one related product line which actively is monitoring the environment for significant diversification opportunities either internally through new products or new businesses or externally through acquisitions. A 2(N) company, on the other hand, would be situated similarly in more than one related product line but would be satisfied to remain at the present level of diversification.[4]

A company may change categories. Indeed, a company which has been narrowly managed and suddenly decides to diversify into new industries must implicitly switch management styles for such a transition. Once the diversification is complete, say from Stage 1 to Stage 2, the company may revert to a narrow management scope (N) for its expanded group of businesses.

Figure 3 shows some characteristic patterns of evolution. For example, Wm. Wrigley is a large company still at the first stage of development. Although the dominant firm in its industry, Wm. Wrigley is a company with only one product line and no apparent interest in expanding beyond it. (Figure 3a) Other companies in this initial stage of growth include such well-known names as Crown Cork and Seal, Maytag, Polaroid and R. R. Donnelley & Sons.

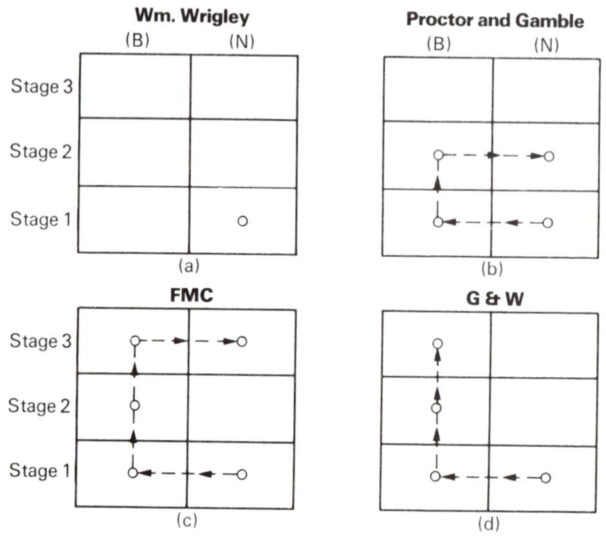

Figure 3. Selected examples of corporate evolution.

Procter and Gamble is an example of a company that has diversified from its basic business of soap and detergents into a number of areas related to a consumer household goods orientation: coffee (Folger's), foods (Duncan Hines) and paper (Charmin) (Figure 3b). But these acquisitions are more than a decade old. Having moved from 1(N) to 1(B) to 2(B), P & G is seemingly settled for the moment to manage the businesses it has and is thus placed in category 2(N).

FMC is a firm which has diversified beyond stage 2 into a number of product areas unrelated to its original business of food machinery equipment (the old name being the Food Machinery Corporation. Figure 3c). It is a highly diversified stage 3 company. However, its diversification is also behind it. According to FMC's president and chief executive officer 'We don't have any major acquisitions in mind, and we're not looking very hard. We've concluded that the internal opportunities are sufficiently challenging to concentrate our efforts on.'[5] Thus, one of the early conglomerates has joined the Establishment of mature yet highly diversified industrials.

Finally, there is G & W, a company which has reached the ultimate level of growth, yet is still actively buying into and out of companies (Figure 3d). Beatrice Food is another diversified major which has made significant recent acquisitions as has Colgate–Palmolive and R. J. Reynolds. These companies are all very diversified yet retain an open and broad management style in terms of leaving options open for opportunities to change the existing structure.

These examples illustrate how individual companies have followed a 'normative' pattern of growth according to the criteria of stage of growth and management style reflected in Figure 2. For each change in corporate strategy, indicated by a shift within the planning matrix, specific strategic plans are implied. These plans may be formal and explicit, as in a detailed plan supported by voluminous data. Or they might be intuitive, with the moves dictated by judgement rather than factual analysis. It is entirely possible and rational for planning to range from the intuitive to the scientific. But it is irrational to assume one plan is the same as any other, or that a single plan can be formulated to suit all companies regardless of complexity of structure or philosophy of managing. It is also unlikely that one type of planner is equally suited for each level of planning need.

Planners to Fit the Planning Matrix

Plans change as strategies change. Planners must change because differences in strategy require different planning skills. We have already designated six possible planning modes a company may occupy. We can now proceed to examine the qualifications a planner must possess in order to fulfill the planning function in each planning mode. We can, in other words, associate planners with plans.

Figure 4 indicates three varieties of planner according to the requirement of each planning mode. The three types of planner are traditionalist (T), specialist (S) and generalist (G). For example, a traditionalist (T) would fill the requirements of a 1 (N) company while a specialist (S) would be the type of planner best suited for a 3 (N) company. In broad scope firms, more than one set of planning skills, or type of planner, is indicated. For instance, both a specialist's and a generalist's outlook on planning would be desirable for a firm in category 3 (B).

Stage of Development	**Planning Scope** Broad (B)	Narrow (N)
Diversified (Stage 3)	G + S	S
Related Products (Stage 2)	G + (T or S)	T or S
Single Product (Stage 1)	G + T	T

Figure 4. Identification of three types of planners within the planning matrix.

The duties and skills implied for each category of planner are perhaps best explained within the framework of the different styles of management. Also, it will facilitate the analysis to begin with the simpler planning needs of companies having a passive or narrow management scope.

Narrow Scope Management

Stage 1

The first level in a firm's life cycle requires the most fundamental variety of planner: the traditionalist. By a traditionalist (T) is meant a planner with a narrow functional range and where the emphasis is on planning through budgeting. The planner's functions are limited because of the company's narrowly defined mission. A company dedicated to a single product line, for example, need only plan for growth within that limited perspective. There is no need for evaluation of potential acquisitions or divestments or internal diversification into new businesses. This type of analysis would go beyond the policy determination of such a company to remain within its primary area of expertise.

The planning method is budget-oriented because this remains the principal formal approach to planning among small or simply structured firms. At this stage of development the capital budget is probably the major 'programmed procedure used in the determination of strategy'.[6] Capital budgeting integrates the projects competing for funds submitted by various departments and evaluates each project on a cost–benefit basis. Planning in this sense has been around practically since the adoption of a formal set of accounts. It requires that the planner be skilled in handling tasks traditionally of an accounting nature.

This narrow interpretation of planning is rational if the company's view of its future growth is also restricted.

For a company satisfied with its one business, the planner's function of choosing among familiar types of budget alternatives is relatively simple. Using the conventional approach of ranking investments by expected return on investment, and subject to overall budget restraints, the planner can decide which of the competing spending requests should be undertaken. The process soon becomes routine. Once the procedure of financial evaluation is formalized, the creative demands on the planner are few.

Indeed, in this environment, there is no need for a separate planning department. Since this type of financial evaluation is within the controller's area of responsibility and skills, there is similarly no need for a separate organizational title of planner. In effect, the president of the company is also its chief planner. Planning is basically geared to day-to-day operational decisions with the budgeting process providing the formal apparatus for planning. The chief accountant or financial officer of the company would undertake the required staff activities of planning although his primary function and responsibilities would be within traditional accounting/financial areas. Strategic planning, such as it is, would be based primarily on the president's intuitive judgement and experience. Since the business has a closely prescribed mission, the following analysis of the strategic planning process in small or uncomplicated firms seem reasonable:

> All in all . . . . the potentials of management science for strategic purposes seem limited to use in large companies that possess considerable technical resources for their development and use. For the foreseeable future, managements in medium-sized and small companies will have to use the generalizing, inductive, empirical method which has evolved out of the old, size-up approach. And this approach remains more an art than a science.[7]

Stage 2

The main differences between a stage 1 and a stage 2 company are complexity and size. A stage 2 company has diversified beyond a one-product orientation. It is probably larger in size. Thus, the stage 2 company would benefit more from a specialization of effort. This would be reflected in specialization of staff functions: legal, finance, marketing and personnel departments, for example. Planning would be no exception. What could formally be handled as a relatively small piece of the controller's primary function may, in a more diversified organization, be more efficiently controlled through development of a new position in the organizational structure.

A qualified 'may be' is used because a definitive answer depends on relative size and degree of operational complexity. In our simplified matrix in Figure 2, only three stages of growth are used. While this captures the essence of the growth process, it obviously masks potentially wide disparities among companies within each of the three categories.

DuPont, for example, is a giant firm which is probably a stage 2 company. Rubbermaid, a leading housewares manufacturer which is diversified into several closely related product lines, is also probably in this category. However, DuPont is roughly fifty times the size of Rubbermaid. It also has many times the number of profit centers which must be accomodated within its planning system. Correspondingly, the sheer scale of the planning function, in terms of coordinating the consistency, timeliness and adequacy of the various planning documents, becomes a considerable undertaking.

Size alone, in other words, can make a difference. Even if the apparatus of planning is budget-based, the sheer magnitute of the task would loom disporopotionately large in terms of the traditional functions of the controller in a small firm. For instance, financial modeling is one of the advanced tools of the planner in large sophisticated companies. The most useful and popular version of the financial model is one which merely consolidates the budgets of various departments or profit centers. While this clearly relies on technical skills within the capability of a modern financial officer, the scale of operations would dictate a relatively more important organizational role, either by forming a new department headed by a planning specialist (S) with separate reporting responsibilities or, if the planner is kept within the finance department, he would be elevated to a more senior position than the traditionalist (T) in our stage 1 company example.

A second factor that may force separation of the planning function within the organization is the complexity of the job. DuPont, for instance, has a relatively wide variety of major product lines, each with its own objectives, policies, strategies and organizational support. Rubbermaid, on the other hand, which may be in the same classification as DuPont, has much less disparity among its business than DuPont in terms of types of manufacturing processes, number of marketing channels variety of technical skills, sophistication in research facilities and so on.

Of these two companies, Rubbermaid may well be satisfied with a traditional planner while DuPont may seek a planning specialist. In comparison to a traditionalist, a specialist would typically be broader in scope and experienced beyond a conventional accounting background. While DuPont's businesses are related, these businesses are sufficiently complex and distinct from each other to require specific information and analysis of each. The more areas, and the more distinct these areas are from each other, the more difficult is the capital allocation process, with increasing reliance placed on non-accounting skills. For example, economic forecasters, social forecasters, technological forecasters, market researchers and market analysts, computer scientists and quantitative methods specialists are some of the advanced job skills employed by planning units in large companies with advanced planning systems. The trend in such companies is unmistakenly toward the application of a wider range of skills with particular emphasis on the application of management science to decision-making. As a consequence the specialist planner must make decisions based on inputs from a variety of disciplines, whereas the traditional planner makes primarily financial decisions using principally accounting-based inputs.

Thus, it may be appropriate for Rubbermaid to opt for a planner (T) while DuPont might choose a planner (S) even though both companies are in the same square of the planning matrix. It also follows that a company such as Rubbermaid may begin with a planner (T) and eventually shift to a planner (S) after the company has become more diversified, even though it still remains in the same classification.

This potential transition from planner (T) to planner (S) represents one of the most difficult and misunderstood organizational aspects of planning. When should the shift be made? When should planning become a separate organizational function and the corporate planner a specialist in his own right? What guidelines exist? As with most prickly questions there are no simple answers. However, understanding relationships between changes in the planning function and changes in corporate structure and strategy should help in appreciating why shifts are necessary. For example, because planning evolves from the controller's office with an accounting orientation, there is often a reluctance on the part of finance officers to give up this area of authority. Also, because analysis of plans still relies on financial inputs, and these may sometimes be the major inputs, it is difficult to convince the finance officer of the need for a separation of functions. Explaining the need is difficult without appreciating the logic behind the planning matrix. With such understanding, a basis for making an informed decision is at least available, although it may prove no more persuasive to an opinionated finance officer.

Stage 3

At stage 3, the planner is unequivocably a specialist (S). Whereas in stage 2 both a (T) and a (S) approach to planning could be rationalized, the choice for companies diversified into several unrelated industries is clear cut. Similarly, the logic of a separate organizational role for corporate planning is compelling. For one thing, the function of allocating funds among a number of disparate businesses, each with its own characteristics and potentially different life cycles, requires a focus and set of skills broader than that of the typical accountant or financial officer. This distinction between resource allocation within a single industry and among many essentially different industries creates perhaps the single most persistent pressure for establishing a separate office of corporate planning. If a company remains dedicated to a single business, there is an experience factor which can substitute for systematic planning. Judgement is the system, if you will.

Development of a sales forecast can illustrate the point. In a small company, an estimate of sales may be derived by marketing or sales personnel based on their knowledge of the customers; approximating a 'normal' increment for next year's sales consistent with the company's historic annual sales pattern. The reasonableness of the forecast can be tested by the president against his personal knowledge of the business and his intuitive judgement for ballpark figures. In a conglomerate organization, the president cannot be so intimately familiar with the variety of different businesses in which the company operates. The planning process (in this case the sales forecast) must be formalized.

An example to illustrate the point might be the development of an economic forecast. In a conglomerate, this would be a typical duty of the corporate planning staff. It could be developed internally, which would imply a commitment of considerable funds and employment of highly trained specialists, or the forecast might be developed with the aid of economic consulting services, such as Data Resources, Wharton Econometric Forecasting Associates, or Chase Econometrics. Once benchmark figures for selected economic variables are established, these become the framework within which the divisions must work. After divisional sales estimates are made, these are checked by the corporate planning staff to assure consistency with the overall growth assumptions and to test the feasibility of the divisional figures. This process may be repeated several times if disagreement persists between the specialists at the corporate level and the various personnel providing input for the sales forecast at divisional and lower levels. The end result of the process leaves little room for executive judgement. What the president eventually sees is the result of an elaborate and nearly impenetrable process, which he must accept largely on faith.

Sales forecasting is only one dimension of planning in a conglomerate organization which will differ from the less complicated world of the first executive. Large diversified firms show steady progress in adopting the more advanced and sophisticated management science techniques to the entire planning process, including such tools as input–output, linear programming, computer simulation and computer modeling. Typically the larger and more complicated the company, the more advanced are the methods.

This evolution of the corporate planner from a planner (T) using the accountant's conventional tools to a planner (S) supervising a number of functional specialists is consistent with Alfred Chandler's observations. As long as a company remains in familiar territory, it can use a traditional and familiar organizational slot to perform a limited planning role. But just as function gives way to product in the organizational structure (see Figure 1), so must a traditional planner give way to a specialist in very diversified companies.

Broad Scope Management

The principal distinction between broad and narrow planning scope is the receptivity to change. The first accepts the challenge of diversification and the associated high risks. The latter restricts its opportunities to those businesses which it now manages and which in its judgement still offer the greatest potential for profitable growth.[8]

The difference between management styles forces a distinction in planning styles. It adds the dimension of creativity to the planner's required set of skills. In Figure 4 this is indicated by the additional role of generalist (G) to that of traditionalist (T) or specialist (S) for each of the three stages of growth for broadly managed companies.

For companies locked into a particular business, the essentials of planning will eventually become formalized and the planner will become familiar with a more or less routine process requiring a specific set of technical skills. Actively managed companies, however, are continually evaluating new opportunities and thus planning for change is part of the planner's job. This involves the ability to create new ideas, new premises and new approaches to doing business. It suggests breadth over depth, vision in place of technique and the ability to think laterally, or creatively, instead of vertically and along traditional lines.

In essence the planner's role in actively managed companies attempts to combine two separate, and conflicting, objectives. The first is to plan the ongoing operations. The second is to consider ways to alter the make-up of these operations. In the first capacity, performance would be enhanced by a stable organizational structure yet in the other capacity the planner's duties work against stability.

The question arises whether an ability to function well in both environments is likely to be found in the same individual. There are reasons to believe the answer is no. First, planning ongoing operations is basically a position that demands a disciplined background, whether the skills are traditional accounting skills or sophisticated management science skills. Planning for change and addressing such questions as 'What type business should be in?' requires an ability to think outside the context of a rigorous and methodical 'learned' technique for problem-solving. Reflecting on this problem, a planner for one large manufacturing company observed that the planning job requires three basic skills . . .

> (1) analytical ability, (2) a strong degree of external orientation (to discern opportunities and problems outside the company), and (3) good communication skills.
> By and large . . . financial people are proficient in the first skill, so-so in the third, but poor in the second — by training and personality they tend to be internally oriented.[9]

These observations seem applicable to technical people generally as well as financial people in particular.

Secondly, the traditional planner and even the specialist tend to work within the system of annual planning cycles, staff-line interaction, scheduled check points and the conventional budget deadline. The generalist must be free from the pressures of coming up with solutions 'on schedule'. His is a less structured role of evaluating new directions the company might take. The decision process involves different inputs, including speculative 'futures' forecasts, special market and customer analyses and in-depth industry studies. These tasks may not easily be fit within the timetable of the annual budget; indeed, they may not fit within a fiscal or calendar year period. If the generalist is obliged to respect the conventions involved in planning the ongoing operations of the business, his creativity and originality will invariably be subordinated to the immediate problem of next year's profits.

In sum, a major organizational dilemma for actively managed companies is how to reconcile these different perspectives. One possibility is a planning officer versatile enough to be both a technician and an innovator. But he would be a rare find. More commonly, companies which have recognized this problem have separated the planning job into two departments with the duties of the generalist (mergers and acquisitions, divestitures, new ventures, analysis of competitors, etc.) separate from those of the traditionalist or specialist. Again, the planning matrix shown in Figure 2 can be helpful in bringing the problem into focus and providing a basis for its resolution.

Choosing the Right Planner for the Job

The planning matrix is designed to separate the job of planning into categories according to corporate needs. Given the types of planners—(T), (S) and (G)—it is then possible to assign the right planners to the right categories. Without the guideline of a planning matrix, mistakes is defining the corporate planning role are commonly repeated.

A familiar mistake is planner overkill. A company decides to establish a new planning department, hires a corporate planner at a high salary and then waits for 'planning' to happen. This is not an uncommon mistake for small to medium size companies to make. They are aware of impressive progress in planning methods and are reluctant to appear backward. The result is to overspecify their need.

Most U.S. companies are neither giant in size nor as complex as major conglomerates. Nor do they have the need for the sophisticated management science tools and specialized techniques on which the planning literature tends to focus. For companies of average size, plus large companies confined to a single business, the planning function should be tailored to these modest needs. A traditional planner, stressing budgets as a primary tool, should be adquate for companies making routine decisions within a fixed and familiar environment.

A mistake in the opposite direction is to stay with a planner who is a traditionalist when a specialist is indicated. Similarly, a specialist or traditionalist are seldom qualified to perform the more creative planning tasks of a generalist. Each of these three types of planners have a unique set of skills, applicable for certain stages in a corporation's life cycle. They are no more interchangeable than other functional roles within the organization. Incorrectly classifying planners and tasks will lead to less effective planning.

Consequences of Not Matching the Planner with the Job

A set of consequences resulting from failure to properly match planner and job are (a) frustration (b) insecurity and (c) misunderstanding of the role of the corporate planner.

Frustration
Frustration is practically built into the planner's job. He bears responsibility for making executive level decisions but lacks the authority of the chief executive officer. A top-notch planner may require the qualifications of the chief executive officer yet must be discrete enough to avoid seeming to infringe on the chief executive officer's authority. When top management is deficient in credentials for long range strategic planning—preoccupied with short-term results, steadfastly conservative or arbitrary in arriving at decisions—the built-in frustrations become even more noticeable.

If, in addition, the corporate planner is the wrong person for the job he will chafe even more. Thus a super planner hired to do a job a competent budget analyst might handle will inevitably be frustrated. Management may have hired him to decorate the company's annual report or to impress the board of directors. Whatever the reason, whether a conscious act of overstaffing or a faulty diagnosis of the company's needs, the end result is soon a planner at odds with the system he is supposed to head.

Insecurity
Planners are a major bellwether of the business cycle. When business is good, the demand for planners is up. When business is bad, planners are among the first to feel the brunt. If the reports and ads of executive search firms can be believed, the job market for planners may be an undiscovered leading economic indicator.

Many reasons contribute to the cyclicality of the job. Among these is the view that planners are an 'affordable' service in good times but, like advertising and R & D, one of the early casualties when business turns bad. In addition, when a planner feels uncomfortable or unsuited to the position he holds it is a pretty safe bet that he does not have too strong a hold on that position.

Misunderstanding of the planning role
A further inherent danger in the planner's job is the human inability to deliver all that management anticipates. Because planning deals with future change, and the future is unpredictable, there is no such thing as the perfect plan or the perfect planner. To the extent that management expects perfection, it is due to be disappointed. And if management is too often disappointed by too large a margin, it may question the ability of the planner rather than the events. For example, few if any planners were able to foresee the extent of the problems in energy prices, materials shortages, general price inflation or sustained unemployment. A mitigating circumstance is that few if any experts of any stripe were able to foresee such major disruptions. Yet if management's expectations are geared to expect more than planners are able to deliver, the planner may be indicted regardless of the circumstances.

Again, the misunderstanding of the planning role is traceable to reasons other than miscasting. However, a planner who is suited to the position he occupies would be better able to fend off such criticisms. He would, for example, be more likely to create unrealistic expectations if he were paid a huge salary but conducted a traditional budget-style plan than if the circumstances were reversed.

The Organizational Strains of Change

Thus far the planning matrix has been used to demonstrate what is intuitively logical—planners differ among companies. It has been useful as a device classifying the three types of planners which have been identified. It has also given some insight into the reasons for familiar complaints of frustration, insecurity and disenchantment on the part of the corporate planner. These symptoms can be traced in part to management's failure to adhere to the rationale of the matrix, such as:

☆ employing a (T) to do the work of a (S), or vice-versa;

☆ employing a (T) and/or (S) to do the work of a (G) or vice-versa.

These are classification errors. The wrong type of planner is placed in the wrong square. Because the planning matrix is basically a static model, it focuses attention on errors of classification. But an overriding organizational dilemma that some corporate planners face is due to the dynamics of change.

For example, a planner who is correctly placed to begin with may have the job description change because the company has changed positions within the matrix. One possibility would be a shift from passive to active management of a company, which would mean leaving one frame of reference and going to another and, as a consequence, shifting from one level of planning need to another. A traditional planner, adequate for a firm at the first stage of development, may be forced into the role as an innovative planner as well, a position for which he is neither qualified, not a position he was expected to fill when first hired.

The pace as well as the direction of change can contribute to the organizational strains on the planner's role. G & W is a company which evolved from a relatively small automotive supply company into a complex conglomerate in a relatively short period of time. The swiftness of the vertical ascent through the various stages of development undoubtedly altered the function of corporate planning, and indirectly the qualifications of the person to hold that position. FMC is a company at the same level of development as G & W, but FMC is a mature conglomerate in the sense of management's election to remain at the present level of diversification. This management decision implicitly redefines the planner's function, according to the matrix, from one requiring a (S + G) capability to a (S) type of planner. It would make obsolete the position of generalist, in other words, as a consequence of the lateral movement from active to passive strategic management. It also provides insight into a unique risk in being a generalist; that is, the cyclical nature of innovative planning: a need arises and a planner is hired, but once the company reaches the desired development stage the rationale for the job disappears, and so, in some instances, does the corporate planner.

The hypothetical planner in either of the above situations would have had to adjust within relatively short time spans to dramatic changes in organizational structure and policy, with each major switch potentially disruptive to the job of the corporate planner. These cases illustrate the potential risks for the corporate planner in fastgrowth success stories. In addition, there is a risk in companies which have grown too fast to last: companies which overdiversified in the '60s, for instance, and were busy returning to their fundamental businesses in the early '70s.

Rohr is a company which began a program of diversification around 1970, including development of rapid transit systems for metropolitan areas, acquistion of an Ohio manufacturer of city buses and acquistion of the U.S. subsidiary of two French companies which was involved in new technology to be applied to rail travel. By 1976 Rohr had decided to leave these new fields, which were providing to be a financial disaster, and return to its original businesses of aircraft and marine equipment. Boise Cascade, American Standard and Westinghouse, among others, also threw their diversification programs into reverse in order to return to a less complicated organizational structure emphasizing fewer major fields.

The planner's job can be inherently unstable if the company continues in flux. The more change, the more likelihood that a planner's job will be redefined in a new organizational structure. Oddly enough, the planner, who is an agent for change, may become its victim. Planners in several corporations have supported the view that turnover in the job may be inevitable; in their opinion, a prognosis that can apply whether the company is swiftly changing or not changing at all.

> As the planning process passes through various stages from inception to maturity, different talents and types of personality are required in the position of corporate planner.[10]

A problem for the planner in the dynamic, actively managed company.

> Boredom or frustration will sooner or later afflict the corporate planner.[10]

A possible problem for the planner in the stable, conservatively managed company.

The planning matrix should permit management to make better choices on job assignments. It will not eliminate job stress for the corporate planner. Nor will the decisions be necessarily easy ones for management to make. Should a generalist who planned a company through a critical expansion phase, and who is consequently now redundant, be callously dismissed for a job too well done? At what point should a traditionalist be replaced by a specialist? Assuming a competent traditional planner, would not a familiar format and a knowledgeable insider offset the risks of hiring an outsider with new ideas? Moreover, the theoretical efficiency gained from a change of planners may not be judged to be worth the practical costs in personnel turnover and dislocations.

The planning matrix does not attempt to deal with the human behavioural aspects of organizational change, although management may decide to ignore the matrix for such reasons. In such instances, the subjective reasoning of management would overshadow the objective logic of the matrix. But the evidence points in the other direction. An absence of literature in this area suggests the reasons for decisions are instinctive rather than methodical.

Conclusion

The normal prescriptions for corporate planning are abstract. They generally ignore size of firm, complexity of structure and style of management. It is therefore not unusual that what works in theory often fits imperfectly in the thousands of firms which are exceptions to the general model.

Two elements are introduced in order to provide a logical framework for identifying levels of planning needs with types of planners to fill those needs. The first is called a planning matrix: a grid with six separate planning modes which identify the level of planning need of a company based on its stage of development and style of management. The second distinguishes among three different types of corporate planners and assigns each to an appropriate square within the planning matrix. These two aids permit management to increase planning effectiveness. They identify the type of planner to do the job and the type of planning job there is to do. They also provide insights into why the nature of the planning function produces a considerable organizational dilemma for individual companies and planners.

References

(1) A. A. Chandler, Jr., *Strategy and Structure: Chapters in History of the American Industrial Enterprise,* Cambridge, Mass., The M.I.T. Press, 1962.

(2) R. P. Rumelt, *Strategy, Structure, and Economic Performance,* Division of Research, Boston, Harvard Business School, 1970.

(3) M. Leontiades, Planning: a reexamination of fundamentals, *Journal of Economics and Business*, Spring–Summer, 1976.

(4) Leontiades, Planning: a reexamination of fundamentals, *ibid*.

(5) *Business Week*, July 12, 1976, p. 23.

(6) H. Mintzberg, The Science of Strategy-Making, *Industrial Management Review*, Fall (1967).

(7) F. F. Gilmore, *Formulative Strategy in Smaller Companies*, Harvard Business Review, May/June, 1971.

(8) Leontiades, Planning: a reexamination of fundamentals. *ibid*.

(9) *Planning and the Corporate Planning Director*, The Conference Board, Report No. 627, 1974, p. 65.

(10) *Planning and the Corporate Planning Director*, p. 63.

How to Integrate Strategic Planning into your Management Process

Thomas H. Naylor, Duke University

The primary purpose of strategic planning is to enable management to make decisions today which will affect the firm over the long run where the long run is characterized by risk and uncertainty. If strategic planning is to be useful to management it must be an integral part of the decision making process and not merely an appendage to the management process. In this paper we shall define some of the problems involved in integrating strategic planning and strategic planning tools into the decision process. We shall also suggest some possible solutions to these problems.

From Entrepreneurial Management to Mature Management

In many companies the principal obstacle to the integration of strategic planning into the management process is the CEO. This is particularly true of entrepreneurial companies which have enjoyed a high rate of growth without the aid of any kind of formal strategic planning system.

Consider the case of McDonald's which has enjoyed a phenomenal growth record during its first 25 years of existence. The company consistently increases its sales and profits by nearly 20 per cent per year. It has no corporate planning department and has never had any type of formal strategic plan. Yet the company's strategic plan can clearly be inferred from a cursory reading of the company's annual report. First, keep the product line simple and resist any significant changes in the product line. Second, do not diversify. Third, spend substantial sums of money on advertising. Fourth, expand the international market. Fifth, open 500 new stores each year.

The author is Director of the Corporate Economics Program, Duke University, Durham, North Carolina, U.S.A.

That this strategy has been successful for McDonald's is an indisputable fact. Indeed, the issue is not whether or not McDonald's should have strategic planning. It has always had a strategic plan—a very successful strategic plan. The real question is 'As the firm continues to grow and mature will it be sufficient in the future for the strategic plan to reside only in the mind of the CEO or will it become necessary to formalize the strategic plan so that it is fully understood by all of the line managers?'

The transition from an entrepreneurial company to a mature company is a difficult transition for many senior executives to make. The degree to which strategic planning will be integrated into the management process will be highly dependent on the CEO's ability to make such a transition. Perhaps some of the arguments set forth in this paper will make it easier for skeptical CEOs to perceive the absolute necessity of their playing a key role in the integration of strategic planning into the decision process.

The Problem of Integration

The problem of integrating strategic planning into the management process has been succinctly captured in George A. Steiner's list of 'ten major traps to be avoided'.[6]

(1) Top management's assumption that it can delegate the planning function to the planner.

(2) Top management becomes so engrossed in current problems that it spends insufficient time on long range planning, and the process becomes discredited among other managers and staff.

(3) Failure to develop company goals suitable as a basis for formulating long range plans.

(4) Failure to assume the necessary involvement in the planning process of major line personnel.

(5) Failure to use plans as standards for measuring managerial performance.

(6) Failure to create a climate in the company which is congenial and not resistant to planning.

(7) Assuming that corporate comprehensive planning is something separate from the entire management process.

(8) Injecting so much formality into the system that it lacks flexibility, looseness, and simplicity, and restrains creativity.

(9) Failure of top management to review with departmental and divisional heads the long range plans which they have developed.

(10) Top management's consistently rejecting the formal planning mechanism by making intuitive decisions which conflict with formal plans.

It goes without saying, that the avoidance of these ten traps will enable a company to make an enormous leap forward in the direction of achieving a truly integrated planning system.

The Problem of Coordination

A problem which is closely related to the problem of integration is the problem of coordinating strategic plans among different divisions, profit centers, or departments. In one company where we helped design a strategic planning system we found no less than ten different mutually exclusive plans—a marketing plan, a real estate plan, a purchasing plan, a new products plan, a store operations plan, an annual profit plan, a personnel plan, and three different long term financial plans. Each of these plans was developed independently of the others. No effort had been made to either coordinate or integrate any aspect of these diverse plans. Obviously strategic plans developed in the manner described above are of limited value since they are not directly linked to overall corporate goals, objectives, and strategies.

One major reason for formalizing strategic planning at all levels within the company is to make sure that all of the operating units of the company are marching to the beat of the same drummer. The coordination of the planning activities of the company represents one of the most important functions of the corporate planning department.

Hierarchical Organization
The coordination of planning activities in a hierarchical organization tends to be somewhat more straightforward than that of a matrix type organization. Even so, for certain types of process industries the problem of coordination can be quite formidable. Electric utilities are a case in point.

Figure 1 contains a flowchart illustrating how the Tennessee Valley Authority[3] integrates the following six functions of strategic planning—load forecasting, power resource planning, transmission planning, construction planning, technology forecasting, and financial planning. Prior to the development of an integrated planning system at TVA each of these functions was carried out by a different department. It is impossible to do strategic planning for an electric utility, if each of the aforementioned planning functions is carried out independently without the benefit of coordination by top management. When Georgia Power Company, a member of a four-utility holding company, set out to develop its own strategic planning system a few years ago, it became necessary to coordinate its activities with its parent company, the Southern Company, and the other three utilities in the group. Developing a stand alone planning system for a single company belonging to an integrated power network is an impossible task.

Matrix Organization
In a matrix organization managers typically have two bosses—a functional manager and a product or business team manager. Accounting, budgeting, and strategic planning are much more complex within a matrix since it becomes necessary to have dual accounting, budgeting, and planning systems for a matrix. That is, we must have a functional planning and budgeting system and a planning and budgeting system organized along product or business lines. Managers must develop dual plans which satisfy both functional and product managers. The coordination and integration of strategic plans within a matrix organization requires considerable patience and skill on the part of the matrix managers and the CEO. A company which has overcome many of the obstacles to planning within a matrix organization is the Shell Oil Company.

The Integration of the Strategic Plan into Project Plans and Operating Plans

Both project plans and operating plans or budgets should be driven by the long term strategic plan. Project plans might inlcude plans to introduce a new product, construct a new plant, or acquire a major piece of equipment. All project plans should be based on goals and objectives which are consistent with the goals and objectives of the strategic plan. Operating plans and budgets should reflect the short term implications of specific project plans.

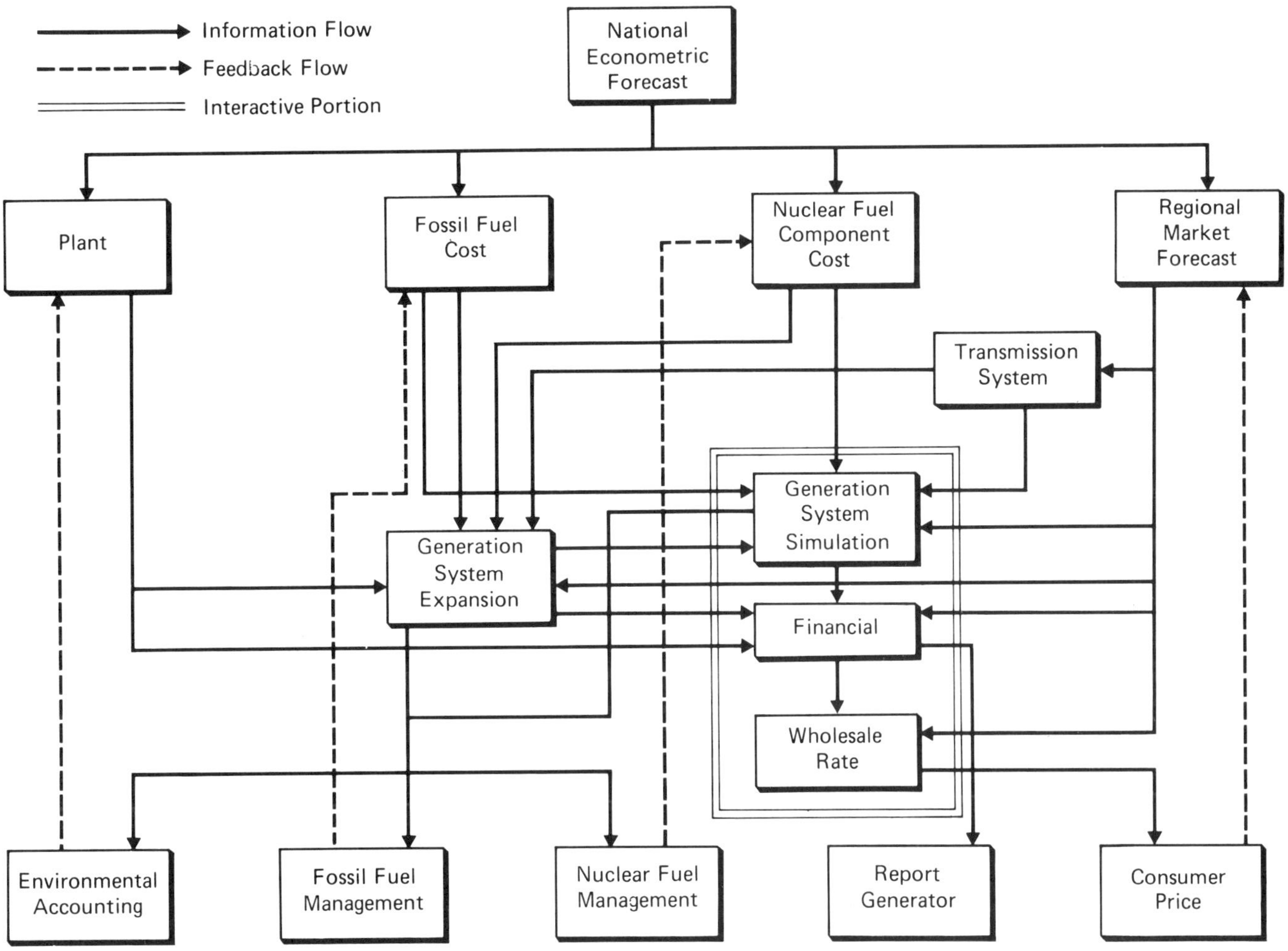

Figure 1. The Tennessee valley authority strategic system

A key role of the corporate planning department is to point out to top management certain inconsistencies which may crop up in both project plans and operating plans in light of given strategic plans. As always, the CEO has the ultimate responsibility for integrating strategic plans, project plans, and operating plans. Hence, the ability of the CEO to accomplish this mission may be strongly influenced by the level of scrutiny provided by the corporate planning department in reviewing the plans of the operating units.

The Integration of Analytical Planning Tools into the Planning Process

Despite dramatic increases in the usage of computer-based planning models since 1970, relatively few corporations have successfully integrated their planning models into the planning process. In many cases, planning models are treated as though they were merely mathematical appendages to the planning process rather than tools to be integrated into the planning process. The failure to integrate planning models into the planning process has severely limited the usefulness of some models as planning tools. All too little attention has been given in the past to the problem of designing planning models to meet the specific planning requirements of a particular company.

A few organizations have been successful in their efforts to integrate business planning models into the planning process. They include Northwest Industries,[4] Ross Laboratories,[4] *The New York Times*,[3] CIBA-GEIGY[3] and Lever Brothers.[2] Without exception, the goal of integrating the business planning model into the planning process was accomplished by each of these organizations only through a deliberate, well-planned effort to implement a truly integrated planning and modeling system. Such a goal is not easily reached.

One of the many benefits of a planning audit is that it provides the necessary information to design computer based planning tools in direct response to the specific needs of senior management. If the analysts know exactly what management wants and expects from their planning tools, then it is indeed quite possible to develop planning tools that will actually be used by management to facilitate the planning process.

This approach was successfully employed with the senior management of Northwest Industries[4] several years ago to develop a corporate planning model. From the outset, management insisted that they were quite satisfied with the existing manual planning system and merely wanted to acquire the capability to answer strategic 'What if?' questions much faster than in the past.

A planning audit was conducted to ascertain precisely

(1) What type of reports management wanted from the computer based model and

(2) what kinds of 'What if?' questions needed to be answered by the system.

Prior to building the model, the design specifications (based on the management interviews) were reviewed with management for final approval. When the pilot model was presented to the executive group, there could be little doubt of its acceptance, since the model had been designed exactly to management's specifications. That the model was used extensively as an integral part of the planning process came as no surprise to anyone.

Figure 2 contains a flowchart of an integrated planning process for a multi-divisional company. We shall briefly indicate how computer based modeling might be integrated into such a planning process.

Computer based planning models can provide management with an effective means of evaluating alternative goals and objectives, testing the feasibility of achieving them, and detecting logical inconsistencies in conflicting goals and objectives.

Many companies employ national econometric forecasting models to generate macroeconomic scenarios describing the economy. Non-economic scenarios must be based on management's experience and knowledge of the firm's social, political and competitive environment. Models may also be used to evaluate the effects of alternative external assumptions on the behavior of a particular division or the company as a whole.

Prior to presenting overall corporate strategies to line management, corporate executives should subject these corporate strategies to some type of 'What if?' analysis. Again, computer based planning models can play an important supporting role.

As the general managers of the divisions develop

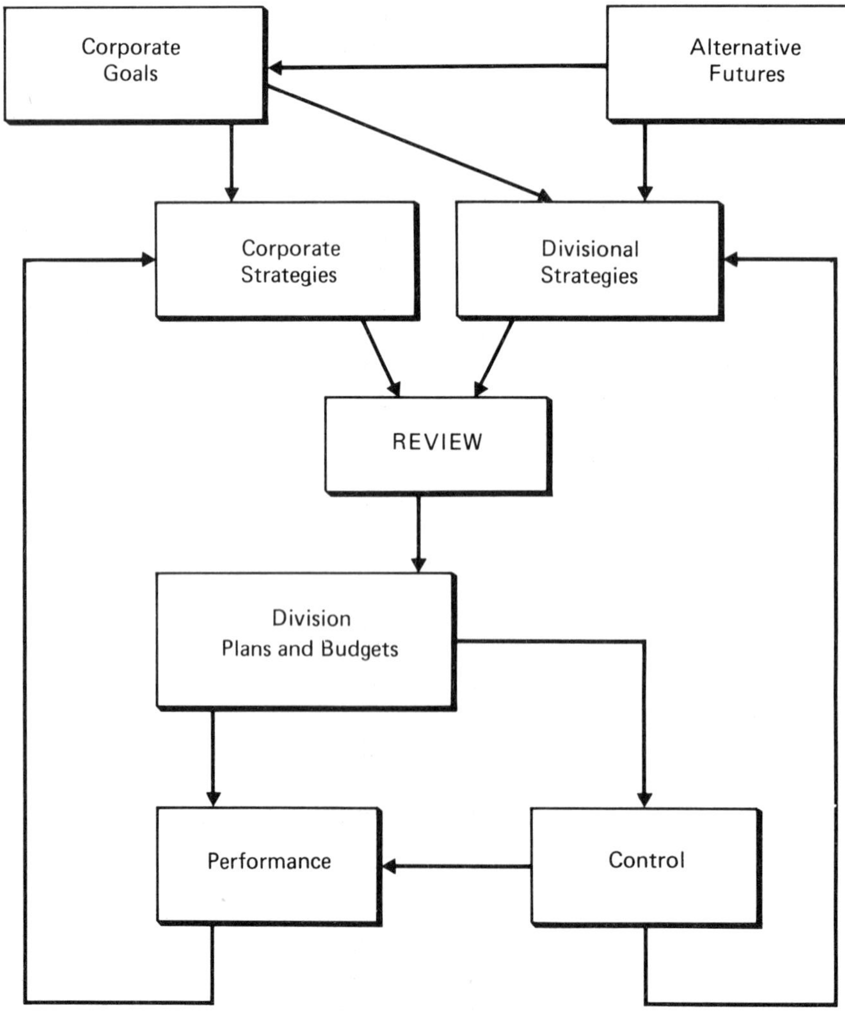

Figure 2. An integrated planning process for a multi-divisional company

their own strategic plans, they too may find it useful to use computer based planning models to evaluate the impact of alternative division strategies in light of given corporate goals and objectives and given assumptions about the company's external environment.

When division plans are reviewed and evaluated by the corporate planning department and by the executive group, then the ability to answer strategic 'What if?' questions again becomes critical.

Companies such as Lowndes-Ajax, *The New York Times*,[3] TRANSCO, Santa Fe Railroad[4] and Canadian National Railways[4] have been introduced to computer based modeling by using computer software systems[3] such as SIMPLAN[1] to help mechanize the budgeting process. Much of the drudgery of budgeting can be reduced through the use of computer based modeling techniques. The new higher level planning languages make it possible to do a wide variety of different types of financial consolidations thus greatly facilitating the entire budgeting process.

Finally, computers are quite useful in producing reports comparing actual results with target results included in budgets and strategic plans. This latter type of information makes it possible to implement the necessary control systems required to make planning effective over the long run.

The Relationship Between Strategic Planning and Decision Making

The most severe test of a strategic planning system is whether or not top management and line managers will actually make decisions based on the strategic plan. If top management consistently ignores the strategic plan when making important operating decisions then the entire exercise may have been in vain.

The role of the 'planning diplomat' is to help motivate senior management not only to participate in the design of a planning system but to use strategic plans as a basis for decisions. One way to motivate results oriented executives that strategic planning is worth the effort required is by constantly reminding them that the existence of a strategic plan will make it much easier to make short run operating decisions. If this point can be sold to busy executives who are preoccupied with the present, then the acceptance and use of strategic planning will have taken a giant step forward.

In the following section we shall outline a number of necessary conditions for integrating strategic planning into the decision making process.

Necessary Conditions for Implementing a Strategic Planning System

There appears to be a number of necessary conditions for integrating a strategic planning system into the management process. We shall find it convenient to classify these conditions as organizational, technical support and communications.

Organizational Development

Top Management Support

That top management support is a necessary condition for integrating strategic planning into the decision making process is so obvious it is almost a cliche. If the CEO is not committed to using strategic planning as a vehicle for improving the quality of short term decision making then there is little point in pursuing the matter further. The CEO has got to believe in planning and must have confidence in its usefulness as an aid to more effective decision making. Georgia Power Company, Northwest Industries and Santa Fe Industries are examples of companies with effective strategic planning systems which enjoy strong support from top management.

A somewhat extreme example of what can happen when the CEO is not committed to corporate planning occurred recently in a large Chicago based company. A planning audit of 24 of the top 25 executives of the company was conducted. The 25th executive, the CEO, refused to be interviewed. The support for the proposed planning system by those participating in the audit was unanimous. A vice president of strategic planning was appointed. A director of planning was hired as well. A staff of five people was put in place. A computer software system and a national econometric model were acquired.

For 2 months the CEO ignored the planning department. Then one day he suddenly and without any warning killed the entire planning project. All of the members of the planning staff were fired and all of the planning systems were put on the shelf. The CEO viewed the planning audit and the planning department which evolved as a type of palace revolt and a threat to his political power.

Albeit a somewhat extreme example, this case once again illustrates the critical role of the CEO in the survival of any type of strategic planning system.

Line Management Support

If, on the other hand strategic planning is viewed entirely as a top down exercise imposed on line management by corporate management, then the planning system is in deep trouble before it gets off the ground. For planning to be effective it must involve the participation and active support of *all* line managers. The planning process must be a joint venture between the corporate executive group and the general managers of the major operating units. Without this type of cooperation, integration of the planning system into the management process is obviously impossible.

The managers who are on the firing line on a day by day basis are the managers of the various businesses of the company. Without their enthusiastic commitment there will be no strategic planning process.

Incentives
In the previous paragraphs we have emphasized the importance of the commitment of top management and line managers to strategic planning. But what will motivate top management and line managers to be committed to strategic planning? This is not an easy question to answer. Ideally managers will be motivated to plan as a means of more effectively coping with the risk and uncertainty in the company's external environment.

If line managers are rewarded for achieving the results promised in their strategic plan, they will be motivated to take planning seriously. Alternatively, if top management appears to be indifferent as to whether targets are met or not, then line managers will surely get the message that planning is not important and is not to be taken seriously. In other words, the incentives have got to be right, if planning is going to work at the operating unit level.

Likewise, top management is not likely to be completely immune to incentives or the lack thereof. Although many CEOs are self-starters and need no further incentive to embrace strategic planning, it definitely helps, if the board of directors is committed to strategic planning. In these days of increased financial liability for corporate directors, one cannot help but wonder why more corporate boards do not participate more actively in the initial stages of the planning process. The number of companies in which board members play a major role in the strategic planning process seems to be quite small.

Relevancy of Issues
It goes without saying that strategic plans must address those issues which are deemed to be important by senior corporate executives and line managers. If strategic planning is perceived as unrealistic, 'blue sky' thinking, then the likelihood of success is virtually nil.

Companies such as Abbott Labs, TVA, Georgia Power, Shell Oil, and Northwest Industries have used a type of planning audit[2,3] to provide input from top management to minimize the risk associated with this type of problem. If the planning audit is conducted properly, then management's priorities concerning the relevant strategic issues should be quite clear.

Technical Support
Another necessary condition for integrating strategic planning into the decision process is adequate technical support from the management science, planning, and data processing staffs. Without good technical support the entire system may collapse thus setting the cause of formal strategic planning back at least 3 years. In many companies the adequacy of technical support for strategic planning is directly proportional to the commitment of the CEO.

Communications
Finally, the degree to which strategic planning can be integrated into the decision process within a company depends to a great extent on the quality of communications between line managers and corporate management. If strategic plans are not properly communicated to decision makers who need this type of information to make operational decisions, then both the decision making process and the credibility of strategic planning will suffer.

References

(1) R. Britton Mayo, *Corporate Planning and Modeling with SIMPLAN*, Addison-Wesley, Reading, MA (1979).

(2) Thomas H. Naylor, *The Politics of Corporate Planning and Modeling*, Planning Executives Institute, Oxford, Ohio (1978).

(3) Thomas H. Naylor, *Corporate Planning Models*, Addison-Wesley, Reading, MA (1979).

(4) Thomas H. Naylor, *Simulation Models in Corporate Planning*, Praeger, New York (1979).

(5) Thomas H. Naylor, *Strategic Planning Management*, Planning Executives Institute, Oxford, Ohio (1980).

(6) George A. Steiner, *Pitfalls in Comprehensive Long Range Planning*, Planning Executives Institute, Oxford, Ohio (1972).

PART TWO

Specific Aspects and Relationships

Corporate Environmental Analysis in Large U.S. Corporations

John Diffenbach, Associate Professor, Northeastern University, Boston

Executives in companies without organized environmental analysis might wonder whether they should implement such activities. Those in companies having organized environmental analysis activities might wonder what they can do to make them more useful. In both cases, the executives would probably be interested in knowing more about the practice of organized environmental analysis in other firms, its usefulness, problems of implementation, and the payoffs. These are the questions addressed in this article.

Corporate environmental analysis has to do with detecting, interpreting and responding to external social, political, technological and economic trends. Most firms practice some form of environmental analysis as part of their strategic management process. Some are quite informal about it, relying heavily on their key executives to keep abreast of the external business environment through newspapers, trade literature and personal contacts. Other firms have organized their environmental analysis effort into structured activities with such things as the formal development of environmental scenarios, Delphi studies and business environment staffs. For the purpose of this article, the latter will be referred to as *organized* environmental analysis.

The findings and conclusions presented here are based primarily on a questionnaire survey of large U.S. industrial firms. Interpretation of the survey data, however, is certainly influenced by other research as well as consulting experiences of the author in the area of environmental analysis.

The survey produced many practical insights. Environmental analysis, it seems, is considered very useful, but it frequently is not done well. Doing a good job is no simple or easy matter. While there are potentially significant payoffs to companies performing environmental analysis, such payoffs are by no means assured. In fact, corporate executives can expect to encounter major obstacles in making their environmental analysis efforts truly effective. Environmental analysis activities appear to be more common in the larger firms. There is also evidence to suggest that the level of effort expended on environmental analysis is highest at the top corporate level of an organization, and higher for short-range than for long-range planning. Depending upon the particular firm, environmental activities served different *uses* and *users*. It also appears that the usefulness of the activity in a firm is positively correlated with the organization level of the primary users. These findings and others will be presented and discussed in more detail later.

The focus of the survey was on *organized* as opposed to *informal* environmental analysis activities by large corporations. The difference is one of degree, and one not always very obvious. Thus, it can be difficult to classify those activities on the borderline of organized and informal approaches, or those containing elements of both.

A brief overview of the evolution of corporate environmental analysis follows, after which the survey findings and implications are discussed.

I. Evolution of Corporate Environmental Analysis

The emergence of the subject of corporate environmental analysis was marked by what might appropriately be labeled as an *appreciation* phase—during the mid to late 1960s. Both professional and academic interest in the subject increased rapidly. There was almost an air of discovery—the discovery of what seemed certain to be an increasingly vital dimension of corporate management. Much of the literature served to instill an

---

The author is Associate Professor at the College of Business Administration, Northeastern University, Boston, MA 02115, U.S.A.
This article is based on research supported in part by grants from Northeastern University College of Business Administration and Boston College School of Management.

appreciation of the total external business environment with its economic, technological, social and political components.[1–5] A common message was to 'remove the blinders' and look beyond short-term market conditions when assessing the external business environment. Such terms as 'business and society', and 'corporate social responsibility' became widespread. And, indeed, these concepts had their roots in the social unrest that swept this country in the 1960s.

As appreciation began to take hold, more attention turned to *analysis* of the environment. Analysis involves finding reliable sources of environmental data, compiling and examining the data to discern trends, developments and key relationships. It also includes monitoring environmental developments and anticipating the future. Thus in the late 1960s and early 1970s, there was an increase in books and articles on environmental scanning,[6–8] scenarios,[9–10] Delphi projections,[11–14] cross-impact analysis, [15,16] input–output analysis,[17] socio-technological forecasting (Abt, 1970) and environmental forecasting.[18] It was clear that corporations had to do more than simply appreciate their environments, they had to increase their environmental intelligence.

As interest intensified in the analysis of environmental information, there evolved the third and current phase—the *application* phase. The challenge here to corporations is one of integrating the results of the analysis with strategic management. All the appreciation and analysis will not make a difference if executives cannot apply or relate it when making strategic decisions. Too often studies of the environment were prepared by corporate staff groups who were not familiar with the information needs of the line executives who ultimately decide corporate strategy. It was not surprising, then, that thick, broad-ranging, futuristic reports of environmental trends and information often received little more than cursory glances by the latter.

It was perhaps natural that the early interest in application focused on developing *long term* strategies which took into account anticipated environmental trends and new developments over the next 5–10 years, or even longer. More recently, however, there has been increased interest in developing short term strategies of flexibility within the context of basic long term directions (see, for example, Quinn[19]). A major reason is the perceived uncertainty of external developments. It seems that to more and more executives, the essence of environmental responsiveness is strategic flexibility, not accuracy of long term projections.

In summary, corporate environmental analysis has exhibited three phases—appreciation, analysis and application. It is important for a company to know which phase it is in. If it is still in the appreciation phase, it must realize that there is much more to be done and that it has not begun to tap the full potential of a mature environmental analysis activity.

II. Survey Findings

The ensuing discussion draws heavily from the author's questionnaire survey* of Fortune 500 firms concerning their corporate environmental analysis activities.

The objective of the survey was to obtain information on *organized* environmental analysis activities, specifically the use, usefulness, deterrents and payoffs of such activities. Organized activity was defined in the questionnaire as 'an organized activity programmed to *scan* the external business environment for information of strategic significance, and to somehow facilitate the *use* of this information by those in the company who are involved in strategic decisions'. 'We mean more than simply planning for economic factors, but planning for some non-economic (political, social and technological) factors as well. We do *not* mean the informal efforts of individuals, acting on their own, to keep abreast of the external environment.' (Note: Such informal approaches might very well be effective, perhaps more so than organized approaches, but for the purpose of this study only the latter were of interest.)

The external business environment was defined as consisting of 'those trends and factors external to your company that have strategic implications for your company'. 'These trends might be of a social, political, technological or economic origin.' 'We are *not* talking about external events that have *only* a day-to-day operational impact upon your company, i.e. events that have an operational impact but are not indicative of a trend of strategic import.'

Eight-page questionnaires were mailed to the presidents of the *Fortune 500* industrials. There were no follow-up inquiries. Twenty companies replied that their policy was not to respond to questionnaires. Twenty-four companies reported that they did not engage in organized environmental analysis as defined. Sixty-six companies responded that they did have organized environmental analysis.

The survey provided information on the following aspects of organized environmental analysis: (1) the number of firms applying it, (2) its perceived usefulness, (3) the process, and (4) deterrents to effective application.

---

*Although the survey was conducted in 1977, more recent research and consulting by the author indicates that these previously unpublished survey findings are still very relevant today with the exception that perhaps a larger percentage of firms are practising organized environmental analysis today.

Number of Firms Applying Organized Environmental Analysis

Seventy-three Per Cent of the Responding Companies Reported that they Perform Organized Environmental Analysis.* Sixteen per cent reported that they do not have organized environmental analysis, but 'they probably should have'. Eleven per cent do not have it and saw no need for it. The remaining 10 firms (11 per cent) did not practice environmental analysis and did not see a need to do so.

This usage frequency indicates that the application of organized environmental analysis is widespread but not close to being a universal practice even among firms in the Fortune 500 size group.

Further, *it appeared that the larger the company in terms of sales level, the more likely it is to do environmental analysis.* Not only was the affirmative response rate higher for the larger firms, but so was the questionnaire return rate higher also. This is probably because a firm *not* engaged in environmental analysis would be less likely to return the questionnaire than one that is.

Perceived Usefulness
The survey findings further suggest that *although environmental analysis is widely practiced and found to be important by a large majority of those who do it, a significant number did not do it or did it but did not find it very useful.* Twenty-five per cent of the firms reporting on 'usefulness of their environmental analysis activity' rated their efforts as *crucial*, 48 per cent as *important but not crucial*, and 28 per cent as only *of some value*.† Future usefulness (next 5 years) was seen as being even greater. From another view, however, it is significant to note that only 44 of all 90 responding firms found the activity to be at least important to them. Further, because of the possible human tendency to justify ongoing practices, it is conceivable that the usefulness ratings are overstated.

Although the larger firms were more likely to perform organized environmental analysis, as noted above, they did not report it to be more useful than did the smaller (under $1m in sales) firms. In fact, the summary of responses in Table 2 suggest that environmental analysis may be more useful to the smaller of the Fortune 500 firms.

Table 1. Summary of survey responses by company sales level

Sales level[2] ($bn)	Total company responses	Number of companies having OEA[1] activities	Number of companies not having OEA[1] activities	Percentage of companies having OEA[1] activities
Over $4·0	20	17	3	85
$2·0–3·9	13	11	2	85
$1·0–1·9	25	22	3	88
$0·5–0·9	18	8	10	44
$0·3–0·4	14	8	6	57
All 90 firms	90	66	24	73

[1]OEA: Organized environmental analysis.
[2]Ranges of sales levels were chosen so that successive higher ranges are approximately multiples of two (except for the highest range).

Table 2. Summary of responses on the perceived usefulness of organized environmental analysis

Sales level ($bn)	Number of companies reporting usefulness	Percentage of companies reporting the three levels of usefulness noted: Crucial	Important but not crucial	Of some value	Total
Over $4·0	16	13	56	31	100
$2·0–3·9	11	27	36	36	100[1]
$1·0–1·9	18	17	61	22	100
$0·5–0·9	8	50	25	25	100
$0·3–0·4	8	38	38	25	100[1]
All 61 firms	61	25	48	28	100

[1]Because of rounding, the percentages of the individual do not add to 100%.

Further insights on 'usefulness' were revealed by the questionnaire comments on *payoffs* of organized environmental analysis. The question was 'what have been the major payoffs, if any, from your company's environmental analysis activity?' *Seven types of payoffs were identified as follows:*

☆ Increased general awareness by management of environmental changes.

☆ Better strategic planning and decision-making.

☆ Greater effectiveness in government matters.

☆ Better industry and market analysis.

☆ Better results in foreign business.

☆ Sound diversification and resource allocation decisions.

☆ Better energy planning.

*There were 90 responding companies which returned questionnaires. Sixty-six (73 per cent) of them reported having an environmental analysis activity.

†Sixty-one of the 66 firms responding affirmatively reported on usefulness.

A representative selection of specific payoff comments is listed in Table 3. There is a wide variety of examples, ranging from the intangible (e.g. disposition to acting in advance of change) to those that relate to specific actions (e.g. development of new energy-efficient glass-forming process). Obviously, many of the payoffs cannot be easily quantified in dollar value. Thus, it makes no more sense to judge environmental analysis in terms of dollar payoff than it does corporate R & D. In a practical sense, the value of environmental analysis will be a matter of how much more confident it makes executives in their strategic decisions.

The Process

The questionnaire solicited information about various aspects of the organized environmental

Table 3. Representative comments regarding payoffs of organized environmental analysis

The following list incorporates a representative selection of the questionnaire comments on the payoffs of organized environmental analysis. The actual comments have been paraphrased and grouped into categories.

Increased general awareness by management of environmental changes

- ☆ Improved ability to anticipate long-term problems and make adjustments earlier than otherwise
- ☆ Increasing responsiveness of operations programs to environmental concerns
- ☆ Awareness of top level management to a range of possible futures and how they might affect the company
- ☆ A noticeable tendency for managers to ask themselves if the same approaches used in the past will work in the future
- ☆ Disposition to acting in advance of change

Better strategic planning and decision-making

- ☆ Plans and decisions that reflect a greater awareness of political events and economic cycles, and therefore more flexibility and adaptiveness
- ☆ Development of contingency plans
- ☆ More disciplined planning
- ☆ Broadened scope of perspectives, so that one can understand the relevance of external conditions to the business of the company
- ☆ Lengthened planning/decision horizon
- ☆ Gradual and continued incorporation of environmental factors into the corporate decision-making process
- ☆ Improved ability to allocate strategic resources to opportunities created by environmental change
- ☆ Improved ability to anticipate long-term problems and make adjustments earlier
- ☆ Divisions' product plan awareness of social trends, ecology, shifts in population age profile, geographic migration, and the position of women
- ☆ Wide acceptance of the necessity for a common set of environmental assumptions as a basis for formal planning activities
- ☆ Avoidance of crises

Greater effectiveness in government matters

- ☆ Better government relations and understanding of the role of government
- ☆ Greater success in winning government contracts
- ☆ Ability to take proactive (rather than reactive) positions on government regulatory matters earlier
- ☆ Time to adapt products to noise and pollution regulations
- ☆ Anticipation of government restrictions on medical equipment led to extra effort to develop foreign markets
- ☆ Orderly response to federal legislation and reporting requirements

Better industry and market analyses

- ☆ Higher quality of predictions in market and product forecasts
- ☆ Greater confidence in product forecasts
- ☆ Recognition of possible declining markets and resultant rejection of capital investment for manufacturing facilities to supply those markets
- ☆ Early detection of developing shifts in trends from either excess capacity or insufficient capacity in an industry
- ☆ Stimulus for corporate and groups to assess more variables which affect product lines
- ☆ Identification of changes in buyer criteria due to social changes
- ☆ Reorientation of marketing program to reflect sun belt growth
- ☆ Ability to anticipate future needs for new products, e.g. increasing oil and gas exploration creates need for (drilling) systems usable in a wide range of water depths and operating environments
- ☆ Research efforts toward products filling needs created by government and social pressures (e.g. development of diagnostic tests as hedge against malpractice litigation)

Better results in foreign businesses

- ☆ Major investments in foreign countries
- ☆ Positive results of overseas investment and market participation
- ☆ Ability to anticipate changes in international markets and ways of doing business in foreign countries

Improvements in diversifications and resource allocation

- ☆ Ability to concentrate our resources in businesses that will be attractive to the corporation in the long term
- ☆ Shifts in product portfolio—away from those products subject to increasing government and social pressures (e.g. 'polluting' processes, 'dangerous' products) toward those less vulnerable to such pressures
- ☆ Guide to acquisitions process
- ☆ Contributed to policy development with respect to expansion and allocation of capital funds
- ☆ Major diversification which helped company ride out rough time in the aluminium business

Better energy planning

- ☆ Ability to predict economic dislocations resulting from OPEC embargo and to deal flexibly with exchange rates
- ☆ Better energy planning for production facilities
- ☆ Correct anticipation of energy trends in the mid-1960s and consequent development of new energy-efficient glass forming process
- ☆ Identification of potential impact of energy shortage over 6 years ago (about 1971) and the development of marketing programs and product lines around ability to help customers reduce energy consumption—action led to strengthened market position
- ☆ Development of additional back-up energy sources

analysis process. There were questions about the level of effort of the environmental analysis activity, the planning time horizon, the techniques employed, the mode of application of the results, and the ultimate users of the results.

Several general observations can be made about the level of environmental analysis effort. *First, higher levels of effort seem to be associated with higher levels of perceived usefulness.* This can be seen in Table 4. This could be because greater perceived usefulness spurs increased effort *or* because increased effort leads to greater usefulness. *Second, the level of effort is highest for short-range (0–3 years) planning, and drops off successively for mid-range (3–8 years) and long-range (8+ years) planning.* The only exception to this pattern was at the corporate level (as compared to division and sub-division levels) for those firms that perceived the usefulness of their activity as at least important; for these groups of firms, roughly equal effort was allocated among short- and mid-range planning. *Third, the drop-off in environmental analysis effort for longer time horizons is markedly less at the corporate level. Fourth, except for short-range planning, the higher the organization level, the higher the level of effort*, i.e. there is more effort at the corporate level than at the division level, and more at the division than at the sub-division level. For the short-range time horizon, however, the efforts at the corporate and division levels are about the same. This latter finding is not consistent with Fahey and King's[20] conclusion that environmental analysis was practiced more at the division than at the corporate level. *Finally, it did not appear that level of effort or time horizon was correlated with the size of the firm.*

Table 4. Differences in indices of environmental analysis effort by organization level and time horizon and for three levels of perceived usefulness

Level of usefulness and level of organization	Time horizon Short-range 0–3 years	Mid-range 3–8 years	Long-range 8+ years
Crucial			
Corporate	2·4[1]	2·6	2·0
Division	2·5	2·1	1·2
Sub-division	1·8	1·2	0·6
Important, but no crucial			
Corporate	2·1	2·1	1·6
Division	2·2	1·5	0·8
Sub-division	1·2	0·6	0·3
Of some value			
Corporate	1·8	1·5	1·3
Division	1·9	1·7	0·6
Sub-division	0·9	0·5	0·1

[1]This 'effort index' is a weighted average of the responses to the level of effort question, where:

Major effort	=3
Some effort	=2
Very little effort	=1
No effort	=0
(No indication of level of effort)	=0

Clearly, the less complex techniques received the widest use, e.g. expert opinion, trend extrapolation and scenarios. This was revealed in responses to a question on which environmental analysis techniques were used, as summarized in Table 5. Interestingly, although expert opinion was checked off in 86 per cent of the 66 affirmative questionnaires, only 29 per cent of these firms reported using the Delphi approach, one type of expert opinion technique. This could be because the Delphi technique was perceived as too complex or as requiring more effort than it is worth, or because the technique simply was not very well known. Generally, *larger firms reported the use of more techniques than did smaller firms;* in particular, the simulation, Delphi and cross-impact techniques exhibited a positive correlation with size of firm. Because cross-impact and simulation techniques are relatively complex, and because the Delphi technique is associated here with them, there is reason to hypothesize that (1) the use of more complex techniques falls off with smaller firms, and (2) that the Delphi technique is often perceived as complex also. Finally, *the choice of techniques did not appear to be related to level of perceived usefulness of the company's environmental analysis activity.*

The surveyed firms also asked how they used the environmental analysis results: (1) for *conditioning* the thinking of individuals? (2) to provide general *background* about the environment to be used as needed? (3) for specific tasks or problems? (4) to *update* company personnel on environmental trends and signals of change? and (5) as part of a *formal planning* cycle? A summary of the responses is given in Table 6. It was found that the above modes of application varied with the level of the organization, but did not vary consistently with the size of firm or perceived level of usefulness. Generally,

Table 5. Use of environmental analysis techniques by large industrial corporations

Technique	Percentage of companies reporting use of techniques
Expert opinion	86
Trend extrapolation	83
Alternate scenarios	68
Single scenarios	55
Simulation models	55
Brainstorming	45
Causal models	32
Delphi projections	29
Cross-impact analysis	27
Input-output analysis	26
Exponential forecasting	21
Signal monitoring	12
Relevance trees	6
Morphological analysis	5

[1]Percentages are based on the responses of the 66 firms that reported having environmental analysis activities.

conditioning, background and formal planning modes were less frequent for successively lower levels in the organization. The *specific tasks and update modes were most frequent at the division level.*

Firms were also queried about who were the ultimate users of their environmental analysis products: board of directors? president? corporate executive committee? top level line executives? and staff personnel? The responses are summarized in Tables 7(a) and 7(b). *Boards of directors and corporate executive committees were more frequently reported as users in larger than in smaller firms* (see Table 7(a)). Further, *more users were reported for higher levels of perceived usefulness.* This was especially true concerning the president, corporate executive committee, and top level line executives. Whether perceived usefulness leads to more frequent use by top level management, or vice-versa, is a matter of conjecture but certainly is not of trivial concern.

Deterrents to Effective Application

A primary motivation for the survey was to identify why firms either do not engage in or experience difficulty in practicing environmental analysis. Survey participants were asked to cite their 'single greatest' and 'second greatest' deterrents 'to making environmental analysis effective for your company', and to give an example of each. The responses, which understandably varied in levels of specificity, were subsequently classified into one of six major groupings as follows:

Table 6. Applications of environmental analysis by level of organization for different levels of perceived usefulness

Categories of applications specified in questionnaire:

(1) *For conditioning* the thinking of individuals
(2) To provide general *background* about the environment to be used as needed
(3) For *specific tasks* or problems
(4) To *update* company personnel on environmental trends and signals of change
(5) As part of a *formal planning* cycle

	Percentage of companies reporting the three levels of usefulness noted			
	Crucial	Important but not crucial	Of some value	Total
Corporate level				
(1) Conditioning	67	34	35	43
(2) Background	60	69	76	69
(3) Specific tasks	33	31	24	30
(4) Update	33	38	41	38
(5) Formal planning	87	66	59	69
Division level				
(1) Conditioning	33	21	18	23
(2) Background	40	45	24	38
(3) Specific tasks	53	62	35	52
(4) Update	40	45	29	39
(5) Formal planning	60	48	65	56
Sub-division level				
(1) Conditioning	20	7	0	8
(2) Background	20	28	6	20
(3) Specific tasks	47	38	24	36
(4) Update	13	17	6	13
(5) Formal planning	47	24	18	28

Table 7(a). Ultimate users of environmental analysis

	Percentage of firms reporting the specified ultimate users of environmental analysis—by sales level categories					
	Sales level categories (dollars in billions)					
	I	II	III	IV	V	Total
Ultimate user	Over \$4·0 (%)	\$2·0 –3·9 (%)	\$1·0 –1·9 (%)	\$0·5 –0·9 (%)	\$0·3 –0·5 (%)	(%)
Board of directors	35	36	18	25	0	24
President	65	73	68	75	63	68
Corporate executive committee	88	73	73	63	38	71
Top level line executives	82	82	95	88	100	89
Middle management	47	64	50	63	38	52
Staff personnel	47	64	41	38	12	42

Table 7(b) Ultimate users of environmental analysis

	Percentage of firms reporting specified ultimate users of environmental analysis—by level of perceived usefulness of the firm's environmental analysis effort			
	Perceived usefulness			
Ultimate users	Crucial (%)	Important, but not crucial (%)	Of some value (%)	Total (%)
Board of directors	27	17	24	21
President	80	66	59	67
Corporate executive committee	87	79	59	75
Top level line executives	100	86	82	89
Middle management	60	62	35	54
Staff personnel	33	52	29	41

Number of times this type of deterrent was cited	Deterrent
21	*Interpretation:* The problem is that of interpreting the results of environmental analysis into specific impacts on the company's businesses and into specific

responses to be made by the businesses. Included is the problem of the results not being in sufficiently precise form.

16 *Inaccuracy/uncertainty:* The problem is that either the output of the environmental analysis is inaccurate too uncertain to be taken seriously, or both.

13 *Short-term orientation:* The problem is that the preoccupation with short-term matters preempts attention to environmental analysis.

9 *Lack of acceptance:* The problem is that environmental analysis is not accepted within the company.

6 *Diversified businesses:* The problem is that diversified businesses mean multiple relevant environments which make environmental analysis too complex.

4 *Misperceptions:* The problem is one of executives having a narrow, limited or invalid perception of the external business environment.

Specific comments on deterrents are listed in Table 8.

Any firm that plans to begin organized environmental analysis would be wise to become familiar with this list of common deterrents, and think ahead on how to avoid or minimize them.

III. Management Implications

Just what do these survey findings mean to the executive considering whether to implement organized environmental analysis or the one wishing to make his company's existing environmental analysis activities more useful?

The fact that a lot of large corporations have organized environmental analysis and report that it is very useful seems reason enough for those who have not yet tried it to give it serious consideration.

Similarly, executives who have become frustrated or disappointed with their company's environmental analysis activities should not give up too quickly. If other firms find it useful, why can't they? There are, of course, a number of deterrents to effective environmental analysis. The executive who is aware of these common deterrents will be better equipped to avoid or deal with them should they occur.

The many different reported deterrents were classified into six major groups environmental earlier: interpretation, inaccuracy/uncertainty, short-term orientation, lack of acceptance, diversified businesses and misperceptions. A review of these deterrents certainly gives one an idea of what problems might arise in implementing organized environmental analysis, and for this reason their specifics are appropriate reading for the corporate executive. On the other hand, it is important in avoiding or minimizing these deterrents that the specifics do not distract one from appreciating the problem in more fundamental terms. Although varying in detail and type, the many different deterrents are essentially problems of (1) education, (2) information content and (3) motivation.

Consider the problem of inadequate 'environmental' education. Most executives are familiar with their immediate market and competitive environment. But they may not be so well versed in the broader social, political and technological environment in which their market is evolving. For example, how many anticipated the environmental movement and social unrest of the 1960s in the U.S., let alone the second-order consequences on their own industry? How many are capable today of assessing the potential impacts of advances in computer and communications technologies on their markets and competitors? Education *vis-à-vis* management development programs and executive seminars have been used to increase the sensitivity of executives to their external business environment. Sessions designed around participative, mind-opening exercises are usually more effective for this purpose than the sit-back-and-listen presentations by experts. A session could include Delphi and scenario exercises performed by the participants who then attempt to relate the results to their own particular divisions.

But, according to the survey, even executives sensitive to the potential far-reaching implications of environmental trends and developments do not always give high priority to organized environmental analysis. One reason is the lack of real motivation, although it may be denied. If the corporate culture and reward system lean heavily to short-term results, it is understandable that individual executives may create little demand for environmental analysis activities. The environmental analysis and longer view can always wait until the more immediate problems are solved. Simply urging and admonishing executives to give more attention to the long term, in itself, cannot be expected to change behavior very much. Companies have and are increasingly incorporating long-term performance considerations in executive appraisal systems. A division manager's compensation, for example, could depend in part upon the comprehensiveness of the division's environmental analysis and contingency plans.

Also, the uncertainty of the external environment may kill motivation for environmental analysis. The attitude of 'the future is beyond our control, but we and our competitors are all in the same boat', can certainly stifle any serious commitment to environmental analysis. Rather than go through the 'futile' effort to anticipate the environment, the focus will be on flexible strategies with an ability to move fast when developments occur. The flaw in

Table 8. Deterrents to effective environmental analysis

Interpretation: The problem is that of interpreting the results of environmental analysis into specific impacts on the company's businesses and into specific responses to be made by the businesses. Included is the problem of the results not being in useful or sufficiently precise form.

- ☆ Difficulty of structuring studies in a way that results can be seen to be relevant and meaningful to decision-makers today
- ☆ Difficulty of reacting because information from environmental analysis is so intangible with regard to timing and impact
- ☆ Difficulty of assessing the implications of general environmental trends for our specific businesses before they exert themselves
- ☆ Difficulty of translating environmental analysis into relevant business terms, e.g. ROI impact
- ☆ Difficulty of quantifying the impact of major threats and developing alternatives to these threats
- ☆ Difficulty of developing the path from assumption to implication to action, e.g. the tendency to relax or stop after stating the assumption, rather than follow through to an action program
- ☆ Difficulty in seeing the impact of environmental trends on short range operations, i.e. the gradual, accumulative nature of trends can be deceptive
- ☆ Lack of sufficient involvement by top management for them to not only understand the conclusions of environmental analysis but also to internalize them and change behavior accordingly
- ☆ Difficulty of translating potential opportunities into action plans, e.g. conversion of traditional furniture ideas into new lifestyle furniture concepts
- ☆ The time and analysis required to apply information to our specific situations, e.g. impact of probable energy shortages or price increases on our market for automotive components
- ☆ Difficulty of institutionalizing environmental planning into the formal planning processes of the company so that division strategies reflect the process
- ☆ Difficulty of follow-up planning, e.g. we have pushed ahead on programs in spite of warning signals that should have alerted us to severe problems
- ☆ Identifying impacts on businesses, particularly when negative

Inaccuracy/uncertainty: The problem is that either the output of environmental analysis is inaccurate, too uncertain to be taken seriously, or both

- ☆ Uncertainty due to the dynamics of the market place
- ☆ Inaccurate depicting of environmental events
- ☆ So many false predictions
- ☆ Inability to predict the future, e.g. past experience revealed inability of experts to predict the extent of inflationary forces
- ☆ Difficulty of properly characterizing uncertainties in understandable and meaningful terms
- ☆ Difficulty of forecasting the magnitude of the impact of a future trend
- ☆ The moving target syndrome, e.g. especially regarding government activity
- ☆ Difficulty of predicting social aims, e.g. no-growth vs continuing growth, etc.
- ☆ Discontinuities in environmental forecasting for which no company can make satisfactory assessments

Short-term orientation: The problem is that the preoccupation with short-term matters preempts attention to environmental analysis

- ☆ Pressure of short-term events, which tend to soak up some of the resources nominally or usefully committed to environmental planning
- ☆ Dislike for spending money today to help solve a speculative problem tomorrow
- ☆ The reluctance to consider more than the short-term because that is where the rewards are
- ☆ Competition between short- and long-term, i.e. most environmental problems emerge slowly and require solutions which only become effective over similarly long periods of time
- ☆ Organization structures and tasks that force managers to focus on the immediate, short-run elements of their jobs, e.g. budgets are for limited periods of time and encourage concern with this year's results, and maybe next year's

Lack of acceptance: The problem is that environmental analysis is not accepted within the company

- ☆ Some degree of skepticism as to the possibility of success with environmental analysis—more so at lower levels than at the top
- ☆ Lack of understanding of the usefulness of environmental analysis
- ☆ Difficulty of environmental analysts convincing line managers that the former's output is applicable to the latter's problems
- ☆ The 'we already know our business' attitude on the part of operating management
- ☆ A suspicion in the practical world of business decisions that scenarios and possible occurrences are impractical and somehow dangerous
- ☆ The 'we have been successful without it' attitude
- ☆ A resistance to change in forecasting methods
- ☆ The presumption by too many executives that each of them can be their own expert in assessing environmental impacts upon the company
- ☆ Lack of commitment and personal involvement of line executives
- ☆ The difficulty of breaking the patterns of thinking in the past.

Diversified businesses: The problem is that diversified businesses mean multiple relevant environments which make environmental analysis too complex

- ☆ Difficulty of applying corporate expertise in environmental analysis at the operating level due to the great diversity of our operations
- ☆ Complexity due to multiple and decentralized organization
- ☆ Need for too large a corporate staff to keep abreast of environments for decentralized, autonomous businesses, and unwillingness of line managers to support a fulltime staff for environmental surveillance at the division level

Misperceptions: The problem is one of narrow, limited or invalid perceptions of the external environment shared by executives

- ☆ Tendency of managers to think in non-discontinuous terms
- ☆ Unpreparedness of managers, because of education or basic interest, to deal with social, political, and cultural aspects of a rapidly changing environment (many managers are knowledge reductionists rather than holistic)
- ☆ Traditional inability to think in world market terms (instead of 'plant countries') when considering trends and factors of a social, political, technological and economic origin

this rationale is not the belief that the future cannot be predicted but rather that the implication that better environmental intelligence cannot improve the company's ability to posture itself flexibly for surprises. This, of course, is the idea in planning for alternative scenarios and 'what if?' exercises. Further, some environmental trends, especially those based on demographic change, can be projected with a useful degree of accuracy. This problem may not be unrelated to that of inadequate 'environmental' education mentioned above. The executives might have to be shown that there are aspects of the environment that do follow some fairly predictable patterns or do exhibit some degree of order. For example, if history is a good indicator, we know that it takes more than just a few years to bring a major new energy technology to widespread commercialization; it usually takes decades. We also can project the percentage of the population entering the 'new household formation' phase for 20 years on the basis of fairly safe assumptions.

Usually it is the line executive decision-maker, not the staff analyst conducting the environmental study, who is most skeptical of the value of environmental analysis when the environment is highly uncertain. The executive will become all the more disbelieving if the study contains specific predictions about uncertain developments. It is important that those producing the environmental guard against high expectations in terms of predictive accuracy. In fact, it is sometimes wise to downplay the predictive aspects of environmental analysis.

Finally, lack of motivation can be linked to the third fundamental problem, that of poor information content. This is discussed next.

Poor information content has to do with inaccurate, incomplete and irrelevant information generated by the environmental analysis. Even a 'motivated' executive may give up on the organized environmental analysis activities if the information generated is repeatedly of little or no value in making strategic decisions. Probably the most common problem here is that environmental analysis information stops short of offering implications to the particular business of the executive for whom the information is intended. Consider, for example, the executive having to decide whether to remain in the diagnostic imaging business. An environmental analysis study that reports on expected technological advances in this field, the possibility of national health care legislation, and trends in health care costs, may not be very helpful. There remain unanswered questions concerning the implications of these developments and trends. What does a rapid succession of more advanced imaging devices mean in terms of the industry and competitive structure? What will be the impact of national health insurance on purchase and usage of CAT scanners by hospitals? Would continued escalation of health care costs curb hospital investments in imaging equipment? Etc. The dilemma here is that the party preparing the environmental study may not be qualified to draw such implications for the executive decision-maker, and that the latter sees little value in a report without such implications. In such a situation, it would be important to build a closer relationship between those generating environmental studies and the intended users of the information. If practical, the user should be brought into the process of generating the information. Working together with the staff analysts in assessing the broad environmental trends and developments, the executive 'user' can steer the study to the more specific questions of interest. In fact, assuming the 'two heads are better than one' such a joint effort could be very beneficial. Even when external consultants are the source of the environmental information, there are ways of facilitating interaction between the consultants and the company executives and generally such should be encouraged. Of course, such arrangements must be handled carefully to prevent release of proprietary company information.

Poor information can also be a result of misapplication of the various techniques used for anticipating future developments. An executive presented with the results of a Delphi study, for example, may discover nebulous conclusions. A report, for example, that experts believe there is a 90 per cent probability that fusion power will be available by 2010 is meaningless without a more precise definition of 'available'. Widespread commercialization of fusion reactors may not occur for 10 years following a successful experimental demonstration of fusion power. Does 'available' mean experimental feasibility or commercialization? Similarly, future environmental scenarios developed for strategic planning purposes may contain assumptions that while independently plausible are just not mutually compatible. Both these examples of poor information are avoidable with proper application of the respective techniques.

There are many different approaches and techniques for implementing environmental analysis—the survey data in this study do not indicate which are better or worse. It could well be that what works for one company does not work for another, and that each company's activities must be tailored to its own situation and needs.

The 'tailoring' should be oriented to the needs of those executives making the strategic decisions, and not to the expertise and resources of the analysts. In interviews independent of the survey research, the author found that it was not uncommon for a corporate staff group to claim to have a sophisticated environmental analysis program although line executives in the same firm considered the staff's efforts to have little value in making strategic decisions. Some caution must be used in giving the line executive simply what they *want*. What they want and what they need may not be the same. The corporate planner can and should be continually trying to make the line executive aware of the information needs and availability for different strategic issues as they arise.

It is critical then that effective communication and mutual respect exist between the staff analysts and the decision-making executives. The former must learn the language of the latter, and not expect the opposite. The analysts must strive to make their environmental analysis product 'user friendly' and not expect the users to decipher annalytical procedures and display formats unfamiliar to them.

More generally, the evolutionary phases of corporate environmental analysis posited at the outset of this paper suggest why some firms are more successful with environmental analysis than others—why some presumably encounter fewer or less severe deterrents than others. It is reasonable to hypothesize that those firms that have moved beyond the appreciation (and perhaps initial fascination) and analysis phases into the application phase will apply environmental analysis more effectively than others. This is because many of the reported deterrents to effective use indicated a problem in relating the environmental analysis effort to strategic decision-making. Accordingly, it would be important for a firm to recognize the phase it is in, and if not in the application phase, to take measures to advance to that phase as quickly as possible.

References

(1) Daniel Bell, The corporation and society in the 1970s, *The Public Interest,* Summer (1971).

(2) Keith Davis and Robert L. Blomstrum, *Business and its Environment,* McGraw-Hill, New York (1966).

(3) William R. Dill, The impact of environment on organizational development. In *Concepts and Issues in Administrative Behavior,* pp. 94–109. Sydney Mailick and E. H. Van Ness (Eds.), (1962).

(4) F. E. Emery and E. L. Trist, The causal texture of organizational environments, *Human Relations,* February (1965).

(5) Shirley Terreberry, The evolution of organizational environments, *Administrative Sciences Quarterly,* March (1968).

(6) Francis J. Aguilar, *Scanning the Business Environment,* Macmillan, New York (1967).

(7) General Electric Company, *Our Future Business Environment* (1968).

(8) The Institute of Life Insurance, Case distributed by the Intercollegiate Case Clearing House, Soldiers Field, Boston, MA, ICCH 9-371-380 (1971).

(9) Rene D. Zentner, Scenarios in forecasting, *Chemical and Engineering News,* pp. 22–24, 6 October (1975).

(10) Herman Kahn and Anthony J. Wiener, The next thirty-three years: a framework for speculation, *Daedalus,* Summer (1967).

(11) Alan R. Fusfeld and Richard N. Foster, The Delphi technique: survey and comment, *Business Horizons,* pp. 63–74, June (1971).

(12) Harold Sackman, Toward more effective use of expert opinion: preliminary investigation of participatory polling for long range planning. RAND Paper P-5570, pp. 1–7, October (1976).

(13) A think tank that helps companies plan, *Business Week,* pp. 70–71, 25 August (1973).

(14) William L. Brockhaus and John F. Mickelson, An analysis of prior Delphi applications and some observations for its future applicability, *Technological Forecasting and Social Change,* **10,** (1977).

(15) George S. Campbell, Relevance of signal monitoring to Delphi/cross-impact studies, *Futures,* pp. 401–404, December (1971).

(16) Selwyn Enzer, Cross-impact techniques in technology assessment, *Futures,* pp. 30–51, March (1972).

(17) Input–output: management's newest tool, *Dun's,* pp. 57–58, March (1971).

(18) Theodore J. Rubin, Toward information systems for environmental forecasting. In *Perspectives in Planning,* pp. 285–303. Erich Jantsch (Ed.), (1969).

(19) James Brian Quinn, *Logical Incrementalism,* Richard D. Irwin, Homewood, Ill. (1980).

(20) Liam Fahey and William R. King, Environmental scanning for corporate planning, *Business Horizons,* pp. 61–71, August (1975).

The New Marketing—Developing Long-term Interactive Relationships

Evert Gummesson

This article places emphasis on relationships and interaction in marketing, an emphasis which has developed out of new theories of services marketing and industrial marketing and also out of practical experience. Building and maintaining relationships have significant long-term implications and therefore affect the strategic and long-range planning of the firm's marketing. In the author's view, the present Marketing Concept, as it appears in research, textbooks and seminars, is unrealistic and needs to be replaced. One reason is its inability to absorb new developments in marketing and its rigid attachment to traditional consumer goods marketing. The conclusions can be seen as part of a progress report from an ongoing research project which aims at developing a New Marketing Concept, that draws both on theory and on the views of practitioners.

Current Approaches to Marketing

The present Marketing Concept states that firms should investigate needs and wants in the market-place. From their findings, they should develop market segments, products to serve those segments, and the necessary production and administrative resources. The firm then stands the best chance of making a profit and surviving in the long run. For the practising marketing manager, the Marketing Concept becomes concrete through a set of theories, models, concepts and techniques that are applied to daily decision-making and implementation. Marketing is used here in its wide sense, i.e. also including sales, and 'Marketing Concept' is used to signify the marketing philosophy as well as its transformation into decisions and activities.

Marketing as a subject for research, textbooks and classrooms operates under self-imposed limitations. Its theory is primarily built on research in the area of packaged consumer goods and consumer durables; for example, in general marketing textbooks, services are only mentioned in passing although they constitute 50–70 per cent of the GNP of developed countries. The present Marketing Concept favours an approach where the mass market is manipulated through a marketing mix, usually associated with the 4 Ps: Product, Price, Promotion and Place. If personal contacts are discussed, it is in a salesperson–consumer relationship in areas where mass marketing is insufficient, e.g. the sales of life insurance or cars.

Dr. Evert Gummesson is Senior Partner and Co-founder of the Stockholm Consulting Group. He is also Associate Professor at the University of Stockholm, Sweden.

Marketing theories developed for consumer goods marketing emanate almost exclusively from the United States and are based on unique conditions there, among them a huge domestic market of 240 million consumers, nationwide coverage by commercial television and radio, and a large number of distribution options. The U.S. theories have been adopted by other countries as well, at least partly due to convenience. In a recent article, experienced international marketing consultant R. J. de Ferrer[1] (p. 227) expresses his dissatisfaction with European reverence towards U.S. marketing thinking and its preachers:

> they are teaching us lessons that emanate from a specific market environment. . . . We are gawking bystanders . . . we fail to notice how much is not relevant to us, or how much that is of vital importance to Europeans is not treated at all. . . . We have been let down, but only by ourselves: we should be developing with greater purpose our own European management craft.

There is no doubt that consumer goods marketing has developed some powerful tools. However, when applied to other areas than consumer goods, the theories are only partially valid, sometimes even destructive, as they fail to recognize the unique features of services marketing and industrial marketing. Moreover, companies are seldom clearly just consumer or industrial or goods or service companies. Their output is both goods and services but in varying proportions. They frequently serve both consumer and industrial markets, sometimes with the same product, sometimes with different products. By studying companies where services or industrial marketing is predominant certain facets of marketing may be observed more clearly. On the basis of these observations, we should then be able to develop a more realistic Marketing Concept. Although marketing may be rich in research and data, it is poor in theory. The theories, models etc. that constitute the present Marketing Concept are too limited in scope, exaggerating some aspects of marketing and suppressing others. The Old Marketing Concept needs to be replaced.

How then could the Old Marketing Concept be renewed. The key words are already found in the title of this article. At the end of the title, *relationship* is mentioned. Marketing can be seen as relationship management: creating, developing, and maintaining a network in which the firm thrives. The next word is *interactive*, i.e. bilateral and multilateral supplier–customer activities to produce and deliver goods and services, primarily in a person-to-person communication with less left to mass communication. The last expression is *long term*, stressing that relationships need time to be built and need time to be maintained. They thus become central in strategic planning, both at the corporate and marketing level.

New developments in services marketing and industrial marketing have a stronghold in Scandinavia. 'The Nordic School of Services' is a designation for independent researchers, primarily from Sweden and Finland.[2] In industrial marketing the 'IM (Industrial Marketing) Group' with its roots in the University of Uppsala, but with ramifications to research institutions around the world, advocates an interaction/network approach to industrial marketing.[3] The Scandinavian research is highly empirical, based on broad case studies for theory generation rather than statistical testing of narrow hypotheses. This requires a symbiotic relationship between academia and industry and respect from academia for the practitioner's experience as an input to theory and vice versa. The Scandinavian researchers as well as practitioners follow closely the developments in the United States and the United Kingdom attempting to integrate those contributions into their own thinking. Partly due to language barriers, the reverse is seldom true.

Services marketing has during the past few years developed some interesting contributions to marketing theory. It is mainly based on consumer services like airlines, hotels, car rental, etc. but also on special fields like health services and professional services. Industrial services are not yet in focus. There now exists a rich literature on services marketing and the references in the English language alone approached 2000 in 1985[4] and 3000 as of September 1986.

Industrial marketing received widespread attention earlier than services. We will distinguish between consumer and industrial marketing using a definition advanced by Cooke[5] (p. 16): 'Industrial marketing is marketing to the organizational buyer as contrasted to consumer marketing, which is marketing to the ultimate consumer'. The organization can be a corporation, a public authority, a reseller, a hospital, etc. Alternatives to the term industrial marketing are business marketing or business-to-business marketing. (It feels a little strange to talk about the sale of biscuits to a wholesaler or a university canteen as industrial marketing; the term feels more natural when applied to nails and screws, machinery, heavy equipment, and the like. But as no real consensus exists on these terms we use industrial marketing as defined above.)

The ideas from consumer goods marketing have been taken over and applied to the industrial stage. In this way, similarities between consumer and industrial marketing have been emphasized but unfortunately important differences have been blurred. One important contribution, original to industrial marketing, is the development of models of organizational buying behaviour. As early as 1976 more than 1000 references existed in the English language.[6]

Through a series of thought-provoking books by practitioners Iaccoca (Chrysler), Geneen (ITT), Rodgers (IBM), Carlzon (SAS, Scandinavian Airlines), McCormack (IMG, International Management Group), and others, a new and rich dimension of marketing has become accessible to researchers. Most of our knowledge in marketing is based on practical experience and intuition, supplemented with results from scientific inquiry. Therefore, if the marketing presented in textbooks and classrooms only draws on fragmented scientific research, the presentations will become lightweight and misleading (even if descriptive cases are added). It is essential to fill the gaps—those areas not (yet) properly researched—with the best knowledge available, namely from those who are where it all happens. Science certainly needs the contribution from what Schön describes as 'the reflective practitioner'.[7]

Although the new marketing theories, combined with views of practitioners have broadened our knowledge of marketing, this knowledge has not yet been exploited in general marketing theory. In general textbooks on marketing, the new approaches are added as 'patches' to the traditional treatment of marketing. These patches may appear as a collection of odd aspects of marketing in an extra chapter at the end of the book but have had no direct influence on the way the general Marketing Concept and its applications are presented.

In this paper, the significance of supplier–customer interaction and long-term relationships will be emphasized. This will be done through references to current theories and models derived through research but also with reference to seasoned practitioners, executives as well as consultants. Naturally other perspectives need also to be explored in order to make the New Marketing Concept realistic, e.g. the global perspective, marketing as investment, the significance of image and positioning.

Relational Aspects of Marketing

In the new theories of services marketing and management, certain unique characteristics of services have been brought out. These unique traits greatly affect the way a service firm designs its marketing strategy and organization. Relationships and interactions are of central importance. The emphasis is on person-to-person interaction and the fact that marketing, production, delivery and also consumption and service development are partly carried out in direct interaction with the customer. The internal relations are stressed as a prerequisite for successful external relations. The significance of the external relations are reflected in the expression 'moment of truth' that has become part of services marketing jargon and which stresses that each customer contact creates a moment that influences the firm's relations and reveals its ability to keep a customer.[8]

In the new theory of industrial marketing called the network/interaction theory, marketing is defined as:[9] 'all activities by the firm to build, maintain and develop customer relations' (p. 10). It further states: 'It is not until one has built a sufficient number of customer relations that one can consider oneself established on a market' (p. 40). Marketing, with reference to industrial and international operations is thus not primarily concerned with the manipulation of the 4 Ps from consumer goods marketing. Instead, it is to reach a critical mass of relations with customers, distributors, suppliers, public institutions, individuals, etc.

Marketing consultant Regis McKenna[10] emphatically points to the need for building relationships. Based on his long experience of the 'fast-changing industrial markets' of Silicon Valley, he claims that personal relationships are more lasting than product or brand loyalties. He states that his experience with computers, semi-conductors, and the like have taught him

> a new approach to marketing, an approach that takes into account the dynamic changes in industries and markets. It is an approach that stresses the building of relationships rather than the promotion of products. . . . (p. 4)

The marketer must

> gain understanding of the market structure, then develop strategic relationships with other key companies and people in the market. They must build relationships with suppliers and distributors, investors and customers. Those relationships are more important than low prices, flashy promotions, or even advanced technology. Changes in the market can alter prices and technologies, but close relationships can last a lifetime, if not longer. (p. 15)

Both services marketing theory and the network/interaction theory emphasize the long-term perspective: it takes time for sellers and buyers to establish a smooth working relationship. Firms need to enter wedlock rather than one night stands. This is particularly obvious when a product requires complex technology and customized design as well as when R & D, production and installation involve active participation from the buyer. It is also obvious in such service relationships as, for example, with a life insurance company, a psychiatrist, an accounting firm, etc. where it is desirable for the customer to deal with the same individuals; the organization to which these individuals belong may be less significant.

The Japanese are known to take a long-term perspective on building market share, seeing it as an investment and not as a temporary campaign. Successful companies in the West are also skilled practitioners of the long-term perspective. Former IBM vice president of marketing, 'Buck' Rodgers describes the IBM strategy in this way[11] (p. 45):

> Successful salespeople understand the importance of long-term customer connections. The size of their paycheck is determined to a large extent by their ability to develop sound, lasting relationships with enough customers.

Nine Issues that Challenge the Present Marketing Concept

Basic concepts in marketing are customer, buyer, seller, competitor, marketing department, consumer goods, services and service firms and industrial marketing. When marketing is approached as interaction and relationships these concepts are challenged. We have to ask whether they have any meaning except as rather general terms in everyday conversation. Or have they just become stereotypes that obscure important issues? Those questions may sound trivial, ideally suited for members of the academic community and their scholarly (read: impractical) arguments. In my opinion practice says differently: the prevelant attitude in economics and marketing to take these words for granted deprives much marketing research of meaning.

In order to display the ambiguity of the above-mentioned basic concepts, nine issues will be presented below. These issues have emerged strongly in theories of services marketing, industrial marketing, and in the practice of marketing. This does not mean they are all new. It just means that they are exposed more explicitly and their impact on the New Marketing Concept is made more evident.

1. *The Many-headed Customer and Seller*
When using the words customer and seller we are often not very clear about what we mean. The terms lead our thoughts to one individual, to a grey mass described through a few socio-demographic variables, or maybe to an organization. Especially in industrial marketing both the seller and the customer are many-headed. This is also pointed out in models of organizational buying behaviour. The best known is probably the Webster–Wind model[12] which identifies the customer as a buying centre consisting of a number of individuals and representing five major customer roles: decider, buyer, user, influencer and gatekeeper.

The network/interaction theory identifies relationships between many individuals from the selling firm's staff and the customer's staff plus relations to other entities such as the seller's suppliers, trade associations, political bodies, public authorities, etc.

Figure 1 illustrates that a multitude of relationships can exist between a supplier and its customers, for example in a company selling high tech equipment in the international market. The marketing department is just one unit from which several employees may enter into contact with several departments and individuals in the buying organization. The design department, the factories, etc. might also establish relationships and the CEO may be involved as well. But the figure is highly simplified: the web of relations can be very complex, and, for example, the intensity and the length of the relationship can be introduced.

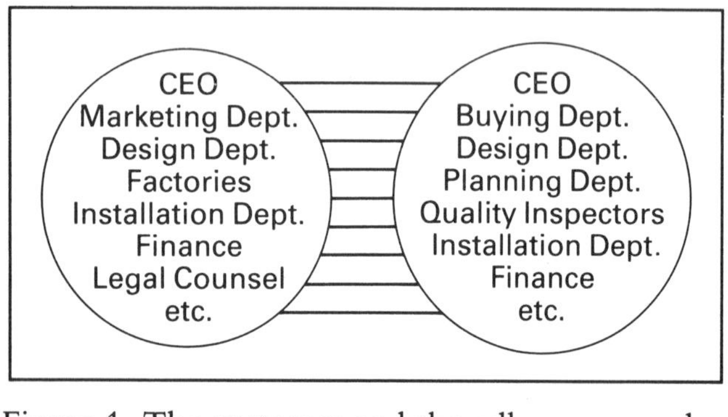

Figure 1. The customer and the seller—a complex relationship. The customer and the seller are often a number of individuals who enter into complex relations with one another

Conclusion: in order to identify a 'customer' and a 'seller' a complex web of relationships has to be described. To find one's way in this web is a job that requires concepts, systematic research, long-term planning of the marketing plus a lot of patience and stamina.

2. *The Real Customer Does Not Necessarily Appear in the Market-place*
In many types of business, the major battle is not in the market-place but elsewhere. In order to open up a market, one might have to receive a blessing from higher up in society. One example is selling equipment of infrastructural character such as nuclear reactors, telephone systems and defence products which affect the country's economic performance, employment levels, financial status and political sympathies. Another example is trade agreements and quotas which are common for agricultural products, or the bilateral trade between a western country and an East European communist country. But it exists for packaged consumer goods as well, for example when getting Coca-Cola into China.

The first step in marketing in these cases are negotiations with presidents, ministers, financiers, politicians, civil servants, trade unions, etc. This is illustrated in Figure 2 which is an extension of Figure 1. Only when a blessing and the necessary permits are issued from one or several of these, can the actual work with the consumer marketing mix start. In order to consider this aspect within the traditional 4 P framework, the Ps have sometimes been extended, adding for example public opinion and politics.

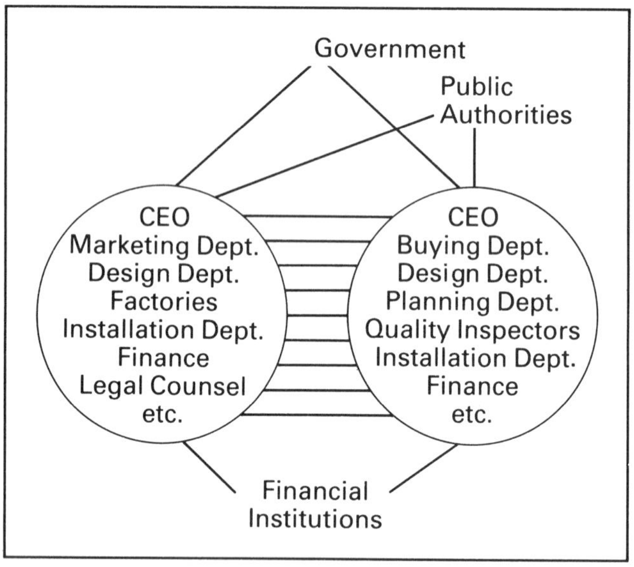

Figure 2. Where is the customer? The real customer, the actual decision-maker, often does not appear in the market-place

Conclusion: attacking the consumer with a marketing mix if the stage is not set first will lead nowhere. The real decision-maker to be addressed is usually not identified in marketing theory as being part of the market.

3. *The Customer as Co-producer*
In services marketing interaction is a key word. At first sight, one might classify this as similar to what we have already presented in the network/interaction theory. However, the unique features of services turned out to render a different meaning to the interaction concept. A distinction is made

between interactive marketing (sometimes called relationship marketing) and non-interactive (mass) marketing.[13] The interactive relationships are not only marketing interactions, they are also interactions during which the service is produced. Moreover, the customer starts to consume the service during the marketing and production process.

The following interactive relationships have been identified (Figure 3):

☆ Interaction between the buyer and the seller's contact persons, e.g. the interaction between a doctor and a patient, an advertising agency and a product manager, a passenger and an air stewardess. If the customer does not co-operate—the patient not taking the prescribed medication, the product manager not briefing the agency properly, the air passenger not appearing at the gate on time—the service cannot be produced. The customer is a co-producer.

☆ Interaction between the buyer and the seller's systems, machinery and routines. This man–machine or man–system interface is equally important as the person-to-person interaction, e.g. a bank customer and a cash machine, the taxpayer and the taxation system.

☆ Interaction between the buyer and the seller's physical environment. One example is a supermarket where the positioning of the merchandise, the way it is displayed, and the attractiveness of the premises, including the parking lot, influence the buyer's behaviour. The marketing director of a U.S. hamburger chain once stated that his most important marketing staff were a group of architects, who designed the physical environment of the restaurants.

☆ Interaction among buyers who produce the service between themselves if the seller provides the right systems, environment and supportive personnel. An obvious example is a dance restaurant: if the customers refuse to dance with each other there will be no service produced. Customers who line up in a queue, travel First Business Class, listen to a concert in the Albert Hall, interact and influence the production of the service.

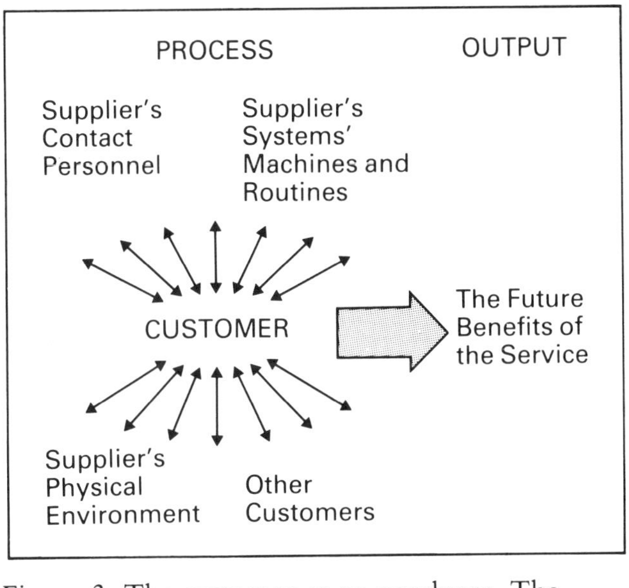

Figure 3. The customer as co-producer. The customer can be a co-producer and enters into relationships not only with individuals

In services, the interactions during the production process provide opportunities for marketing the service by the creation of favourable 'moments of truth' that will encourage the customer to return and give referrals to his friends. For example, consulting services usually improve in quality if they are produced in close interaction between buyer and seller personnel. The shared experience can also cement long lasting relationships. The customer's 'participation style'[14] becomes important as well as the seller's ability to design and produce the service so that the contribution from the buyer becomes a good one.

As most of the companies traditionally labelled as manufacturing companies also provide services, the aspects of interaction learnt from studies of more pure service firms are of general interest.[15] These interactions add a new dimension to the previously presented issue on the many-headed customer and seller.

Conclusion: it is essential to recognize that a service is partly produced, marketed and consumed in an interactive relationship between the customer and the selling firm and that the quality of this relationship as well as the quality of the service is the result of efforts from both sides. The marketing that takes place during the interaction is often the most important, sometimes even the only marketing that a service company does.

4. *Market Mechanisms are Controlled Outside the Firm*

According to representatives of the network/interaction theory of industrial marketing[16] (pp. 26–27):

> A company can be viewed as a node in an ever-widening pattern of interactions, in some of which it is a direct participant, some of which affect it indirectly and some of which occur independently of it. This web of interactions is so complex and multifarious as to deny full description or analysis. Indeed, the interaction between a single buyer and selling company can be complex enough. . . .

These webs woven between companies take many forms. The seller and the buyer may be in all sorts of dependent positions, not covered by the cases of monopoly, oligopoly, etc. so favoured in traditional economic theory. But the market economy may not necessarily exist outside the firm even in economies that are basically capitalistic. There exist legal as well as covert trusts and cartels which create interdependencies between firms in a market. There are a large variety of ownerships, joint ventures, and unions through banks, persons or families. These private networks—the 'old boy network' or 'invisible colleges'—may be locked to the non-member. In addition one could mention the 'facilitating payments' which are sometimes crucial, most often illegal but accepted under a variety of disguises in many markets. These personal networks, payments, etc. help to cement a very strong kind of relationship. Competitors co-operate on certain issues but may be fierce combatants in others. Suppliers are part-owners of customers and vice versa. Companies may even own one another. Many sorts of mixes between private ownership and government ownership may exist. Industrial policies may provide subsidies through direct payment but also through indirect channels such as research institutions or large orders to domestic suppliers. Business consultant Ohmae[17] points to the necessity for global companies to establish a foothold in the 'triad' of the world economy—America, Western Europe, Japan—and how this is done through various connections between competing firms. He provides illustrations from firms in the car industry, in computers, robotics, etc. concerning both technical, marketing, and financial co-operation. All these relations can be quite hard to survey and evaluate for the outsider. Finally, there is a 'black economy' built on more or less secret networks which is estimated to account for 10–20 per cent of the GNP of industrialized countries.

Conclusion: the complex network of relations that exist in the market means that buyer–seller interaction takes many forms which are institutionalized and which curb the market mechanisms. These networks have to be analysed in order for the seller to assess his market opportunities and develop his strategies.

5. *Market Mechanisms Are Brought Inside the Firm*
Even if the market mechanisms have been curbed outside the firm they have been let loose inside the firm. In its pure form, a company can be seen as 'a planned economy' where clearly defined activities are co-ordinated towards clearly defined goals. This paradigm is reflected in textbooks. However, planned economies, as we know them from whole nations, have efficiency problems: rigidity, lack of initiative and difficult to manage. Companies, being

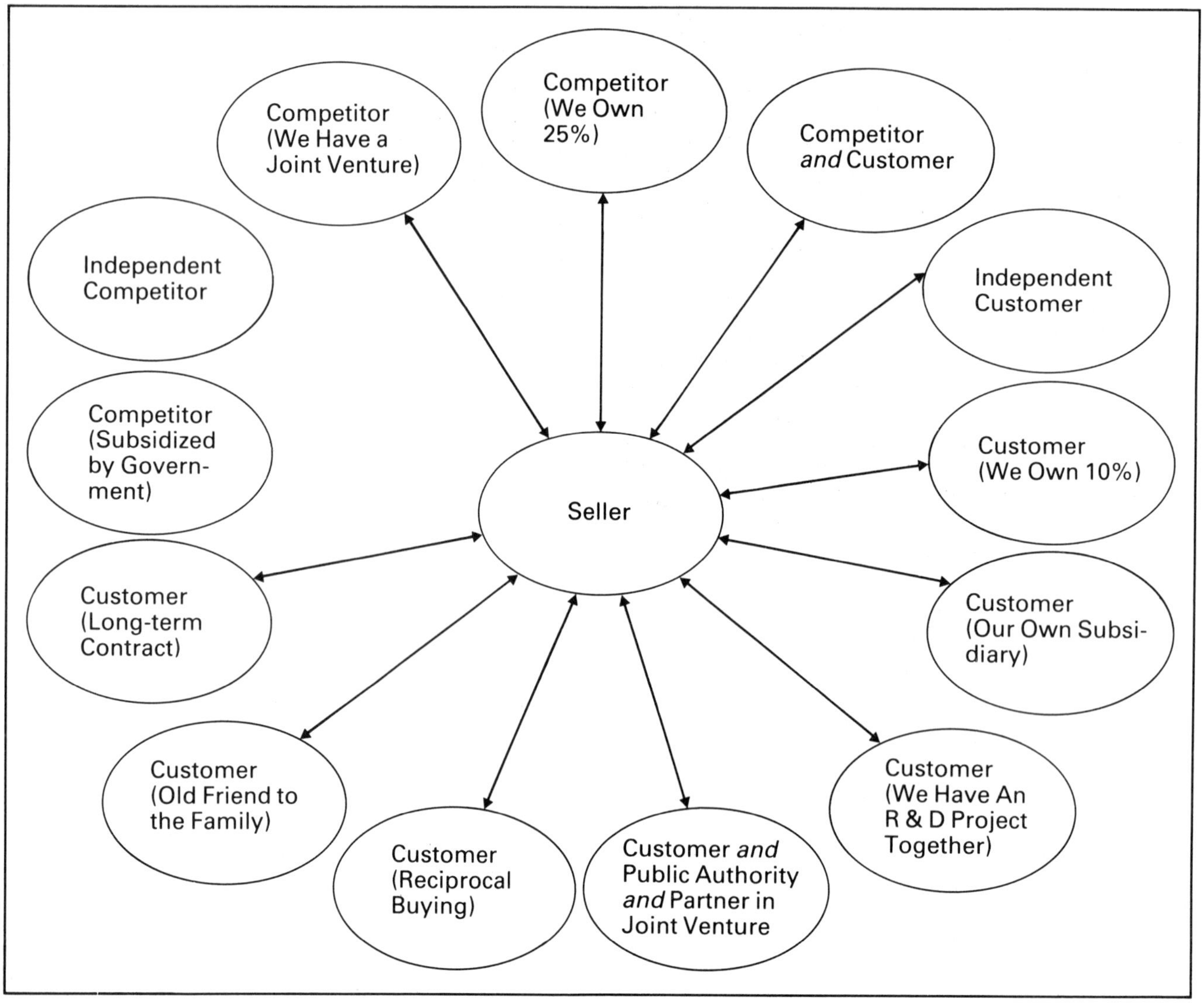

Figure 4. How market mechanisms are modified. The figure shows how market mechanisms can be controlled through different types of relationships

usually smaller than nations, have found the same problems and therefore tried to create a competitive and dynamic environment inside the firm, an internal market. The trend towards 'a market economy' inside the firm has been strong and it is probably the most common way for firms to reorganize when profits are low. The market economy inside the firm is often some variation of the following:

☆ The firm is organized in four parts: CEO and executive committee, operational units with production and/or marketing in its core, internal service units, and staff units.

☆ As many units as possible are made profit centres (separate companies, business areas, divisions, etc.). These are the operational units and the internal service units.

☆ The delineation between staff units and internal service units is not entirely clear. Staff units can be seen as the extension of management of different levels. As such they are treated as cost centres even if they serve others. If possible, and in order to gain the advantages of the market mechanism, as many units as possible are turned into independent service units and profit centres.

☆ A profit centre is made as independent as possible meaning that, for example, a production unit may supply a marketing unit, but the marketing unit may use an outside supplier if it does not find that its brother or cousin in the family can offer the right conditions. An internal service unit may supply services together with outside suppliers and the operational unit's own specialists, but also sell its services to other firms.

Other forms are also possible: licences, franchises, co-operatives, intrapreneurship, and most likely structures that have been invented by individual firms and which have not even got a name.

Conclusion: as the market mechanisms have been brought into the firm, replacing the planned economy, it is not clear who is a seller, a buyer, or a competitor. The boundaries between 'us' and 'them' are not clear and marketing strategies have to be developed to handle this type of internal market relations.

6. *Interfunctional Dependency and the 'Part-time Marketer'*

When Iaccoca arrived at Chrysler as its new CEO and saviour, he met with a nightmare[18] (p. 162):

> Nobody at Chrysler seemed to understand that interaction among different functions in a company is absolutely critical. People in engineering and manufacturing almost have to be sleeping together. These guys weren't even flirting. . . . The manufacturing guys would build cars without even checking with the sales guys. They just built them, stuck them in a yard, and then hoped that somebody would take them out of there. We ended up with a huge inventory and a financial nightmare.

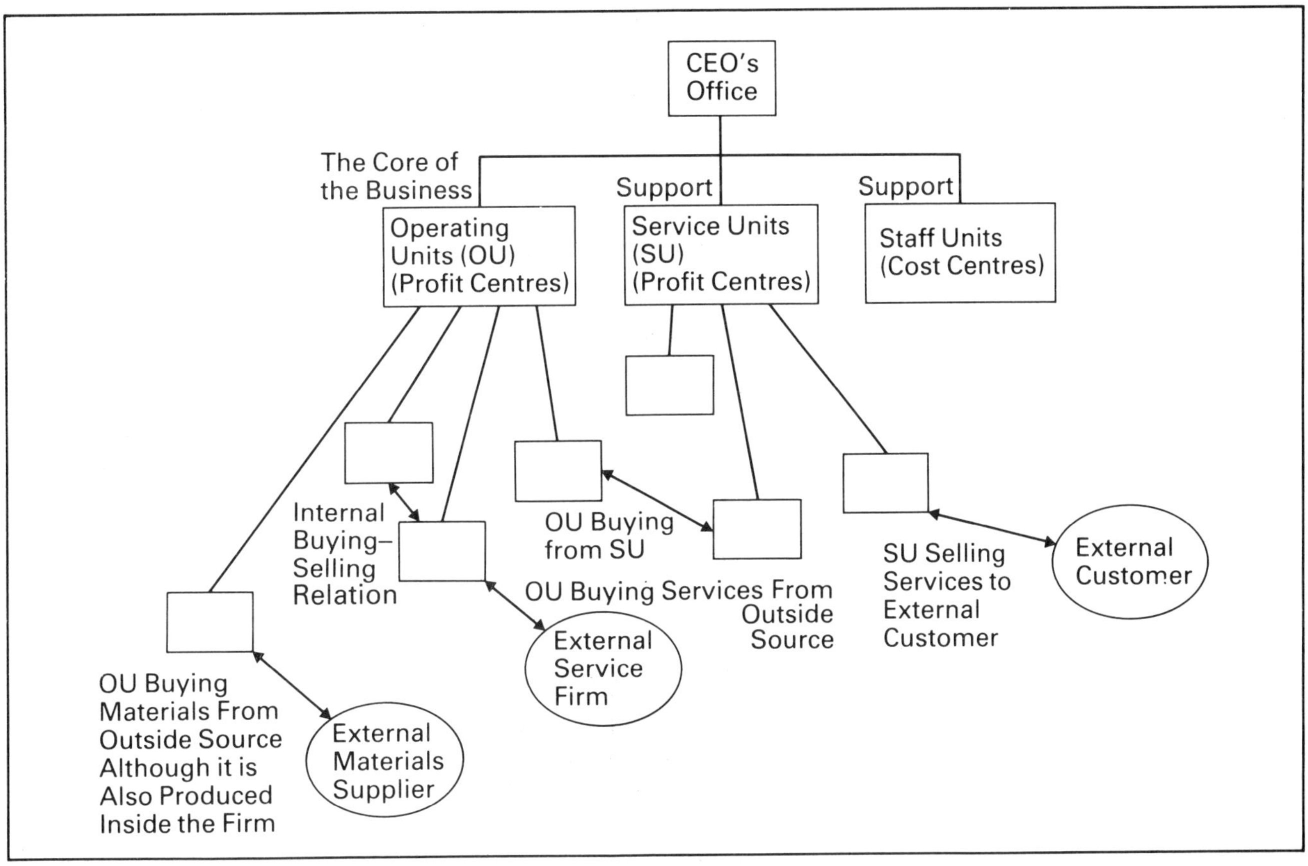

Figure 5. Markets inside the firm. The figure shows market relationships that occur when market mechanism are brought inside the firm, a divisionalized firm with profit centres

Let this quotation serve as an introduction to another relational aspect which is omitted by traditional marketing theory, namely the interdependency between functions. Marketing cannot live an isolated life, it is intertwined with all other functions of the firm. One of the pillars of the network/interaction theory is marketing's dependency on technology both in R & D, purchasing and manufacturing. This is particularly obvious where complex, customized equipment is produced. Services marketing theory has found that production, marketing, and even service development are largely handled by the same people. As a result the marketing function is spread throughout the firm; the marketing department sometimes becoming insignificant or even non-existent. Everybody is 'a part-time marketer'.

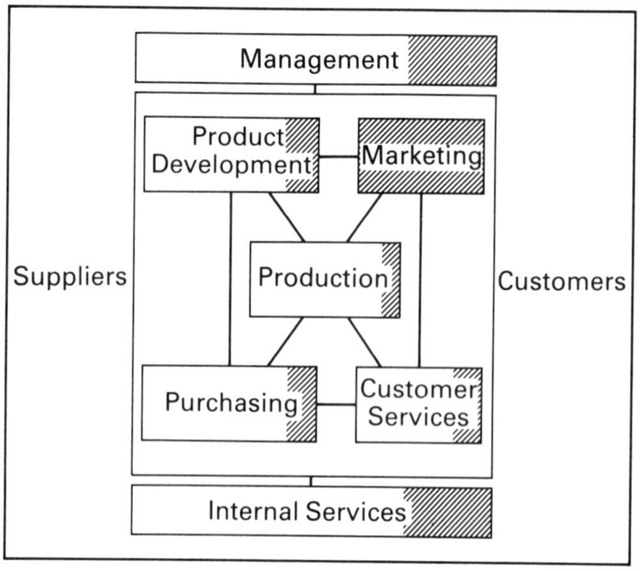

Figure 6. Interfunctional relationships and the distribution of the marketing function. The figure points to interfunctional dependency where full-time marketers appear in the marketing department and 'part-time marketers' are found in all other functions (shaded areas)

This conclusion has vast implications for the approach to marketing. It indicates that customer relations are influenced by everybody. The general manager negotiates big contracts and appears as a goodwill ambassador to customers, the telephone operator and the receptionist give the customer the vital first impression of the firm, the designers meet with customers to draw up the specifications that create 'fitness for use', those in charge of the firm's property management create a physical environment which influences the customer touring the supplier's plant, etc. The sales people are the professional 'contact persons' who build relationships. But they can never do it on their own. The problem, if marketing is unsuccessful in an industrial firm or a service firm, is often not the marketing department and its specialists, it is the marketing function as a whole and its integration with other functions.

Conclusion: the boundaries of marketing responsibility are dissolved and are no longer identical with the marketing department. The work to create and maintain market relationships is divided between the full-time professional marketers in the marketing department and the omnipresent (non-professional) 'part-time marketers'. The network of contacts inside the firm, the formal as well as the informal, the professional as well as the social, are part of marketing.

7. *Process Management and the Internal Customer*
The concept of the internal customer brings customer–supplier relationships inside the firm. It means that everybody should see himself as a customer of colleagues, receiving products, documents, messages, etc. from them, and that he should see himself as a supplier to other internal customers. Only when the customers are satisfied—it is the satisfied customer that counts irrespective of whether he is external and internal—has a job been properly executed. Ishikawa, one of the fathers of modern quality thinking, used the slogan 'the next process is your customer' back in the 1950s 'to resolve fierce hostility between workers from different production processes of a steel mill . . .' and 'still uses it today in his lifelong effort to break through the barriers of sectionalism in business organizations'[19] (p. vii). By making everybody a customer in his relations to others inside the organization we begin to see what happens in a firm as a proper process. Principles of process management have been used for many years in manufacturing and these principles are now also being applied to services and administrative operations, e.g. at IBM[20] (p. 329).

However, we must not fall into the trap of seeing internal relationships as simple. Once again a web is woven between many-headed internal suppliers and many-headed internal customers, a co-production relationship that establishes formal as well as informal links.

The concepts of the internal customer and process management have arisen in the area of quality, an area which is gradually being recognized as part of marketing and top level management. This recognition is due to a combination of Japanese and U.S. quality gurus and Japanese practitioners rather than marketing theory and practitioners in the West.

Conclusion: the customer–supplier relationship of process management links everyone together inside the company. They need to follow the golden rule of Christianity: 'Do unto others as you would have them do unto you'.

8. *Internal Marketing*
We have so far met at least two phenomena that could be labelled 'internal marketing': the fact that marketing takes place between units inside the same

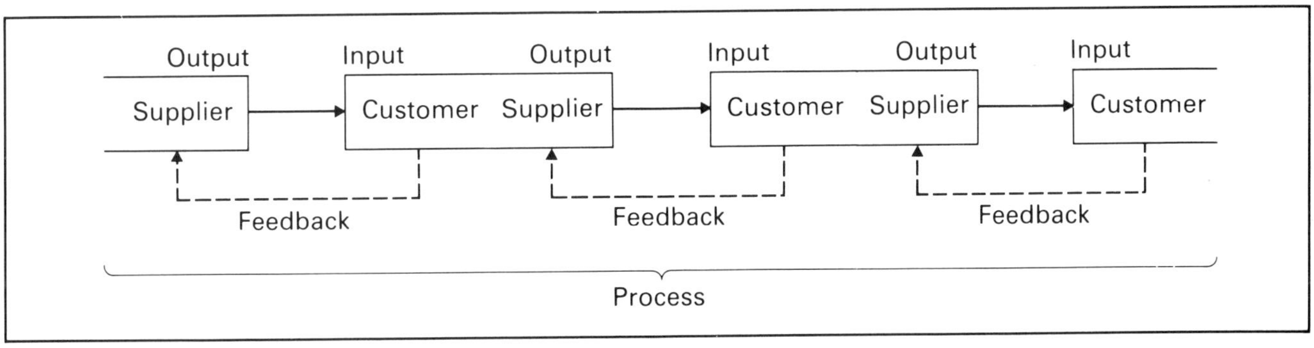

Figure 7. Process management. In process management everyone in the firm is linked with one or more individuals or groups in an internal customer relationship

firm, and the notion of the internal customer. Current terminology, however, as it appears in services marketing, reserves internal marketing for a third phenomenon. In internal marketing we apply marketing know-how, originally developed for the company's external marketing, to the 'internal market' as well. In service firms, where the interface with the customer is particularly broad and intense, it is essential that all contact personnel are well attuned to the mission, goals, strategies and systems of the company. Otherwise they cannot represent their firm well and successfully handle all those crucial 'moments of truth' that occur in the interaction with customers. It is equally important that management and supporting personnel are well informed or the internal customer–supplier relationship will be inhibited.

Internal marketing stresses that human resources are a key factor in the development and maintenance of a successful service business. Efficient internal marketing becomes a prerequisite for efficient external marketing.

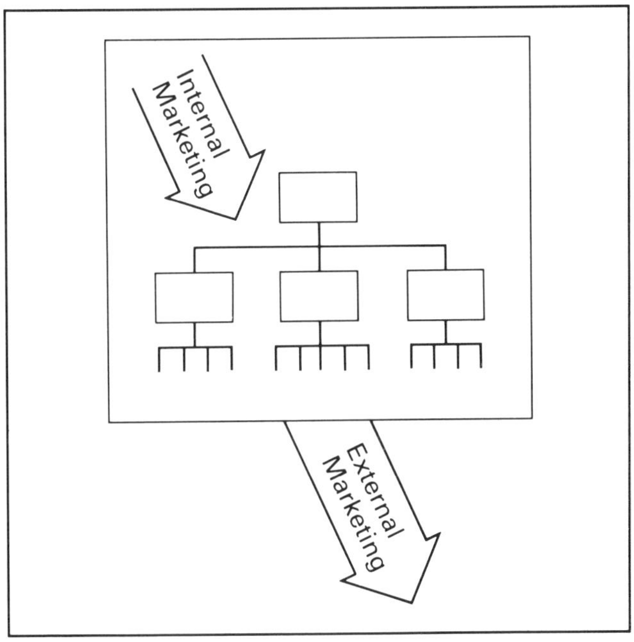

Figure 8. Internal marketing. Internal marketing, directed towards a company's own personnel is a prerequisite for successful external marketing

Internal marketing as a concept has emerged out of services marketing. However, there is no reason to see internal marketing as limited to service firms although it becomes more visible in a clear service setting. The interface between a firm's employees and its customers can be extensive even though the firm is not traditionally thought of as a service firm *per se*. This is particularly true of firms that market complex equipment or systems, whether it is to consumers or to businesses. But even if the interface is limited, companies desperately look for better ways of preparing their employees for organizational changes, the introduction of new products and services, new technologies, new routines, etc. Traditional ways of reaching out, using internal memos and magazines, meetings, training courses and recently to a greater extent video and computer techniques, leave a lot to be desired.

Conclusion: the personnel constitute a market inside the firm and this market has to be reached efficiently in order to prepare the personnel for external contacts. Know-how from external marketing can also be applied to the internal marketing.

9. *Relational Quality*

Quality is in vogue. Hopefully it will stay in vogue for a long time. Quality used to be an empty word that littered marketing textbooks, strategy statements, and advertisements, and was a cliché used in bombastic speeches by salesman and executives. During thg 1980s, quality is finding an identity. The definition which is gaining acceptance is that quality equals customer-perceived quality, or 'quality is in the eye of the beholder'. This is a market-oriented approach. Quality thinking has gone all the way from inspection in the factory to spot defective products before they are shipped, to the total quality concept of today which involves everyone, everywhere in the company seeking to continuously develop better quality through prevention—'doing it right the first time'. Quality is thus built into the product or service at the development and design stage.

Quality is important for marketing people. Understanding quality means that marketing people must become interested in technology, both design and production, be it a service firm or an industrial firm or a consumer goods firm. In 1984 when the author published a new book on marketing and had included 10 pages on quality, a critic in a professional journal grumbled that the quality pages were way out of place because 'this is not a book on manufacturing'. Today the book would have had a full chapter on quality and on marketing's contribution to quality, to the internal customer as well as to the external customer.

The marketing function contributes to quality in many respects. Acting as a spearhead to the market, it provides an input to the design department on market needs, wants, opinions, etc. It is expected to give accurate forecasts to engineering, production, personnel and other departments. Salesmen should not oversell, promising features that do not exist, or delivery times that are uneconomical.

Finally, we come to one area where the marketing department has a unique competence: relations to customers. If a delivery is late, or a product is defective, a good salesperson can handle the situation so that the customer eventually becomes satisfied. But we have said that almost all people are 'part-time marketers', meaning that they create and maintain relations and interaction. As the way we handle relations is part of the customer's (subjectively) perceived quality, we all contribute to his perception through high quality of relations. In a recent project on quality,[21] the term *relational quality* was coined in order to draw attention to the fact that relations are part of customer-perceived quality. This is alien to the engineer's approach to quality but it has emerged strongly in studies of services marketing where the notion of functional quality —how a service is delivered—is balanced against the traditional technical quality of the service[22] (pp. 38–40).

Conclusion: relational quality is a concept which has been formed to stress that skilled handling of relations between buyer and seller is part of customer-perceived quality. High relational quality contributes to positive customer-perceived quality and thus enhances the changes for a long-term business relationship.

Marketing Theory Goes Realistic—Towards a New Marketing Concept

The complex web of market relations that needs to be created, maintained, and also dissolved has been presented in words and figures. An attempt to integrate the relational aspects into a 'metafigure', has not surprisingly failed. The New Marketing Concept, as far as relational aspects are concerned, recognizes that:

- ☆ the terms buyer and seller can refer to any number of contacts between representatives from buying and selling organizations,
- ☆ the real customer does not necessarily appear in the market-place,
- ☆ the customer can be a co-producer who interacts with the seller as well as with systems, the physical environment and other customers, and that marketing can become an integral part of the production as well as the consumption process,

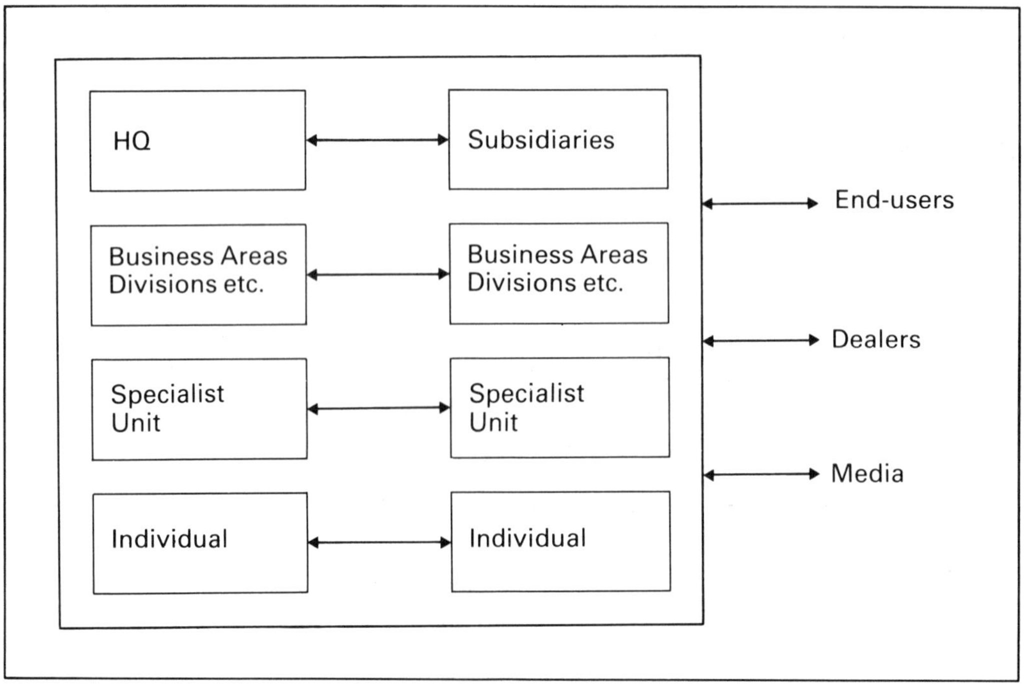

Figure 9. The quality of relationships. The quality of relationships, 'relational quality', affects the customer's perception of quality

☆ market mechanisms can be curbed in the external market, but also

☆ the market mechanisms have been brought inside the firm,

☆ customer relations are influenced by 'part-time marketers' from all sorts of functions within the firm, and consequently the interfunctional dependency in the firm must be emphasized,

☆ the internal processes can be better handled by introducing the notions of the internal customer and process management,

☆ efficient internal marketing is a prerequisite for successful external marketing, and finally

☆ relational quality is part of customer-perceived quality.

The interim conclusions in the research project on the New Marketing Concept can be summarized as follows:

> The importance of these nine issues does not follow the demarcation lines between consumer goods marketing, services marketing and industrial marketing. Their significance has been revealed by empirical research and practice, with the purpose of generating concepts and theories instead of verifying established 'myths' (or marginal variations of these 'myths'). They have emerged through the study of services and industrial marketing but to a large extent also build on previous know-how and the experience of practitioners, which have so far not been properly integrated into general marketing theory as presented in textbooks. Some aspects are seen better when services are studied, others when consumer goods are studied, or in an industrial setting. Some insights may be made by systematic academic researchers, while others are provided by 'reflective practitioners' through their direct involvement in actual events. Finally, few marketing situations are clear cut cases of consumer/industrial, or goods/services; those dichotomies are arbitrary and only temporarily useful as vehicles for thought. More often a firm's marketing is a blend of all of them in a unique combination.[23] Consequently: each marketing situation should be treated as unique and in its own right, drawing on all the available knowledge that may help in handling the situation.

The New Marketing Concept aims at integrating major aspects of marketing and alotting them proper weight. As was pointed out earlier, relational aspects are not the only ones that need to be integrated. International aspects are another example. This article should be read as a progress report from an ongoing research project that seeks to create a New Marketing Concept, which will be more realistic than the prevailing concept.

References

(1) R. J. de Ferrer, A case for European management, *International Management Development Review*, **2**, 275–281 (1986).

(2) C. Grönroos and E. Gummesson (Eds.), *Service Marketing—Nordic School Perspectives*, Research Report No. R 1985:2, University of Stockholm, Department of Business Administration (1985).

(3) H Håkansson (Ed.), *International Marketing and Purchasing of Industrial Goods*, John Wiley, New York (1982).

(4) R. P. Fisk and P. S. Tansuhaj, *Services Marketing—An Annotated Bibliography*, American Marketing Association, Chicago (1985).

(5) E. F. Cooke, What is business and industrial marketing? *Journal of Business and Industrial Marketing*, **1**,(1), 9–17, Fall (1986).

(6) J. N. Sheth, *Recent Developments in Organizational Buying Behavior*, Working paper, University of Illinois at Urbana-Champain, August (1976).

(7) D. A. Schön, *The Reflective Practitioner—How Professionals Think in Action*, Basic Books, New York (1983).

(8) R. Normann, *Service Management*, John Wiley, Chichester (1984).

(9) K.-O. Hammarkvist, H., Håkansson and L.-G. Mattsson, *Marknadsföring för konkurrenskraft*, Liber, Kristianstad (1982).

(10) R. McKenna, *The Regis Touch*, Addison-Wesley, Massachusetts (1985).

(11) F. G. Rodgers (with R. L. Shook), *The IBM Way*, Harper & Row, New York (1986).

(12) F. E. Webster and Y. Wind, *Organizational Buying Behavior*, Prentice-Hall, New York (1972).

(13) C. Grönroos, An applied theory for marketing industrial services, *Industrial Marketing Management*, **1** (1979).

(14) J. R. Lehtinen, Improving service quality by analyzing the service production process, in C. Grönroos and E. Gummesson (Eds.), *Service Marketing—Nordic School Perspectives*, Research Report No. R 1985:2, University of Stockholm, Department of Business Administration, 110–119 (1985).

(15) C. Grönroos and E. Gummesson, Service orientation in industrial marketing, in M. Venkatesan, D. M. Schmalensee and C. Marshall (Eds.), *Creativity in Service Marketing: What's New, What Works, What's Developing*, American Marketing Association, Chicago (1986).

(16) D. Ford, H. Håkansson and J. Johanson, How do companies interact? *Industrial Marketing and Purchasing*, **1**, (1) (1986).

(17) K. Ohmae, *Triad Power—The Coming Shape of Global Competition*, The Free Press, New York (1985).

(18) L. Iaccoca (with W. Novak), *Iaccoca*, Bantam Books, New York (1984).

(19) K. Ishikawa, *What is Total Quality Control? The Japanese Way*, Prentice-Hall, Englewood Cliffs, New Jersey (1985).

(20) E. H. Melan, Process management, ASQC Quality Congress, Anaheim, U.S.A. (1986).

(21) E. Gummesson, *Quality—The Ericsson Approach*, Ericsson, Stockholm (1987).

(22) C. Grönroos, *Strategic Marketing and Management in the Service Sector*, Marketing Science Institute, Cambridge, Massachusetts (1983); also Chartwell-Bratt, London (1984).

(23) E. Gummesson, Applying service concepts in the industrial sector—towards a new concept of marketing, in C. Grönroos and E. Gummesson (Eds.), *Service Marketing—Nordic School Perspectives*, Research Report No. R 1985:2, University of Stockholm, Department of Business Administration (1985).

Coordinating Business Strategy and Technical Planning

Alan L. Frohman, Associated Professor, Boston University and
Domenic Bitondo, Executive Officer, Bendix Corporation

Business managers face the decisions discussed in this article regularly. Without a systematic framework, the business context for these decisions is more difficult to establish and to communicate in a company. Where technology is the life-blood of the company, the strategic decision-makers can ill-afford to have the technological resources allocated in a sub-optimal fashion. Nor can they afford a business strategy which does not recognize the implications of their technological assets. This article describes an approach to technological strategy formulation that has successfully achieved this.

1. The Traditional Approach to Functional Decision-making

Traditionally, each functional sub-unit uses its own expertise to decide how to allocate resources. The Marketing Group will usually request what is most likely to satisfy the current demands of customers. Manufacturing will strive for a stable, balanced and efficient production process. R & D usually operates in the same fashion. A coherent approach makes more visible each functional unit's requirements and determines the trade-offs between achieving functional, sub-unit goals and overall business goals.

Functional and business managers wrestle with the decisions discussed here regularly. However, without a systematic framework, the business context for these decisions is more difficult to establish and to communicate in a company. Where technology is the life-blood of the company, the strategic decision-makers can ill-afford to have the technological resources allocated in a sub-optimal fashion. Nor can they afford a business strategy which does not recognize the implications of their technological assets. In this article we shall describe an approach to technological strategy formulation that has successfully achieved this.

Alan Frohman is Associated Professor, Center for Applied Social Science, Boston University Graduate School, 197 Bay State Road, Boston, MA 02215, U.S.A and Domenic Bitondo is Executive Officer with Bendix Corporation.

2. Strategic Technological Issues

To develop the technological strategy, the manager of a business or company must address how much to spend, on what efforts and when relative to the competition. They require knowledge of numerous factors such as:

(1) What are the key performance parameters of the product as seen by the customer?

(2) What are external technological sources doing, and how are we keeping up?

(3) What manufacturing processes have or could have a serious impact on the product?

(4) What technical competencies, if used differently, could result in new products for new markets?

(5) What new and/or different technologies are superseding existing technologies in products? And are we keeping up?

The list could go on-and-on.

The development of the technological strategy requires the leadership of the chief operating executive or manager, assisted by his planner, and the joint participation of Marketing, Manufacturing, Engineering and Research & Development. The determination of the technological strategies can be focused through joint discussions centered around the above sample questions.

3. Understanding the Interaction Between the Business and Technical Strategies

The technological strategy for a business unit depends upon the business strategy. A business strategy for a rapid growth market in which the unit's position is strong may require major support from R & D. On the other hand, support for R & D will be considerably less and very selective if the R & D is for a product with low growth and the unit's competitive position is considered weak. Digital Equipment Company's position in the field of minicomputers is an example of a company in the first category. American Motors is an example of a company in the second category.

In developing the process for the effective determination of the technical strategies, we start with the business strategy developed from the product portfolio analysis methods of the Boston Consulting Group[1] and the strategic marketing planning analyses described in Abell and Hammond.[2] We will use these references in defining a business strategy for purpose of illustration in this paper. Other methods can be used with only slight modification. The market and investment strategy for a typical product portfolio is summarized in Figure 1. The summary represents the product lines of a typical business unit of a corporation.

The determination of a business strategy is also based on a number of additional factors subject to high degrees of uncertainty such as economic and market forecasts, competitive developments and financial constraints. Account of one's own strengths and weaknesses also contribute to the development of the strategy. Examples of strategy statements are listed in Figure 2.

No attempt is made here to detail the methods used for this kind of analysis. They are well documented by the Boston Consulting Group,[1] Abell and Hammond[2] and similar sources.

This brings us to the identification of the implications of the business strategy for the technological strategy. While it is clear from the previous discussion that the business strategy heavily influences the technological strategy, the

Product Line	Market Attractiveness	Business Position	Relative Market Share and Trend	Sales Growth Rate and Trend	Forecasted Market Share Strategy	Product Line Needs	Product Life Cycle and Forecasted Position	Investment Strategy
Mechanical Product (M)	Low	Strong	4 X ↓	3% ↓	Give up Share	Existing	$ → $	Harvest
Solid State Product (SS)	Medium	Strong	0.3 X ↑	≈10% →	Increase Share	New	? → ☆	Aggressively Invest to Replace M Product
Aviation Product (A)	Low	Weak	0.2 X ↓	2% ↓	Divest	Existing	X → OUT	Harvest by Divesting
Health Product (H)	High	Medium	0.9 X ↑	12% →	Increase Share	Improved and New	☆ → ☆	Invest to Improve Business Position
Chemical Product (C)	Medium	Strong	1.5 X →	6% ↓	Maintain Share	Existing	$ → $	Harvest but Hold Share
Advanced Chemical Product (AC)	High	Medium	4 X ↓	12% →	Capture Dominant Share	New	☆ → ☆	Aggressively Invest to Replace C Product
Industrial Chemical Product (IC)	High	Weak	0 ↑	20% →	Capture Dominant Market	New	? → ☆	Aggressively Invest to Penetrate Market

Figure 1. Summary of market and investment strategy for a typical product portfolio

1. Aggressively Support the Newly Introduced AC Product (Which Replaced the Obsolete C Product) to Ensure Dominance
2. Maintain Performance and Price Strategies of S Product to Insure Share of Market as it Phases Out and AS Product Replaces it
3. Gain Share of Market for IC Product with Aggressive Development of New Product Based on New Technology
4. Gain Share of Market for SS Product as it Replaces M Product Which is Losing Market Share and Maintain Total Share of Market for Both Products Combined. Consolidate Models of M Product and Aggressively Apply Technology to SS Product
5. Gain Share in Market for H Product by Acquisition of Products to Round out Product Line

Figure 2. Summary of investment strategy

exact dimensions of the influence have gone relatively under-defined until recently. In the next section, we shall look at translating the Business Strategy (Figure 1), into a technological strategy with the proper fit.

4. Developing the Technological Strategy

The technological strategy appropriate for each business strategy can vary along a number of dimensions:

☆ Positioning the R & D strategy from defensive to offensive, depending on the Market Attractiveness and Business Position (Figure 3).

☆ Posturing of the R & D effort within the spectrum from state-of-the-art research (technology invention) to prototype development (minor application of existing technology), depending on product line need and Market Share Strategy (Figure 4).

☆ R & D meeting objectives ranging from eliminating products to developing new products to new specifications[3] (Figure 5).

☆ Matching the needs of the product, depending where it is in the life cycle requiring R & D from product innovation to cost reduction (Figure 6).

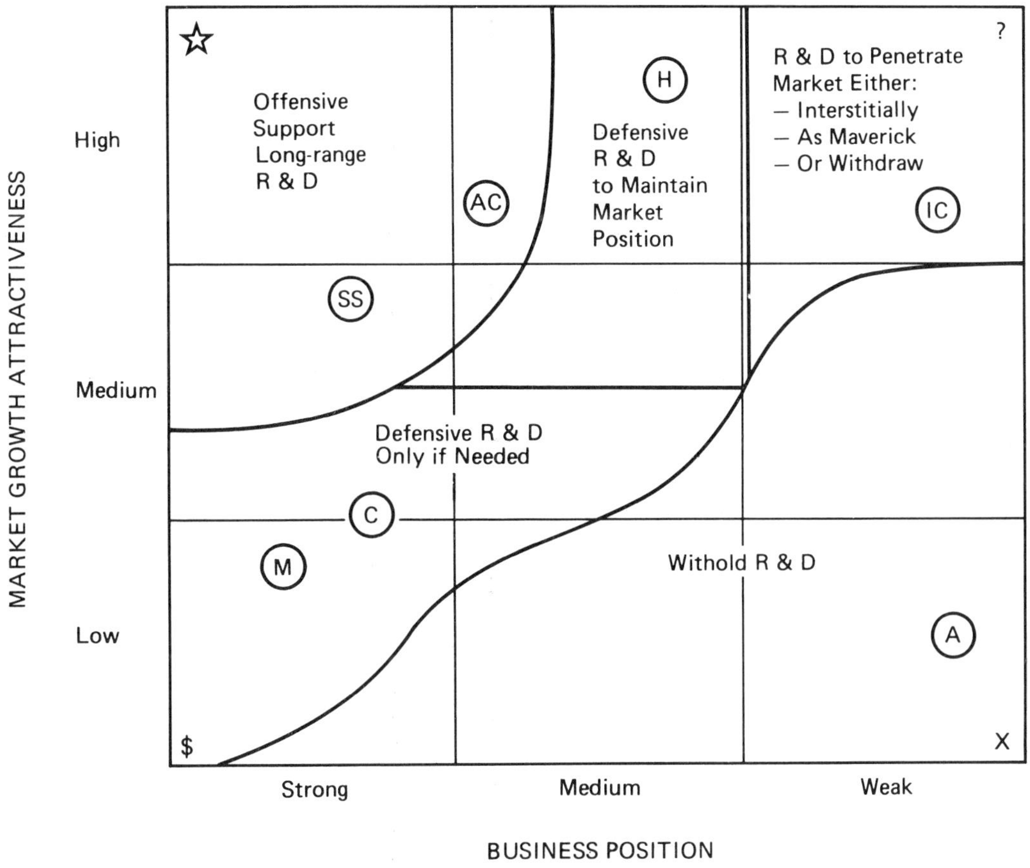

Source: Adapted from Henderson – Reference 1.

Figure 3. Research and development strategy correlated with relative investment opportunity

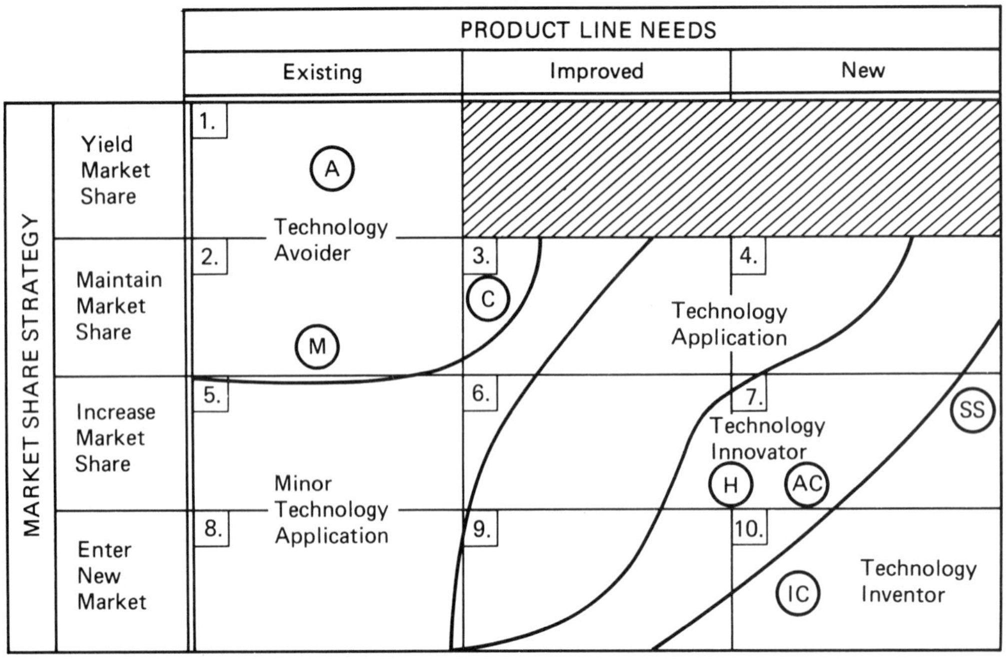

Source: Adapted from Johnson & Jones – Reference 3

Figure 4. R & D posture for each product line

☆ The maturity of the technology in its own life cycle from new to stagnant (Table 1).

☆ The strategy for acquiring the technology ranging from internal development of technical capability to licensing (Table 2).

After the investment and product line needs have been defined, the functional responsibility for reaching the goals and the role of R & D must be determined. Note that from Figure 5, for a product strategy relying on existing products, a market strategy is mainly required. For improved or new

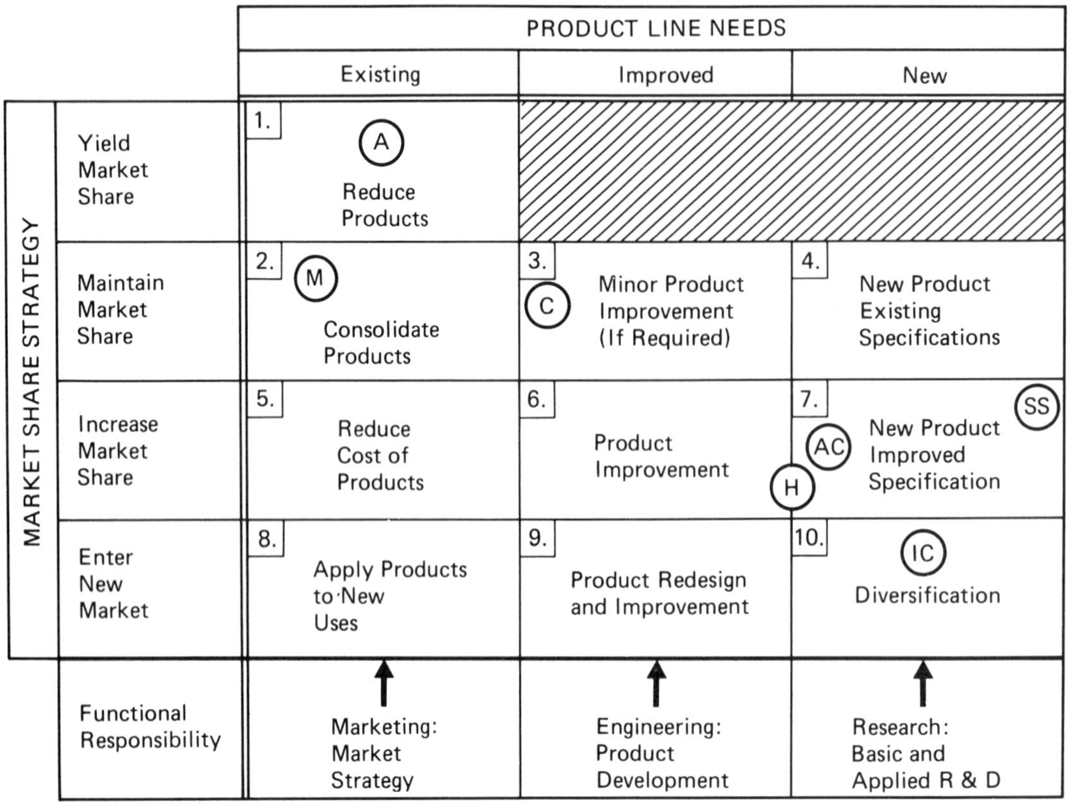

Source: Adapted from Johnson and Jones – Reference 3.

Figure 5. Product line strategy

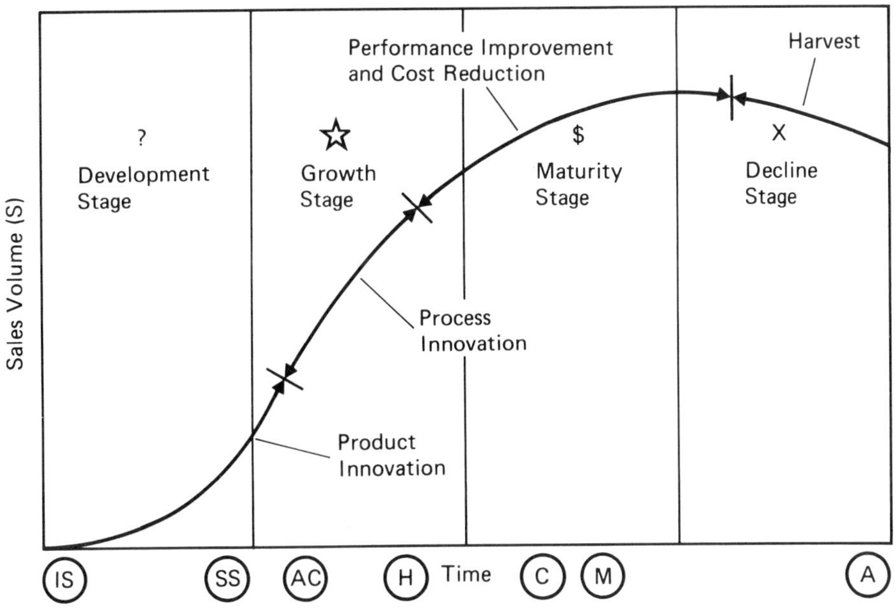

Figure 6. Product life cycle and R & D match

Table 1. Technology cycle

New
Rapidly advancing
Evolving normally
Stagnant

Table 2. Technology acquisition strategy

Leader—internal capability
Follower—awareness - limited effort
Subcontracting—within
—outside
License
Joint venture
Acquisition

products, the emphasis is placed on the technology strategy for each product. What function is responsible in leading and developing the specific strategy for each product will depend on the emphasis of the strategy. The implications of the investment strategy for the R & D strategy is shown on Figure 7. This chart is intended for the purpose of general positioning and getting correlation and agreement on the R & D strategy as it relates to market share and sales growth rate (Figure 7).

The Technological Strategy derived from Figures 1–7 and consistent with the Business Strategy of Figure 1 is summarized in Figure 8. The summary of the results in Figure 8 helps the business unit to address the more specific questions that have to be answered in a technology strategy. Some of these questions are listed in Table 3.

5. Formulating the Technological Strategy: R & D Strategy Workshop

Deciding on the resources and determining the technological strategy can be accomplished by means of an organized R & D Strategy Workshop where the data and the analyses represented by Figures 1–8 are presented and the questions of Table 3 (plus other questions) are used to stimulate the thinking of the participants in preparation for their participation in the R & D Strategy Workshop.

Experience suggests that such a meeting is most successful if attended by Planning, R & D, Engineering, Marketing and Manufacturing; two to five from each function. Specifically, this group should include:

- ☆ The Head of Marketing and selected Marketing people who are visionary rather than sales-oriented.
- ☆ The Head of Engineering and selected engineering people who are oriented toward technology changes important to business interests rather than protective of past design.
- ☆ The Head of Manufacturing and selected manufacturing people who are familiar with division manufacturing capabilities and the direction these capabilities should take.
- ☆ The Head of R & D and the top R & D people who are most prolific idea generators and contributors.
- ☆ The Chief Executive of the business unit and the planning director who can act as secretary.

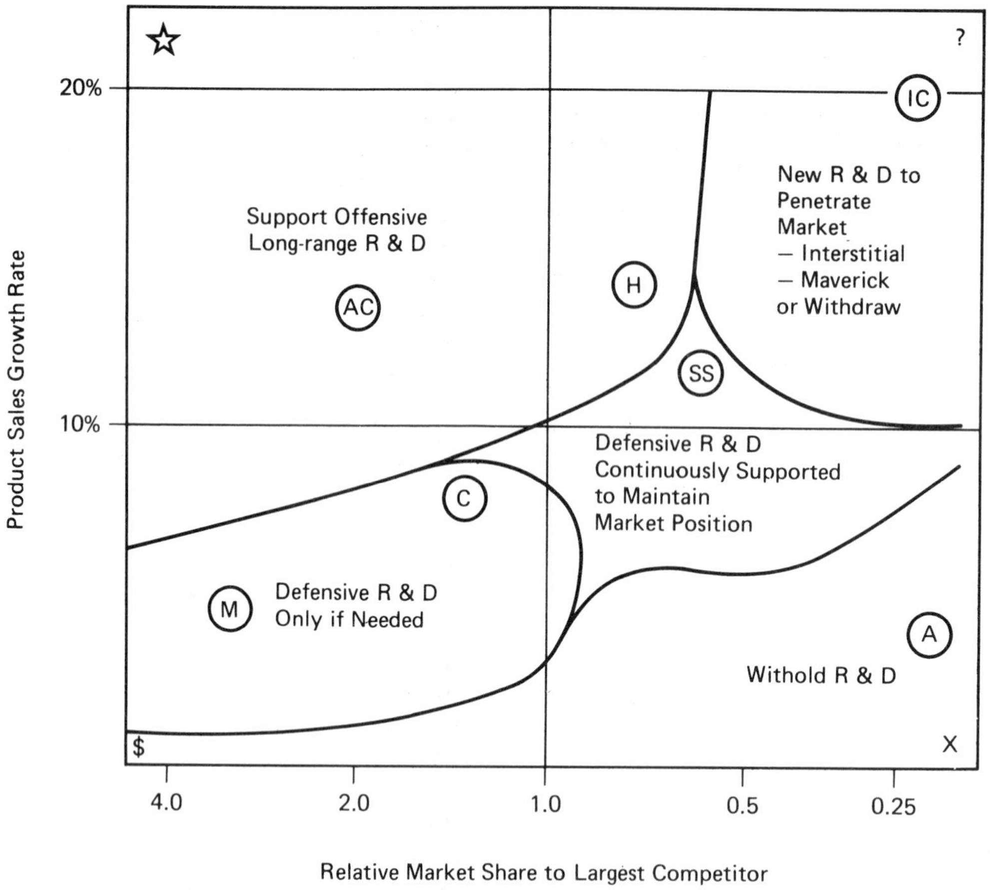

Figure 7. R & D strategy as it relates to relative investment opportunity

During the workshop, the participants in response to the questions in Table 3, provide information suitable for discussion and debate which eventually brings out the R & D strategies for each of the product lines and identifies the distinctive technical competencies (DTC) important to the product lines.

6. Formulating the Technological Strategy: Analysis

The allocation of resources in Figure 9 can now be analyzed from the standpoint of the product line or along the distinctive technical competencies (DTC). Andrews,[4] whose early book still is one of the most valuable in the field, has used the phrase 'distinctive competence' referring to business strategy. We shall adopt that phrase to technological strategy formulation and call it 'distinctive technical competence' (DTC).

Distinctive Technical Competence(ies) (DTC) are what the organization is particularly good at. It includes the skills, know-how and expertize of the people as well as other resources of the organization such as its reputation, patent position and capital equipment. A competence is a demonstrated and potential ability to accomplish against the opposition of circumstances or competition what a company sets out to do technologically. An example of an organization's DTC in 'Precision Small Mechanisms' is:

> Our engineering ability in the field of precision manufacture of high quality mechanical products containing numerous small parts is one of our DTC's. We have no particular talent for low cost manufacture. Our competence lies in the field of products where quality is relatively more important than low manufacturing cost.

Figure 9 identifies the allocation of R & D resources to each of the product lines spread by distinctive technical competencies (DTC). The Other Technologies are the remainder of the R & D programs that are in support of the DTC's. During the R & D Strategy Workshop the allocation of resources in Figure 9 are analyzed as a function of the Technological Strategy outlined in Figure 8. A discussion along one product line and one DTC will illustrate this point.

The mechanical product utilizes two DTC's (Figure 9)—precision small mechanisms and plastics—the other two are not applicable to this product line. Since this product line is in its maturity stage of Product Life Cycle (Figure 6), only defensive R & D is planned if needed. In this case, in order to maintain market share as its shrinks, reducing costs by incorporation of plastics for metal parts is required. If R & D on behalf of this product line had been planned for Precision

Table 3

A. Technology objectives
● Is it our objective to apply technology for product innovation; for process innovation; for product performance improvement; for cost reduction? ● Do we need to replenish our technology (i.e. advance and/or catch-up with the state-of-art?
B. Technology selection
● What technology(ies) to invest in for current products? ● What future technology(ies) to invest in to provide opportunities for future growth? ● How to exploit existing technological capability for maximum return and/or new products for new markets?
C. Technology investment level
● How much to invest in each technology? ● How stable to maintain R & D investment?
D. External intelligence
● How much effort to expend obtaining knowledge of competitive and external direction? ● How to organize the technological surveillance effort?
E. Technological posture
● How close to the state-or-the-art should the firm's technology be? Should we be the leader or just maintain an awareness? ● What should the balance be between basic approach, applied approach, development and applications engineering?
F. Technology acquisition
● To what extent should internal vs external sources of technology be relied on? (licensing, joint venture, acquisition, other divisions, central research organization, contract research (government and outside companies), and internal development are possible options)
G. Technology organization and policies
● How to organize technology in the business (e.g. centralized vs decentralized)? ● Should a project, functional or matrix organization be used? ● Is a 'dual ladder' necessary? ● Should R & D facilities be established in other countries? ● Are the hiring and reward practices consistent with the strategy?

Small Mechanisms, an explanation would be required.

Now, let us look at the resources allocated for the Precision Small Mechanism technology. There is no need to expend any effort for the Mechanical Product Line and the Aviation Product Line while the Chemical Product Line needs defensive R & D to reduce the cost of the product either through product redesign or process improvement as shown in Figure 8. Also, since all three product lines are either in the declining stages of the product life cycle, or very close to entering those stages, there is no need to advance the state-of-the-art in this DTC. Therefore, no funds are allocated to replenish this competency (Figure 9). If this strategy continues over several years, the DTC will die as a strength of the organization. On the other hand, since it has been and still is a very strong capability, management should explore the advisability of exploiting the DTC for new products and new markets. Some resources should be allocated to 'R & D for Studies' to exploit the DTC for new products. If no new products are forthcoming after sufficient exploration, this DTC should be closed down as all the products depending on it move into the 'Dog' stage of their product life style. Other product lines and other DTC's can be analyzed in the same way.

Examples

In another company whose sales had stabilized at \$40m for several years, at a technical strategy workshop it was brought out that the design and assembly of precision small parts into an intricate and accurate mechanism was a strong distinctive technical competence (DTC). However, the DTC was in support of two major product areas both of which were being replaced by semiconductor technology. Once the DTC was highlighted, discussions ensued about exploiting this DTC in new products for new markets. Since the DTC was almost close to being proprietary in the sense that other organizations could not build up the skill, products based in this DTC could have a competitive edge. The company decided to be more aggressive in exploiting the DTC to develop new products. A brainstorming session was held, and out of over 90 ideas presented 12 were recognized as having considerable potential for the company's growth.

In a review of the technical strategies of a company whose products were designed of exotic materials to withstand extreme environments of temperature, vibration and stress, it was determined that one of their DTC's was Advanced Manufacturing processes. Sales based on these products totaled \$100m. The present capability of the Manufacturing Department was based on several advanced processes developed over the past 15 years in their R & D program. However, during the last recession, arbitrary cuts of the R & D budget resulted in almost a complete elimination of this DTC. At that time their technical strategies were not well defined, nor were they based on the analysis of their DTC's and consequently no one could defend this area. As a discussion of their future position continued, it became obvious that the advantage they had built up with their exotic manufacturing processes had deteriorated, and if allowed to continue, would make them less capable than their competition. Now that this DTC was made visible to management, it was decided to strengthen this DTC and to build up their processing capability.

Product Line	R & D Strategy	R & D Posture	Product Line Strategy	R & D and Life Cycle Match	Lead Responsibility for Strategy	Technology Cycle of Prime DTC	Technology Acquisition
Mechanical Product (M)	Defensive R & D if Needed	Technology Avoider	Consolidate Products	Cost Reduction	Marketing	Stagnant	Internal Capability
Solid State Product (SS)	Offensive Long-range R & D	Technology Inventor	New Product to Improved Specs.	Product Innovation	R & D	New and Rapidly Advancing	Central Lab then Internal
Aviation Product (A)	Withold R & D	Technology Avoider	Eliminate	No Investment	Marketing	Mature	Eliminate
Health Product (H)	Offensive Long-range R & D	Technology Innovator	Product Improvement and New Products	Product and Process Innovation	Engineering and Manufacturing	Mature	Awareness
Chemical Product (C)	Defensive R & D if Needed	Technology Avoider	Consolidate Products	Performance Improvement	Engineering	Stagnant	Awareness
Advanced Chemical Product (AC)	Offensive Long-range R & D	Technology Innovator	New Product and Improved Specs.	Product Innovation	R & D	Rapidly Advancing	Internal and Assist from Central Lab
Industrial Chemical Product (IC)	R & D to Penetrate Market — Maverick	Technology Inventor	New Product in New Business	Product Innovation	R & D	Rapidly Advancing	Internal Capab. and Assist from Central Lab

Figure 8. Technological strategy

Product Line \ DTC	Precision Small Mechanism Technology	Chemical Technology	Plastics Technology	Semiconductor Technology	Other Technologies	Total R & D Funding	Sales	Profit
Mechanical Product (M)	0	—	$ / $ / $	—	0	$ / $ / $	$	$
Solid State Product (SS)	—	—	0	$ / $ / $	0	$ / $ / $	$	($)
Aviation Product (A)	0	—	0	0	0	0	$	($)
Health Product (H)	—	$ / $ / $	$ / $ / $	—	$ / $ / 0	$ / $ / $	$	$
Chemical Product (C)	$ / $ / $	0	$ / $ / $	—	0	$ / $ / $	$	$
Advanced Chemical Product (AC)	—	$ / $ / $	0 / 0 / $	—	$ / $ / $	$ / $ / $	$	($)
Industrial Chemical Product (IC)	—	$ / $ / $	0	—	$ / $ / 0	$ / $ / $	0	($)
Research Replenishment	0	$ / $ / $	0	$ / $ / $	0	$ / $ / $	0	($)
Exploitation Studies	$ / $ / 0	0 / 0 / $	0	0 / $ / $	0	$ / $ / $	0	($)
Totals	$ / $ / $	$ / $ / $	$ / $ / $	$ / $ / $	$ / $ / $	$ / $ / $	$	$

Key: — DTC is Not Applicable
0 DTC is Applicable but Not Funded
$ Funding for this Fiscal Year
$ Funding Plan for Next Year
$ Average per Year Funding for Next Four Years

Figure 9. Distinctive technical competencies (DTC) and R & D investment

In both these cases, by carefully defining the DTC's, management was better able to focus on the technical strategies that were important to their business and determine gaps in their R & D program that would have resulted in deterioration of their technical capabilities in the future.

By being able to link their DTC's to their product lines and relate the technical strategies to the business strategies it became quite obvious which R & D areas needed support.

We recommend that similar analyses be made of the top competitors including a determination of their Distinctive Technical Competencies. It is recognized that the kind of detail required may not be available, or be very sketchy at best, but analyzing a competitor in this way provides a more tractible set of areas (i.e., each DTC) to gather future data in order to determine their technical position.

Further analysis of Figure 9 brings out the fact that Semiconductor Technology, a relatively new field to the company, is applicable to only one product line. Economy of scale may be a problem if the effort under exploitation does not bring forth new products. Also since this is a new DTC, the company needs to catch up and stay ahead, therefore, research funding for replenishing the DTC is required. With only one product having to support all this technical effort, its financial picture may look bad. Since it is a new DTC, funds to exploit its use in new products are allocated. This example illustrates the need for a corporation to see that its DTC's are exploited by a multitude of products. Also, if a new DTC is needed, such as is the case here (to stay in a market because Solid State Product are replacing Mechanical Products), it may be best to review the other alternative to get out of the market and apply existing DTC's to new products as being a more profitable route. Figure 9 presents the data in a compact form, analyses and judgments are required to make the final strategic decision. Many other comparisons are possible from a careful investigation of Figure 9.

7. Technological Strategy and Fit with Other Functions

The strategy of each function needs to be formulated so that it is compatible with the business strategy and with each other. This is true for all functions; Manufacturing and Marketing will be used as examples of this general point. The technological strategy has important implications for manufacturing in the design and pilot manufacture of new products. The technological strategy must also be able to support the implications of the business strategy for manufacturing. For example, is a new process necessary to manufacture the new product and will R & D be required to develop the process? (e.g. Industrial Chemical Product, Figures 1, 8 and 9). Or is cost reduction a requirement thus needing the development of a more efficient process (e.g. Chemical Product, Figures 1, 8 and 9)?

Similarly, the link between marketing and technological strategy needs to be consistent. The product development process embodies the crucial interface between the technology groups and marketing. The technology groups are responsible for determining what is feasible and the cost. The marketing groups are responsible for determining what the market needs are, volume and price. The technological strategy must be able to support and maintain the target position of the product in the market and relative to competitors.

The R & D Strategy Workshop and the questions used by the participants bring out the above concerns (and more), and as a result of the discusion that ensues, decisions and actions are determined.

8. Summary

In business dependent upon technology for their future, it is critical that the technology be strategically managed. We have presented some of the factors and practices we have found useful to organize the thinking and data and to link it to the business plan. Without deliberate management attention to these matters, the life blood of a technology-based business may be slowly drained.

Bibliography

(1) See Bruce D. Henderson, *The Experience Curve-Reviewed, IV. The Growth Share Matrix of the Product Portfolio* (Boston: The Boston Consulting Group, 1973), Perspectives No. 135. Also: *The Product Portfolio* (Boston: The Boston Consulting Group, 1970), Perspectives No. 66.

(2) Derek F. Abell and John S. Hammond, *Strategic Market Planning*, Prentice-Hall, Englewood Cliffs, New Jersey, Dwg (1979).

(3) S. Johnson and C. Jones, How to organize for new products, *Harvard Business Review*, **35**, 49–62, May–June (1957).

(4) K. Andrews, *The Concept of Corporate Strategy*, Dow Jones, Irwin, Homewood, Illinois (1971).

Creating a Manufacturing Strategy to Suit Your Business

A. John Pendlebury

The development of manufacturing strategy requires approaches and techniques different from those used in the past. To play its proper role in establishing competitive advantage, the contribution of manufacturing must be recognized explicitly and exploited in conjunction with marketing, design and purchasing. Strategy and implementation are inseparable, and are a vital force in overcoming resistance to change.

So much has been written, particularly in the American literature, about the way in which we in the West have been neglecting our manufacturing base that it can come as no surprise to learn that many people have been seeking to explain the causes of our relative decline and the reasons for the neglect.

The subject is of vital importance to the health and welfare of us all since it has become the accepted wisdom on both sides of the Atlantic that high value-added activities need to relate to a strong manufacturing base. This has been recognized in places as far apart as the State of Florida, the Scottish Development Agency and the steel towns of the Ruhr.

Manufacturing is a process requiring the organization, creative flair, and sheer hard work of thousands of people to be successful and as such is one of the highest forms of human activity, plainly distinguishing us from the rest of the animal kingdom (a few odd ants and bees perhaps excepted!). Nevertheless, the status of manufacturing remains low in most Western societies and even in the manufacturing company, the manufacturing executive often has lower status than his counterparts in other functions such as marketing or finance.

Too often the manufacturing function has been a passive element in the 'loftier' strategic processes which have frequently been assigned uniquely to other functions or to specialist strategic planners. This state of affairs may have come about for a variety of reasons arising in the past, including:

☆ The prevalence of restricted national seller's markets not placing undue emphasis on manufacturing cost, quality or delivery performance

☆ An emphasis on standardization, thereby simplifying the manufacturing mission

☆ Undemanding customers, unused to international comparisons, strong on brand loyalty and unsophisticated in their buying habits.

As a result there was little demand to make manufacturing the centre of attention and manufacturing management suffered accordingly, both in quality and importance.

The situation really began to change after the first oil crisis in 1973, when the Japanese were particularly hard hit. It was at this time that the Chairman of Toyota, Mr Ono, propounded a strategy for his organization which will ultimately reshape the modern world. He saw that the crisis would kill his company unless they adopted a much sharper approach in manufacturing. Manufacturing became the key to survival and success with issues such as elimination of waste and unnecessary variability of demand being the order of the day. The consequences were phenomenal, so much so that I will never forget my first exposure to the practical implications of these ideas in the French motor industry in the late 1970s. Eliminate complexity, forget detailed control, simplify the organization, and achieve a drastic reduction in stock were the messages from Toyota, taken up also by the remainder of the Japanese auto industry.

In the early 1980s the Japanese had demonstrated success in other equally important areas: quality circles and more general Total Quality Control. Meeting Ishikawa in 1981 (the inventor of the fishbone diagram and other important elements)

John Pendlebury is Managing Director of Coopers & Lybrand Associates Europe.

revealed that it was not an issue of Japanese culture, the whole world could benefit too.

So we find at the present time that the market conditions have changed beyond recognition in that

- ☆ The market is now a buyer's market
- ☆ It is fought for on a global basis
- ☆ More items have become fashion items and therefore customized (e.g. motor cars)
- ☆ The sophistication of buyers has greatly increased.

Yet, paradoxically, many manufacturers are still operating on the basis of the old, more passive, rules of the game as if they were playing three-and-in soccer at one end of the field and someone unnoticed to them had moved the goalposts to the other end.

The important issue now is, therefore, to recognize that changing conditions have brought about a need for companies to place much more importance upon manufacturing so as to meet the rapidly evolving needs in the market-place. This is not a short-term issue: it is strategic, requiring much more active participation of manufacturing in determining the future direction to be taken by the company. From now on manufacturing will have to be given a role nearer to centre stage, otherwise the organization will be threatened as a whole.

In parallel with this development and as a necessary consequence we have seen an explosion in the challenge to conventional strategic approaches in which the Western preoccupation with the short-term non-manufacturing issues (such as financial to marketing linkages) has led to disinvestment and, therefore, decline.

Equally the problems brought on by over-reliance on short-term financial measures and the short-term, 'stock market' orientation of many companies have arguably prevented them from taking the longer-term view for which the Japanese, and to some extent the Germans, have become respected.

Finally and very importantly, we have been experiencing until very recently conditions under which investment in industry was unattractive as compared with leaving money in the bank. Some authors have sought to show that this is the main cause of the difference between the different manufacturing countries. Certainly in the United Kingdom we have experienced some of the worst returns on industrial investment, whilst also having the highest real rates of interest. However, we may need to admit that it is an industrial management problem that creates poor returns on investment and a financial management or political problem that creates dearer money than anywhere else.

In the remainder of this article I shall be describing some of the problems of setting up a manufacturing strategy in more depth and then showing how in my experience it is possible to come up with dynamic, aggressive and change-oriented strategies covering not only manufacturing but also the functions with which manufacturing must most commonly interface, including finance and accounting and the knotty return on investment problem.

It must be emphasized that the experience is very recent, post-dating such new ideas as computer aided design and manufacture, just-in-time manufacturing, computer integrated manufacturing and total quality concepts. This newness is an essential element since it is only with these revolutionary ideas that massive changes in productivity, stock-turnover, design-to manufacture times and other key performance indicators have become foreseeable for most companies within a reasonable period in the future.

This is why manufacturing has become so strategic, since massive changes can now be contemplated and introduced within the space of a few years, even months in some cases.

Priorities, Concerns and Action Plans of Manufacturers

A luxury available to consultants in the large international firms is the ability to draw upon a wealth of client data and attempt to generalize from it. Equally it is possible to draw upon the findings of academic institutions who carry out large-scale survey work in manufacturing companies.

Drawing upon the results of the Manufacturing Futures survey undertaken annually over a period of years by the Universities of Boston (U.S.A.), Waseda (Japan) and INSEAD (France) by Ferdows, Miller, Nakane and Vollman, reveals the plural and multi-disciplinary nature of competitive priorities, areas of concern, and programmes being implemented by the world's leading manufacturing organizations in Europe, the United States and the Far East.[1]

The evidence from the data suggests in my view that the West is generally becoming a follower of Japan in strategic terms which is particularly disturbing. This can be seen as follows:

- ☆ Competitive priorities: Japan is particularly concerned with rapid design change and low prices while the West is still more concerned with quality and reliability issues
- ☆ Major concerns: quality comes out the top concern world-wide, but while the West worries greatly about indirect cost structures and materials and inventories, the Japanese are much more

concerned with process yields and the impact of new technology. A major worry for Europe is that new product introduction is a major issue in the United States and Japan but not in Europe, not, I suspect, because Europe has solved the problem before anyone else

☆ Action plans: there is clear evidence that the Japanese are forging ahead with automation whilst most Western counterparts are primarily concerned with labour motivation and other 'softer' subjects such as planning and control.

My own experience of the strategies now needed by the major companies known to me leads to three interesting conclusions regarding their approach to setting directions for future progress:

☆ They normally require to balance the strategy across the functions, with the functions most often needing to be involved being design/engineering, marketing, purchasing, finance and distribution, although departments such as quality and human resources also need to be heavily involved (and committed)

☆ The areas tackled can be drawn from a very wide range with companies frequently wanting to tackle a subset of the major issues, including: flexibility, working capital, quality, planning and control, new product design and development, service levels, price, automation, productivity, energy, human resources and financial performance

☆ In most organizations, it proves very difficult to transmit to the shop floor strategies decided and agreed upon at the very top.

These conclusions suggest strongly that the existing approaches to strategy determination are both simplistic and not sufficiently sensitive to the times in which we live.

The Problems We Encounter in Manufacturing Industry

There are essentially four different problems encountered in trying to achieve massive change in large-scale manufacturing operations:

☆ The attitude of people and their cultural environment

☆ Taking on board new technology

☆ Putting new management systems and processes in place

☆ Justification of the investment;

each of these areas is discussed in turn below.

People and Culture

The most striking thing about making change is the sheer immovability of most organizations when confronted with it, no matter how good they are as an organization. In fact, it is often the very best organizations which are hardest to change. They become proud of their capabilities and effectively stop listening both to their customers and to the other organizations with which they interface (suppliers, competitors, etc.).

The problem is, in fact, a very old one with a quote from Machiavelli on the subject being my favourite, with words to the effect:

> There is no process more difficult to institute nor more perilous to conduct than the implementation of change; for the new methods have as enemies all those who are beneficiaries under the old order of things, while only lukewarm support from the proponents of the new.
>
> Machiavelli, The Prince

Organization structures create a basis towards incrementalism as can be seen from the way in which similar projects repeat in different areas. Engineers call it the not-invented-here syndrome. Over-rigid and hierarchical structures impose an inbuilt bias against major change since no single function can instigate major change while any single one can block it.

The consequences of a blinkered approach within the function are widespread and ultimately destructive. If the organization does not take a periodic look at itself as a whole, degradation will set in (a preoccupation with short-term efficiency, for example, at the expense of effectiveness through broader more radical reforms).

It is important to delve into the major functions to understand how incremental activities within them can seriously degrade manufacturing performance; some examples are given below:

Marketing. Product proliferation for marginal business (one million options on a European saloon car)
Unrealistic expectations on costs and lead times.

Engineering. Proliferation of similar designs
Overly vertical product structures
Unmanufacturable products
Over-costly and untimely design.

Finance. Emphasizes control at expense of efficiency
Provides wrong information (exactly wrong rather than roughly right)
Cannot cost things properly.

This list is by no means complete, but does give some feel for the real problems the manufacturing function has to face.

New Technology

No matter what we say about the use of advanced new technology the instigators of the new concepts will often pay a high price for their valour. Being first usually costs more than planned and requires relatively rare and precious skills. In many cases the new technologies are only just arriving, so the leaders in the field must be better at implementation and project management than any of their competitors if they are to stay ahead.

Having made these points though, the move to new technology, even when relatively untried, may prove irresistible in situations where a technology-based strategy is so devastating in its market impact that business life with such competition would lead to ruin (examples abound in defence, machine tools and the service sectors of the economy).

In this sense the adoption of new technologies can be seen as a high-wire balancing act, good if you can do it but terrible folly if you are unable or unskilled in the use. Many organizations either duck out altogether by setting unsuitable investment hurdles or move in without sufficient knowledge, thought or experience, thereby condemning themselves to expensive failure.

In any event we should not seek to introduce dramatic new technologies to rejuvenate geriatric management; it cannot work.

Management Processes and Systems

The way in which a business is run is in itself a technology which has evolved over a considerable time. What is new right now is that fundamental questions concerning this technology are being posed, primarily as a result of the astonishing performance observed in leading companies in Japan.

As a result of the oil shock in 1973, Toyota rethought its manufacturing strategy and came up with a production system which has become the model for the world. More surprising still, it overturned most of the theories of scientific management propounded in the West since the end of the war, disposing of many sacred cows.

A comparison of just a few of the differences between the new ideas and the original Western tradition is made in the box.

These differences are so fundamental that they were not understood for several years before they were taken up in the West and demonstrated to be equally valid there too.

Strategy in the manufacturing company must, therefore, pay due consideration to the ways of working to be adopted. It was this appreciation that took the Japanese motor industry to 'least cost operator' position. The same attitudes have percolated through the myriad of suppliers so as to impact upon the whole of Japanese industry.

Western model	*Japanese idea*
Production workers need to be extensively controlled	Make the worker as much responsible as possible
Organizations need to be well-structured, carefully divided and with staff support	Keep structures flat and maximize the responsibilities within the line organization
Quality is a management and staff function	Quality is the responsibility of all
Systems need to be comprehensive and handled by specialists	Simplify the process and look for visibility of control and feedback characteristics
Efficiency is the goal on narrow measures	Effectiveness is the goal on broader measures
Inventories promote productivity	Inventories inhibit productivity improvement
Complex problems must be controlled by complex systems	Simplify or remove the problem at source

Cost Justification

Cost justification methods have come under attack as (particularly U.S.) managements have come to realize that short-term orientation tends to push managements into low investment (and ultimately destructive) paths.

Return on capital employed and return on investment criteria have often been set so high as to prevent investment in technology taking place at all. High finance charges are only one of the reasons for the problem becoming severe, yet:

> We may be getting to the point where business is reluctant to expand plant and equipment with borrowed money for fear that, if investments should not be productive, they couldn't pay the service costs on the money they borrowed.
>
> Alan Greenspan, Chairman Federal Reserve Board, 17 July 1986

If the cost of financing falls, it is likely that an explosion of interest in factory automation will occur as capital becomes more privileged at the expense of labour.

The relationship between the cost of money and the return on industrial investments is in the view of some economists one of the key performance measures of macroeconomics. In this respect the United Kingdom has been just about the world's poorest performer. It is interesting to observe that the interest rate/industrial return rate is far lower in Japan and in West Germany than in the United Kingdom or United States, although whether we are measuring cause or effect is far from certain. In recent times the United Kingdom's economy has shown some improvement, with the average return on industrial investment rising sharply.

The policies of Western governments and local authorities on grants and incentives have over the last few years been oriented towards helping companies over the problem, both in the United Kingdom and overseas. In fact, the U.K. Department of Trade and Industry (DTI) is much admired in other European countries for its strenuous efforts to promote improvements in industry, whether investment or innovation.

We must, however, still question the competence of managements who set targets too high. By doing so they are foregoing profitable opportunities for their businesses without finding alternative ways of sustaining them. Interestingly, high investment hurdle rates are not a universal problem: the process industries, for example, look for much more realistic rates of return on heavy capital investment than their counterparts in mechanical or electrical engineering. Little wonder, therefore, that the chemical industry has outperformed the others in the U.K. economy since 1979.

Existing Approaches to Strategy

From what has been seen above, it is clear that a variety of obstacles are presented to organizations seeking to obtain competitive advantage from their manufacturing operations, many of them self-imposed. A further problem is that conventional approaches to determining strategy assume a passive role for the manufacturing function. In this sense, manufacturing has never in recent times been allowed to play its proper and vital part. Thus as a result, Western manufacturing has been losing its competitive edge.

Even more alarming is that, when finally company managements give manufacturing a real chance, the results are often profound. In one recent case a major manufacturer was on the point of transferring his entire manufacturing process to the Far East, and this would have been the strategy, assuming a passive manufacturing capability.

He developed, however, an aggressive manufacturing improvement programme along the lines to be explained in this article and achieved great results in almost every dimension (productivity, quality, delivery and cost) so that now he is least cost operator world-wide, having reduced his product costs by 35 per cent. Other examples from some of IBM's manufacturing plants have demonstrated the same results, the most well-known example being the plant at Lexington, Kentucky, where an aggressive strategy in manufacturing, including investment in automation, just-in-time manufacturing, product redesign and major redeployment of labour led to a fundamental transformation in competitive performance, again leasing to low cost operator status. Interestingly enough, after much evaluation and adjustment, return on investment criteria was successfully met.

From the point of view of the head of operations, the evolution of approaches to strategy as commonly developed and practised might be seen as follows:

- ☆ Strategies determined primarily at the interface between marketing and finance: these include the activities of portfolio theory adherents, cost cutting specialists and a variety of others
- ☆ Strategies giving recognition to the nature of competitive advantage, in which the cost structures in manufacturing, distribution, supplies, etc. are given more prominence but which remain essentially fixed in the marketing and finance functions[2]
- ☆ The work carried out recently at Harvard by Skinner, Wheelwright and Hayes, giving more recognition to the central and pro-active role of manufacturing in improving competitive advantage, and drawing upon the relative success of Japanese and German companies.[3,4]

It is only in this later work that manufacturing has begun to receive attention more attuned to its potential importance, thereby changing the approach required when setting not only manufacturing but also business strategy.

However, even in this recent work, an important element still does not receive sufficient attention: the contribution of the design and engineering areas, where not only is the company's future market success determined but also 70 per cent or more of final product costs.

In a recent statement made around the time of release of first quarter 1987 results, Mr John Akers, Chairman of IBM, made clear that, apart from cost and expense cutting, the top priority of his organization was faster time to market, a critical area in the design-to-manufacturing interface. This is exactly the priority that many Japanese companies are placing on engineering-related issues, thereby putting design and engineering in their rightful place at the heart of good strategy.

In what follows below I shall be describing how manufacturing and related functions such as engineering and purchasing can be successfully brought out of the cold and into the strategic arena. The emphasis is on vision, planning, implementation, continuous improvement, the achievement of consensus and respect for people.

The inspiration is the recent work of Skinner, Kaplan, Hayes, Porter, Wheelwright and others and the progress made by the Japanese and the people who have learnt from them (companies such as HP, IBM, Ford, Fiat, 3M, Harley Davidson and Philips).

The New Requirement for Setting Manufacturing Strategy

There is almost certainly no universal approach to establishing manufacturing strategy which can meet the needs of the wide diversity of companies having an interest in the subject. Se we need at the outset to document the essential requirements of the majority of organizations wishing to develop radically new manufacturing concepts, recognizing that many organizations will nevertheless slip the net.

Below are summarized my own perceptions regarding the range of issues that need to be covered in the majority of cases:

☆ The strategy must be singular, compelling, visionary and easy to communicate

☆ It must reflect clearly the relations with other critical functions: marketing, design, engineering, purchasing, distribution, spares, quality, finance and personnel

☆ It must address, correctly, fundamental business issues such as profitability, capital structure, ownership, customer service, personnel policy, systems strategy and corporate culture

☆ Competition must be understood, analysed in full and responded to in devastating fashion

☆ It must be implementable by being developed down into action plans which are correctly balanced between people, systems and technology

☆ It must gain the commitment of the organization as a whole

☆ It must be feasible, in terms of what it asks people to do, over the time period in consideration

☆ Incremental tendencies in the different functions must be largely eliminated so as to optimize the whole rather than isolated individual parts

☆ The methods used in cost justification should be developed, defined and justified as part of the strategy itself.

Having laid down these principles, which may seem only too obvious, we can go on to describe how such a process can be successfully developed, based upon having seen and assisted a number of organizations do the same things themselves, while drawing on advanced ideas or technologies to achieve radical change.

In general the following stages need to be undertaken as illustrated schematically in Figure 1:

☆ Establishing the critical business performance requirements to meet the requirements of the owners

☆ Development of a vision of the future (such as low cost operator, fastest to market, most flexible response, leader on service, best product range, technological leadership, etc.)

☆ Forming the new concept, including the new roles of all functions involved

☆ Balancing the concept between the functions, to understand how they will all benefit and checking back against the business requirements

☆ Committing the organization to the concept and particularly to the benefits which can result

☆ Completing the justification process, together with any necessary modifications to be introduced in the evaluation techniques

☆ Setting up the action plans, timescales and priorities for implementation

☆ Balancing the implementation between people, systems and technological factors

☆ Obtaining the resources and skills necessary to implement the plans

☆ Documenting and communicating the strategy and plans

☆ Organizing the follow-up process to make sure that objectives are met in line with commitment.

This process of development has been designed to address some of the basic problems faced by organizations trying to make major shifts in the way manufacturing is carried out and has been exposed to the demands arising in a number of very different situations.

There are several aspects in the development process which are of note.

We balance in two stages: first, at the concept level between the functions (we seek consensus), and second, at the implementation level so as to move the process through the middle management level where many strategies come unstuck (respect for people).

Return on investment (ROI) is sensitive to the two-level balancing, because at the implementation level our hurdle rate depends on the direction of change (there are three possible axes: people, systems, technology, and we can move freely in this space). However, it is at the functional level that our final ROI criteria must be evaluated since not only manufacturing but also marketing, supplies, quality, human resources, finance and accounting, design, engineering, distribution and spares are also potential beneficiaries. Again the target ROI must reflect the nature of the benefits being obtained.

The conceptual development must be carried out by a strong manufacturing and engineering team with responsibility to link with counterparts in all the functions who might be implicated. This stage must have the commitment, support and active participation of the top management.

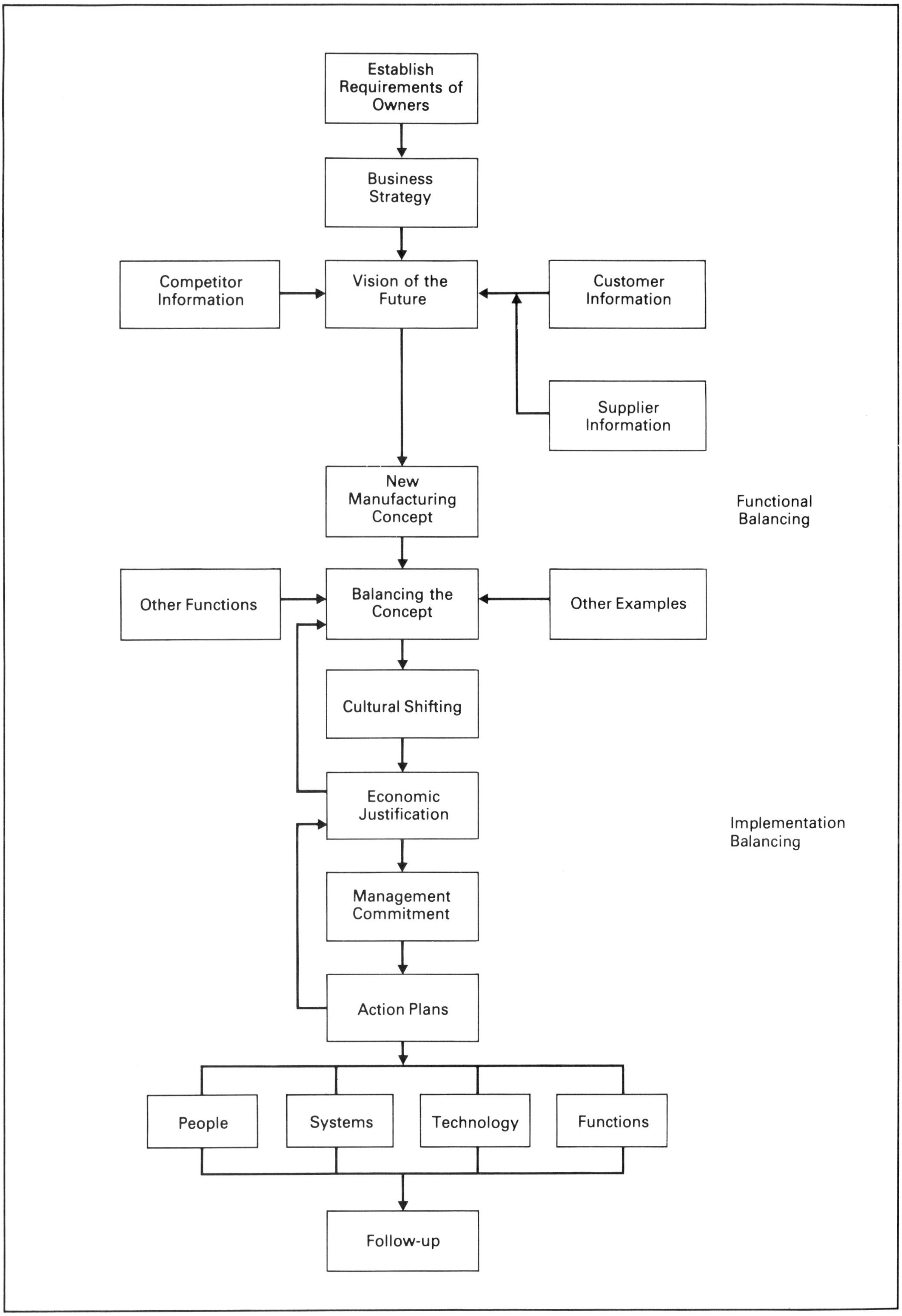

Figure 1. Stages in developing manufacturing strategy

Functional balancing is no easy affair, the kind of manufacturing concepts envisaged are drastic in their impact and result in major shifts proposed for many business parameters. Below are the elements which have appeared recently in representative cases:

☆ Work in progress and lead times reduced 80 per cent

☆ Halving in design time

☆ Reduction in the number of parts in a product by 50 per cent

☆ Reduction in quality related costs by 20–50 per cent

☆ Productivity up 40 per cent

☆ Elimination of finished goods inventories,

all of which in the first place tax the belief of functional and middle managements and to some extent can reflect badly on them or cause them anxiety; hence the need for the balancing process so as to create a shift in corporate culture and attitudes.

Functional balancing requires visits to other organizations who have already to some extent taken the same path themselves and perhaps also a degree of reassurance from independent expertise, of university professors or their staffs, or outside consultants.

The justification process will generally be iterative in nature as we play with the implementation plans and vary priorities. It is quite possible to 'tune' the strategy using ROI criteria as the output variables.

If difficulties are experienced in achieving a satisfactory ROI, it is necessary to examine the directions of change to ensure that the balance is 'optimal' between the possible elements (i.e. people, systems and technology) and to consider whether the hurdle rates are appropriate to the direction of the change taking place.

The idea that hurdle rates are direction-dependent has been successfully put into practice by at least one major multinational corporation, while many others vary the rates according to underlying risk. Figure 2 shows how very different strategies can exist at the implementation level. Direction A is relatively people and systems oriented, while direction B is much more hard-technology driven.

Of great interest are strategies which are unidirectional since it is questionable whether they are ever the optimum route. Examples are so-called IT strategies, isolated AMT applications and people-only strategies. To be effective on one axis really requires consideration of the other two.

If at the implementation level the benefits are not at first apparent, the calculation and structure of product costs needs to be reappraised to ensure that the structure is indicative of real costs (e.g. materials handling, quality costs).

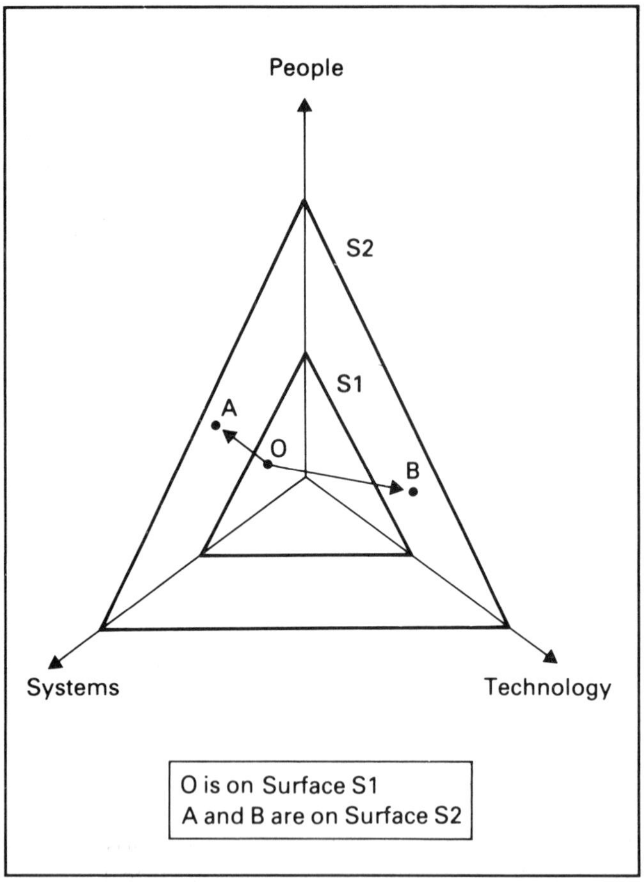

Figure 2. Understanding manufacturing strategy at the implementation level

Once the analyst is sure that implementation level issues have been dealt with in full, he may next wish to examine the issue of functional balance. The idea here is to test how variation between the possible beneficiaries can influence the overall return. An example here might be reduction in finished goods inventories, which, when accompanied by higher flexibility, benefits both sales and manufacturing, if not, one is favoured at the expense of the other.

The message must be that there has to be some (higher) level at which the investment must be justified, otherwise the investment is not viable.

Only one exception to the principle can be tolerated, the one that obtains when the gap between ROI and the (re-evaluated) target ROI is so small as to be compensated by non-tangibles. This situation can come about in infrastructure-type projects such as information technology updating, AGVs, and administrative and accounting systems investments.

Once the strategy represents an acceptable development from an investment standpoint, we will have balanced the plans not only between the main company functions but also between people, systems and technology. After this stage the requirement is to complete the detailing of the action plans and their order of execution and then document the strategy and its implementation.

While it is one thing to make plans it is sometimes more difficult to obtain the resources necessary for execution. In my experience almost all organizations will fail to make the necessary provision of skilled resources to undertake what has been so carefully planned. The difficulty lies as much as anything else in organizations failing to understand where the bottlenecks to change really are. Techniques are becoming available to assess an organization's capacity to undergo radical change.

Once the plans have been finalized and resources identified, the next step is to communicate the plans and strategy to the organization itself. Effective communication will do a great deal to overcome resistance to change, although the process is very dependent upon the leadership given by top management for it to be effective. Top managements sometimes underestimate the importance of their role in making change come about through a process of strong and dynamic leadership.

Execution of tasks must proceed as far as possible to plan and this requires monitoring and follow-up processes to be introduced. Follow-up is particularly important to make sure that business benefits accrue as planned in line with ROI criteria. In general, performance measures are needed specifically to measure achievements against objectives; they may be very different from those used in the past.

Examples

It is not easy to quote the names of the companies who have successfully used manufacturing to create sustained competitive advantage, unless they have been prepared to make such information generally available. Nevertheless, the mixture of anonymous and well-known cases described below are representative of what has been and is being achieved.

IBM—The Lexington plant's recognition of the need to become cost efficient and 'least cost operator' world-wide marked a significant turnround in the design and manufacture of its product. Of particular interest in this case was the effort put into economic justification and the very real emphasis on people and their need for re-training and redevelopment.

UK confectionery manufacturer—In this case there was a clear perception that the interface between marketing, manufacturing and personnel would be critical to the vision of the future. The manufacturing system was reorganized to bring primary materials nearer to sources of supply and finished products closer to market. Factories were focused on one primary mission. Products were rationalized down to perhaps half the original number of brands. Employment was cut via a generous redundancy and re-training package. Plants were modernized by significant investment in new process technologies supported by new working practices. The result was 5 years of Japanese-style annual productivity growth.

General Electric, domestic appliances—This case in the United States has been documented in video as an application of just-in-time and other techniques, but is notable for efforts to simplify the product design and improve reliability. Apart from efficient manufacturing the result was a significant improvement in market share, accompanied by greatly reduced service and warranty costs.

Consumer products, United Kingdom—In another fast-moving consumer goods case, the issue was to convert a well-documented and argued business strategy into a realistic and practical plan, capable of implementation across the full range of company functions. This process required that the business vision be re-interpreted and modified successively so as to meet IRR requirements and produce a devastating competitive edge. Sub-strategies in product development, manufacturing technology, human resources, computer systems, quality, supplier relations and customer service were the result bound together through a major project management and investment programme. A video supports this case.

Electronic systems manufacturer and supplier—The issue here was how to create greater responsiveness to the market in a major supplier with old-established traditions of quality and service. Higher flexibility in the market demanded new concepts for manufacturing very different from those in use in the past. It was difficult for managers to accept that new methods would bring about radical improvements, since radical change implies an unacceptable degree of past deficiencies. The new vision was subjected to considerable discussion and debate with a clear need emerging for a more gradual process of adaptation and change than might otherwise have been contemplated. Initial projects were introduced to validate elements of the new concepts so as to catalyse the introduction of still greater change. Of late the pace of change has accelerated as managers have become aware of the new possibilities open to them. All project targets have been exceeded by the organization so that the company-wide goals set at the outset are being worked to with high hopes of success. This particular strategy is not of itself too investment intensive although the environment is generally one of sophisticated product and process technologies.

Conclusion

The development of manufacturing strategy requires approaches and techniques different from those used in the past. If manufacturing is to play its proper role in establishing competitive advantage, its contribution must be recognized explicitly and in conjunction with the synergies likely to come from exploiting links with the other functions such as marketing, design and purchasing.

Balancing the strategy at two levels is an important part of the process, not only to secure commitment and consensus, but also to understand the impact of investment on the financial and business ratios.

Above all, strategy and implementation are inseparable. Success depends on being able to deliver to plan the vision and concepts established at the outset, and overcome the inevitable resistance to change.

Acknowledgements—I am indebted to a great number of people for their ideas in the area of manufacturing strategy, including colleagues in Coopers & Lybrand, executives in client companies and leading academics who have been prepared to give of their time to discuss their ideas freely, including Professors Ferdows, Skinner, Hayes and Wheelwright.

References

(1) Private communication from Professor Ferdows, 1986.

(2) Michael E. Porter, *Competitive Advantage,* Free Press, New York (1985).

(3) Wickham Skinner, *Manufacturing, The Formidable Competitive Weapon,* John Wiley, Chichester (1985).

(4) Robert Hayes and Stephen Wheelwright, *Restoring Our Competitive Edge, Competing Through Manufacturing,* John Wiley, Chichester (1984).

How Information Technology is Transforming Corporate Planning*

Siegfried Höhn, Director, Strategy and Investments, Volkswagen AG

This article illustrates the importance of the use of information technology in planning and control in an automobile company and outlines the possibilities and limitations in the use of different forms of information systems. It discusses the demands the user places on the new systems and what problems and implementations requirements arise in operational practice, within the framework of planning and control.

Introduction

The growing variety and increasing complexity of requirements for the timely development, manufacture and sales of industrial products, produces an increasing need for information. This applies both to the shaping of such industrial processes and to their sequence. Satisfying the requirement for information is decisive especially for the productivity and flexibility of industrial manufacture. Securing and processing of information thus represents a basic problem in the application of information technology. In the same way, the public discussion is to considerable extent being conducted in a manner related to what is offered, stimulated by the dynamic progress of development in computer technology. If the technical resources and possibilities are changing, the question should be raised all the more as to their use. The BIFOA takes credit for concerning itself at a very early date with the application of this technology to business administration planning and control. My comments below will follow this method from the point of view of the practical user.

Siegfried Höhn is a Director of Volkswagen AG and in his present position is in charge of Strategic and Investment Planning for the Volkwagen Group.

*Lecture held at the Specialist Conference on the occasion of the 20th anniversary of the founding of Business Administration Institute for Organization and Automation (BIFOA), 'Company Management and Information Technology' on 4 October at the University of Cologne.

The application of information technology should be included in the field of the application of overall technology itself. The problem-related, humane use of technology belongs to the elementary strategies of our industries. Planning and control must therefore concern themselves integratively with the realization of this strategy, and become involved in the process of policy-setting in order to solve the conflicts involved. On the other hand, planning and control themselves depend on the employment of information technology. Whereas cost accounting in the sense of rationalization was the initial object of application of the computer, data bases for functions and operation today dominate in the field of producing computer-aided information. This level of development in data processing in the company represents a challenge for business planning and control. The systems of cost accounting are faced with the danger of becoming divorced from the complexity of actual, operational activity, if one restricts oneself only to updating old systems. Operational management of information is required. Here, the beginnings could lie in developed planning and control concepts as part of management organization; cross-linking of management information with the operational data bases must be assured in this context.

The increasing need for company-specific planning control and reference data makes increasing demands on the efficiency of information technology. This is particularly valid for companies with comprehensively interconnected performance and manufacture which transcend natural boundaries, and whose strategic orientation and operational planning are determined by a variety of external and internal factors (Figure 1).

The availability of planning, control and reference information and its user-related transformation is in essence decisive for the efficiency of the operational

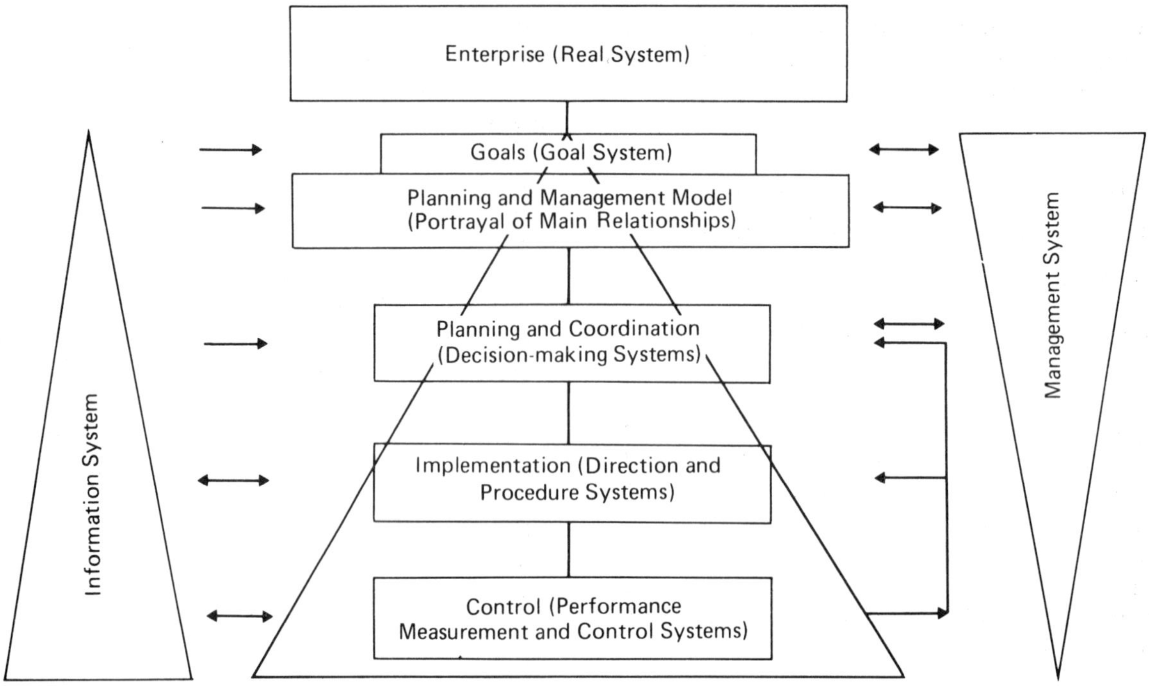

Figure 1. Information, planning and control in the management system of the Volkswagen Group

combination of resources, and thus for the competitive position of the company within the competitive environment. Here, information management occupies a key position; its productivity and possibilities to react can be considerably improved by using new information and communication technologies.

The short- and long-term adaptation of company operational structures to changes in the constellations of competition-determining data has become more and more marked by computer-aided systems, which considerably simplify the process of acquisition, analysis, evaluation and user-related representation of information (Figure 2). Particularly in the process of mastering the large quantity of economical and technical information typical for the wide range of external and internal data bases offered, efficient data acquisition, processing, representation and reference systems tailor-made for specific company needs are essential.

I should like to illustrate the importance of the use of information technology in planning and control in an automobile company. In view of the considerable number of different systems used in planning, direction and control of production programmes, flow of materials, employment, research and development, quality assurance, costing, investment and financing, my treatment of this complex field can only contain an outline of the possibilities and limitations to use of different forms of information technology.

I intend to show what demands the user places on the proficiency of new information systems, and to

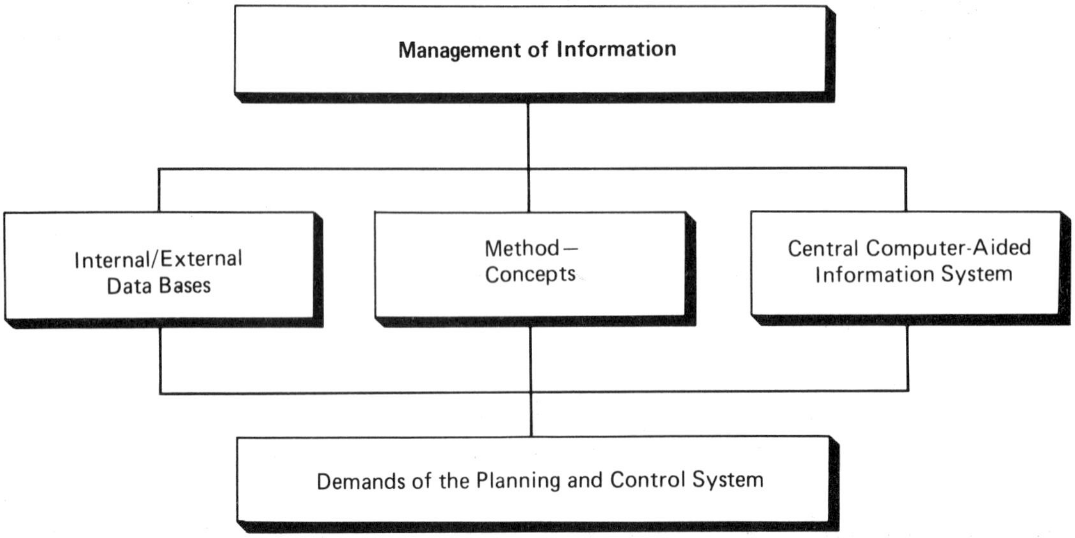

Figure 2. Management of information

discuss what questions and implementation requirements arise in operational practice within the framework of planning and control.

The Importance of Information Technology for Business Planning and Control

The need for businesses to adapt to external and internal changes, makes it necessary to have early-warning information, containing evidence of the probably point of occurrence and the extent of these changes. In addition, by linking the macro-data influencing the company to the micro-structures to be adapted a presentation must be given of what actions are necessary and which alternative concepts in planning and control must eventually be implemented, in order to achieve business goals under the changed conditions.

As information technology must produce data related both to the future and to the past, different demands are made on the process of acquiring, storing, processing and communicating information. This concerns on the one hand methods of acquiring information, and on the other hand the degree of aggregation in planned and actual data.

Deduction of Information Requirements
Building an information system for planning and control requires in the first instance a comprehensive definition of information requirements. This requirement profile results from:

☆ the goals of business policy;

☆ the strategic and operational business concept;

☆ the economic and technical planning of functional areas and overall planning;

☆ the comparisons of target with actual figures for control and the resulting performance data and

☆ company-specific flows of performance and production and of the link in information transcending national boundaries.

Information requirements are assessed according to functional criteria, taking into consideration the requirements of areas and cost centres, in addition to the centrally oriented data requirements for overall planning and business control (Figure 3).

Acquisition of Information
The employment of information technology has taken on increasing importance, particularly in the use of external and internal data bases for planning, direction and control. The demands for current information have led to a world-wide build-up in data base systems containing both data from the past and forecasts of future trends. The majority of database firms have set up information networks operating internationally, and they are offering the broad range of data stocks from the IMF, the OECD, the EEC, research institutes, national statistics offices, important economic associations and consulting firms.

In spite of this comprehensive data service available at short notice on the basis of efficient data transmission and receiving systems, there are considerable gaps in this information—judged against the needs for information in a multinational company (Figure 4). This is particularly true in comparing statistical data from different sources within the framework of analyses, and also when examining information and competition within an industrial sector.

Basic information is available for an assessment of data relating to demand, in the form of trade data bases, but major stocks of data for the analyses of competition in sales are lacking.

In addition to large amounts of quantitative data, external data bases often also supply qualitative information which is important for an evaluation of the opportunities and risks contained in business decisions. This consists predominantly of socio-political, ecological and technological data.

Internal data bases containing data related both to past and future are of considerable importance for planning and control (Figure 5). The acquisition and up-dating of data takes place in the light of the requirements of specialized areas and of the need for

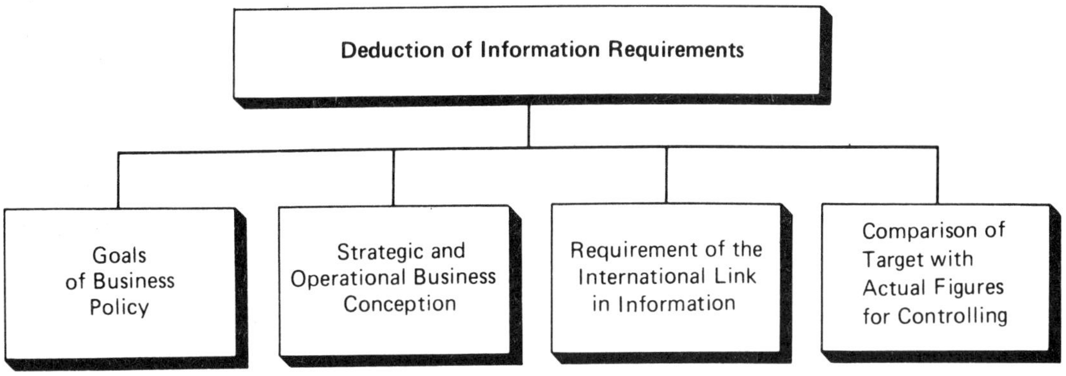

Figure 3. Deduction of information requirements

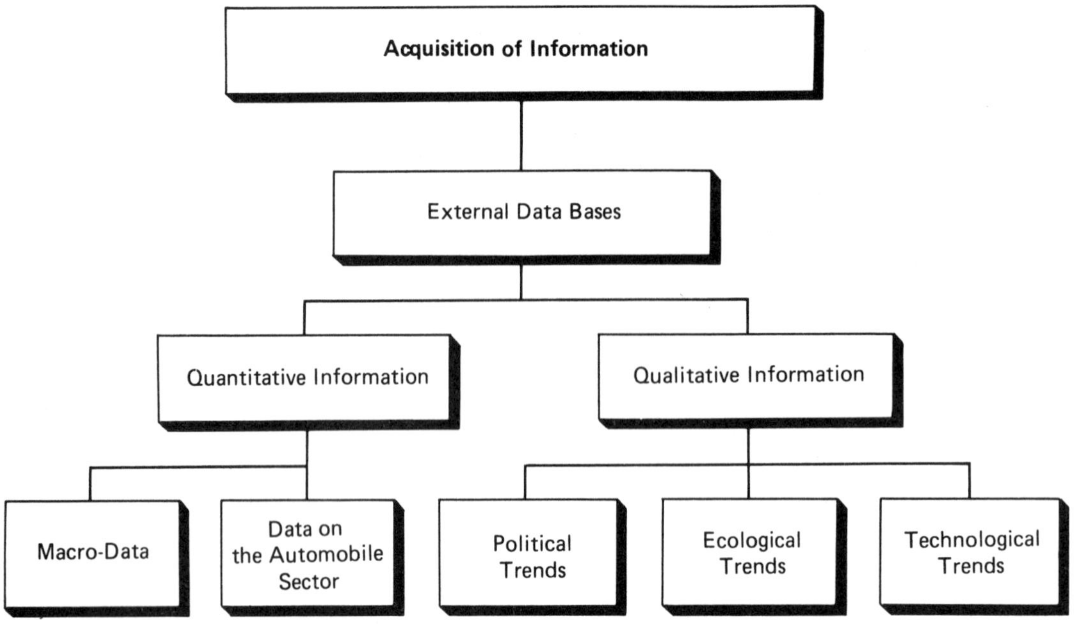

Figure 4. Acquisition of external information

information from functional units. Here, the type of data required is determined by area-related reporting; the criteria for producing the budget, the projected results and the medium- and long-term planning process establish the logic of the system.

The information links between different functional areas require the specification of appropriate interfaces and this in turn places demands on the integration of data bases. Planning and control calculations also require basic data for the assessment of technical and economic trends. The data base system must also be able to analyse performance and cost variables for sub-functions in complex, operational processes.

In addition to determining the data required, the methods, concepts and programmes for the data bases make it possible to carry out time series analyses, seasonal adjustments of data, the calculation of index series, the structuring of report information and the production of diagrams by computer.

Planning and Information Technology
The layout and structure of the information system

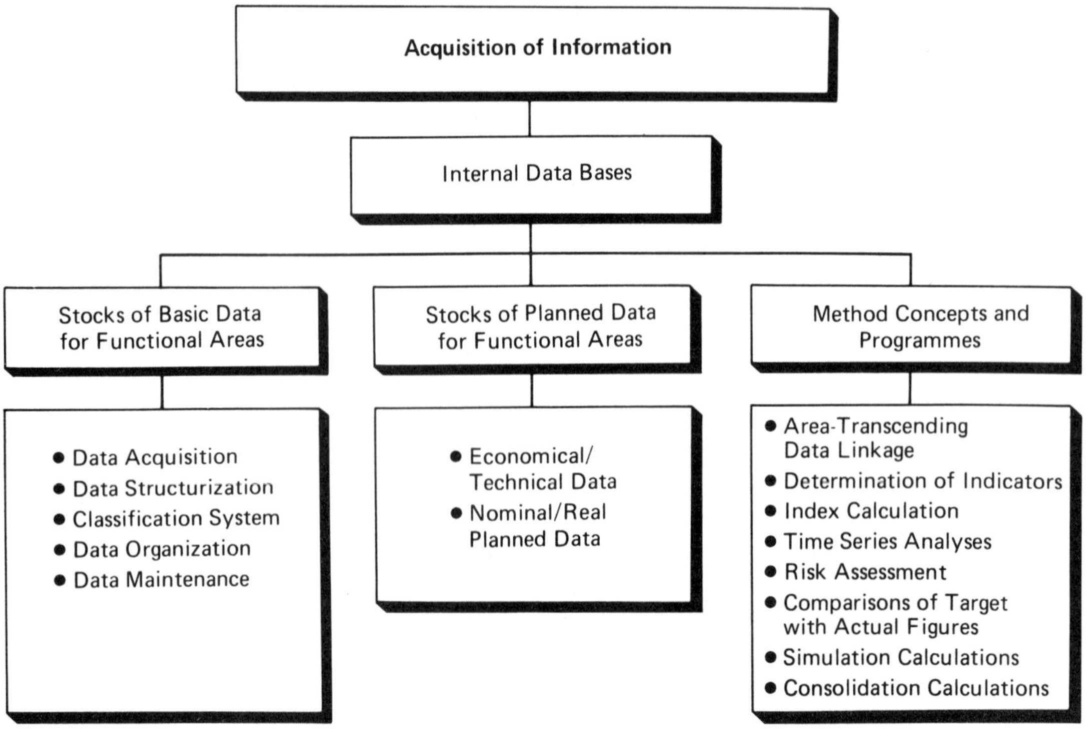

Figure 5. Acquisition of internal information

is of crucial importance for the planning process and for the content of plans. The possibilities of using information technology depend heavily on the formalization of modelling of tasks and sequences involved in planning. However, the representation and linking of complex technical/economic and social sequences in an overall model has so far not been satsifactorily achieved.

Computer-aided systems of planning are therefore used in *partial* models, enabling practical statements to be made for manageable functional areas. These individual models are integrated, taking into consideration the need for consistent overall company concepts and processes. This integration concerns on the one hand those assumptions which are related to overall planning and influence operational and strategic decisions, and on the other hand the coordination of quantitative plans. An efficient control of the exchange of information using new information and communication technologies can improve the quality and topicality of plans. This increases the speed of response by management when it is necessary to make changes in company policy.

To exploit the potential of information, communication and office technologies requires comprehensive analyses and forecasts of information for planning. This involves an investigation of:

(1) the *short-term* effects on the development of the business and

(2) the *long-term* influences on strategy.

Planning information for the short-term range focuses on a variety of factors concerned with turnover and costs. These, as a rule, consist of forecasts with a high degree of uncertainty and it is important to produce statements within acceptable margins of error, making use of statistical forecasting techniques. The following 'early-warning indicators' are usually analysed:

☆ orders received in the automotive sector and the company;

☆ orders on hand;

☆ delivery dates and

☆ stocks in hand.

The following analyses are then made to assess the size, the emerging trend and the causes of changes in indicators:

☆ analyses of deviations from the trend

☆ analysis of time series, taking into consideration the trend, market condition, seasonal and special influences and

☆ processes for exponential smoothing.

To estimate the effects of changed environmental conditions it is necessary to assess not just on the total volume of sales but on the breakdown of sales by product-type.

Owing to the large number of product variants and the different ways of combining products short-range product planning requires comprehensive information which can only be made available by efficient computer-aided systems. The necessary flow of information between Sales, Production, Purchasing and Logistics is achieved by means of a system which spans the different functions.

It is likely that oscillations in demand will increase in the future as volume markets are approaching saturation. This will require further improvement in the external and internal information system as the product range becomes even more complex. Other amendments will be needed to accommodate internationally linked manufacture, and the integration of the computer-aided systems of suppliers into the information systems of the company.

A further area of application and use for new information technologies concerns the analysis and forecasting of information for medium- and long-term planning (Figure 6). The main emphasis of application concern the derivation of planning information for:

☆ future product concepts and product range;

☆ future methods of manufacturing and

☆ the international location of production plants.

The forecasting of medium- and long-term changes in environmental conditions influencing the business is conducted using the scenario technique. This method requires a multi-disciplinary appraisal of future trends. Sub-scenarios on economic, socio-political and technological changes, must be combined into a consistent overall system.

The information requirements of the scenarios for the product concepts and the manufacturing strategy are defined by the functional areas of the business. The ultimate formulation of the scenarios, an evaluation of alternative developments and the selection of the most likely scenario, are made within the framework of overall planning.

Planning of the future product concept begins with a formulation of the requirements in each specification manual, depending on the scenario. This set of goals contains the combination of characteristics for the vehicle to be produced, correlated after the completion of a cost–benefit analysis. The further phases in vehicle development, as far as preparation for launching, are conducted with the assistance of computer-aided systems, within the framework of project control, problem follow-up and schedule monitoring. The parts list systems, structured

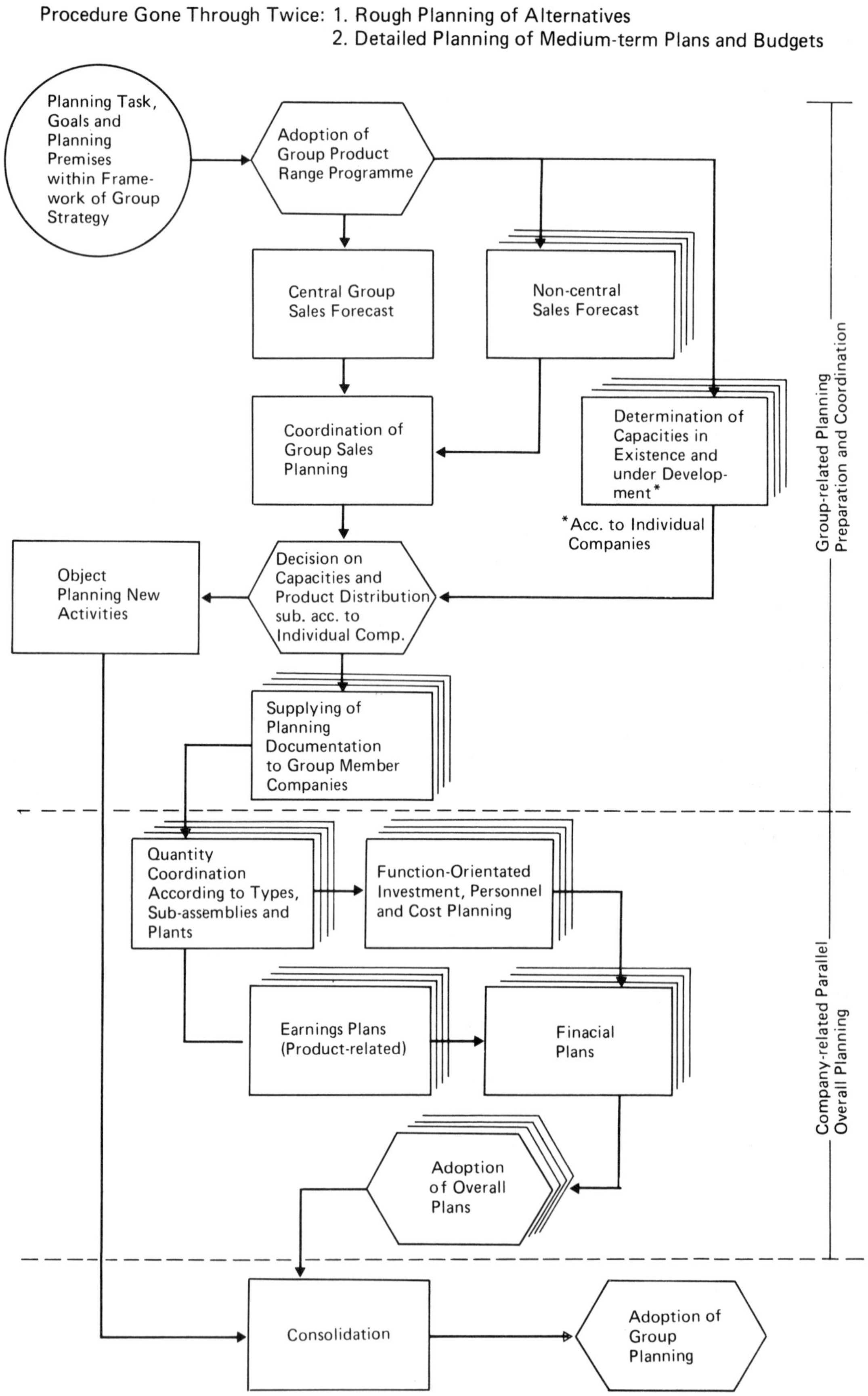

Figure 6. Course of overall planning in the Volkswagen Group

according to technical and economic criteria are especially important in this process.

Planning the product range requires a mass of information on the market segments (Figure 7). The most important information refers to the real earnings of the passenger vehicle customers, and the real value of the vehicles for the appropriate market segment. A customer analysis of value and prices compared with competition is necessary to estimate the volume of sales for each market segment. Price forecasts to determine probable changes in competitive position by market segment, are conducted using a simulation model.

The starting point for forecasting the price policy for individual competitors is an assessment of increases in basic costs, allowing for changes in productivity. An estimate of the volume effects of different price trends is made, allowing for competitors' product strategies. Changes in exchange rates is also included in the simulation calculation for a business which conducts a considerable portion of the automobile business on the world market, and which is subject to severe foreign competition on the domestic market.

The cost-price competition model should therefore be extended in order to make corrections in the rates of exchange. It is important to be able to forecast the effects of revaluation and/or devaluation of currencies, which can have a considerable effect on the competitive position in terms of prices—as the examples of U.S.A. and Japan eminently show. Computer-aided calculations supply important data for the assessment of risks in different states of competition. This helps to determine which locations in the world automobile market can be serviced at competitive prices.

Another field for the application of computer-aided systems concerns the planning of the product range in its multi-layer and complex configuration, according to manufacturing companies, demand markets, engines, gearboxes, body variants, types of steering, equipment and models. Planning a variety of combination possibilities presupposes comprehensive files of technical and economic information, which might not be possible to produce at all without EDP, or would only be possible with considerable manual effort.

The change in customer-specific product requirements, shifts in launching or phasing-out schedules for models, and modifications required by development and production, demand a high degree of flexibility in planning. The use of computer-aided systems has considerable importance in this context, particularly in internationally linked production. The necessity for up-to-dateness in planning data also requires continual updating of files and computer programs within the framework of a revolving planning process. Shifts within the product range, frequently bring extensions to the range of models and to model variants, the possibility of expanding the spectrum of applications is therefore important in applying EDP.

The planning of investments requires the use of computer-aided systems, in order to be able to conduct an assessment of investment projects within the framework of a total investment programme. The following criteria are used in assessing investments:

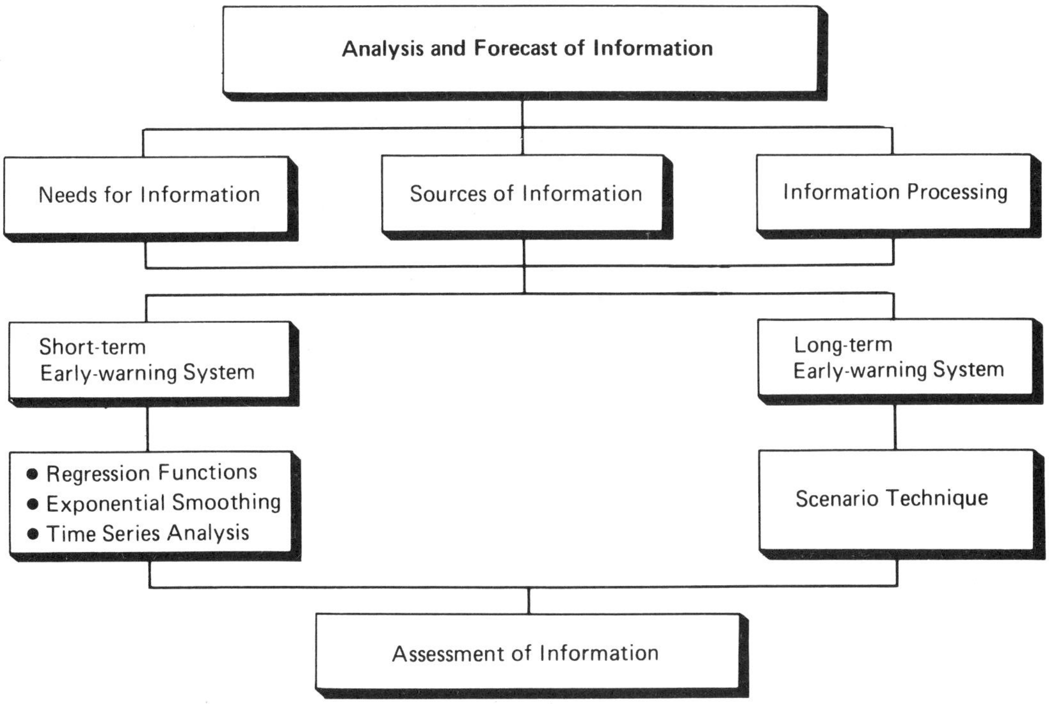

Figure 7. Analysis and forecast of information

(a) *Objectives of investments*

- ☆ meeting customer needs in different markets and complying with legal conditions for new products;
- ☆ meeting company growth targets through an increase in capital investment;
- ☆ increasing productivity through rationalization;
- ☆ keeping equipment and facilities up to date by replacement of fixed assets;
- ☆ meeting legal requirements and wage agreements by 'investments in human capital' and
- ☆ fulfilment of legal regulations for environmental protection.

(b) *Investments by business areas, functions and cost centres*

(c) *Investment according to plans (objects, projects)*

An analysis by this scheme of classification is also used to set priorities within the programme of investment, and to supply important information for operation and strategic decisions.

Computer-aided planning models are also employed in determining future personnel requirements. The aim is to produce a work-force 'balance sheet' for the business. For production activities the total number of employees is determined making assumptions about productivity. For non-production activities the level of future demand is assessed on the basis of function-related targets. The breakdown of this demand is determined, by estimating the impact of new technologies on the qualifications required by individuals involved in production and administration.

The supply of employees is determined, taking into consideration the age structure of the present workforce and their qualifications, together with the probable rate of labour turnover to produce a forecast of the number of personnel available. A comparison between the structure of demand and supply represents the work-force 'balance sheet' for the business. This work-force balance sheet shows where and for which functional groups imbalances are to be expected. Areas of over supply and shortages indicate where there may be a need for recruitment and for training.

The detailed planning of function- and area-related personnel requirements and structure involves the evaluation and analysis of a mass of data and combinations of characteristics. It is only possible to master this information by making use of data processing technology.

Productivity investigations and sensitivity analyses to assess the effects on business policy of different productivity routes form another important application of computer-aided systems in planning. This applies both to the analysis of the productivity of labour and the productivity of capital (Figure 8). EDP is used in this context for the following tasks:

- ☆ Determination of the value added according to the methods of calculation used by official statistics offices, research institutes, the Association of German Motor Manufacturers (VDA) and the company's own concept.
- ☆ Calculations of the value added for foreign companies, which publish their information on a different basis. To make this information comparable with the German information requires comprehensive analysis which can only be made using a computer-aided model.
- ☆ Determination of capital assets according to the 'gross' concept in which an evaluation of the stock of non-monetary capital must be made, taking into consideration the age composition and the function-related structure of a wide variety of capital equipment and buildings.

In order to determine what growth in productivity will be necessary to achieve the required return on the capital employed, requires a number of simulations. This usually reveals the conflict of goals which arises from the requirement to maintain competitiveness, and the demand to maintain a high level of employment. These simulation calculations supply important basic information for management which is necessary to develop a programme for productivity improvement to be implemented in the long term.

The Importance of Information Technology for Controlling

The control function requires a wide range of information for the control, coordination and monitoring of data on the development of costs and profits in the company. Information is needed for the following purposes:

- ☆ the formulation of *standards of performance* to be derived from these goals of the overall business;
- ☆ comparative analyses of planned and actual figures for economic monitoring and reporting;
- ☆ decision-making aids and
- ☆ guidelines for planning and for monitoring results.

This control process is heavily dependent on the use of efficient information, communication and office technologies.

In a decentralized business control is dependent on the availability of data from individual areas, functions and cost centres which influence efficiency. The control process also requires access to

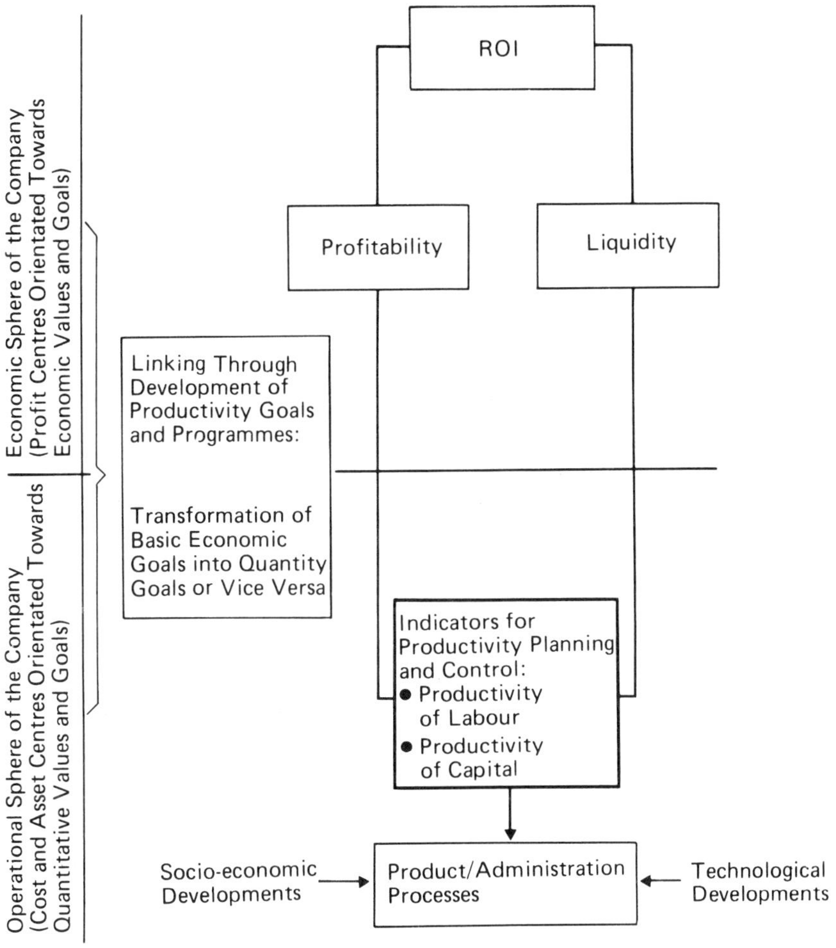

Figure 8. Productivity indicators as supplementary cardinal figures in the ROI/cash flow system

stocks of business administration and technical data which relate to the total company operation. To produce an efficient information and control system to monitor the performance of individual business areas in a decentralized business involves the following requirements:

(i) a unified classification system and the definition of economic and technical data of the company;

(ii) an improved flow of information between the business areas, functions and cost centres by systems of communication aided by EDP and

(iii) the provision of evaluation and processing programs for business areas and functions, insofar as these are necessary for fulfilling the tasks of controlling.

The standardization of definitions for the contents of data and for the methods of classifying stocks of data is an important prerequisite for the joint use of information and for the efficient application of information technologies. A uniform coding system for reporting is crucial in this context. This applies particularly to the comparability of report data from individual companies in a multinational group and the arrangements for consolidation.

The task of control requires detailed information for an assessment of individual functions and organizational units representing cost-/asset- or profit-centres. A performance-related calculation and attribution of costs, of the input of assets and of profits is an important prerequisite for forward-looking control. It is particularly important that results can be related back to functions and the causes of high and low performance can be traced. For planning and control calculations information should be related to the following 'earnings units':

(i) products and product ranges;

(ii) objectives and programmes to achieve objectives and

(iii) functional areas and business areas (Figure 9).

The control and coordination of product planning is carried out by the product controller, taking into consideration the product estimates, which are designed as a flexible system of information, and which supply comparative data for the following causes of variance:

(i) discrepancies in consumption;

(ii) changes in prices for manufacturing materials;

(iii) changes in personnel costs and

(iv) the introduction of new production technologies.

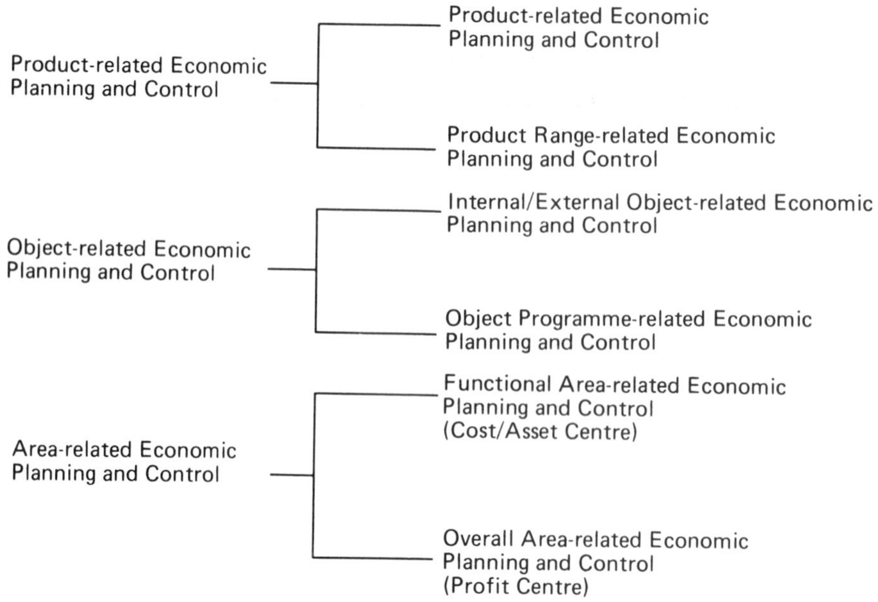

Figure 9. Elements of the system of economic planning and control calculations for the earnings units within the framework of the Volkswagen planning system

The control of the product range focuses on the calculations of earnings and liquidity and produces an analysis of the sources of profit and the input of assets.

Objective related control involves the assessment and control of the individual objectives by the investment controller. In this context, checks how far the planned operational and financial goals have been achieved, and what measures need to be taken to adapt the objective planning to change external and internal conditions.

To control the objective programmes means monitoring and controlling the input of capital for each group, taking into consideration the central goals of the business profitability and liquidity.

Another dimension in terms of control entails the monitoring and control of cost centres and asset centres in the functional areas. The goal of these control systems is to check and regulate variable and fixed costs. The control of functional areas makes it possible to subdivide costs into cost centres for each part of the organization. The classification system thus allows disaggregation of costs down as far as the smallest controlling unit. However, this high degree of detail is only achieved in budgeting. For long-term planning, aggregation is taken down only as far as the cost centres.

The growing complexity of the product range, the heavy investment in new technology, the improvement of manufacturing and distribution logistics and the increases in productivity are producing new needs for information which may require a reform of in-company data collection, of internal accounting and in particular of the calculation of costs and performance. The management of these needs for information requires the application of new information technology. To relate operational and economic data bases, for example places heavy demands both on software and on cost calculation. It is possible that we will be helped by current research into data which is organized on the basis of modular standard calculations and problem-related valuation calculations.

The rapid change in the programs for industrial production on the one hand, and the explosive development of new information technologies on the other hand, do not allow companies to adopt a 'wait-and-see' attitude (Figure 10). The leaps which occur in the level of technology require constant attention to learning and absorption. The current distributions of tasks in information processing represent an unmistakable bottle-neck in this context.

It is only necessary to follow the heated discussion on the future role of central EDP units in the face of increased decentralization of EDP application (Figure 11). These follow the use of such technical resources as PCs and workstations. We require a new business concept designed to integrate this decentralized technology into the system of control, planning, direction and information management.

The Influence of the Future Use of Information Technology in Planning and Control

The introduction of new information technologies has radically changed the process of compiling plans and the possibility of control. The trends of future development in data processing, communications technology and office automation, as far as they can be foreseen, indicate that this movement will

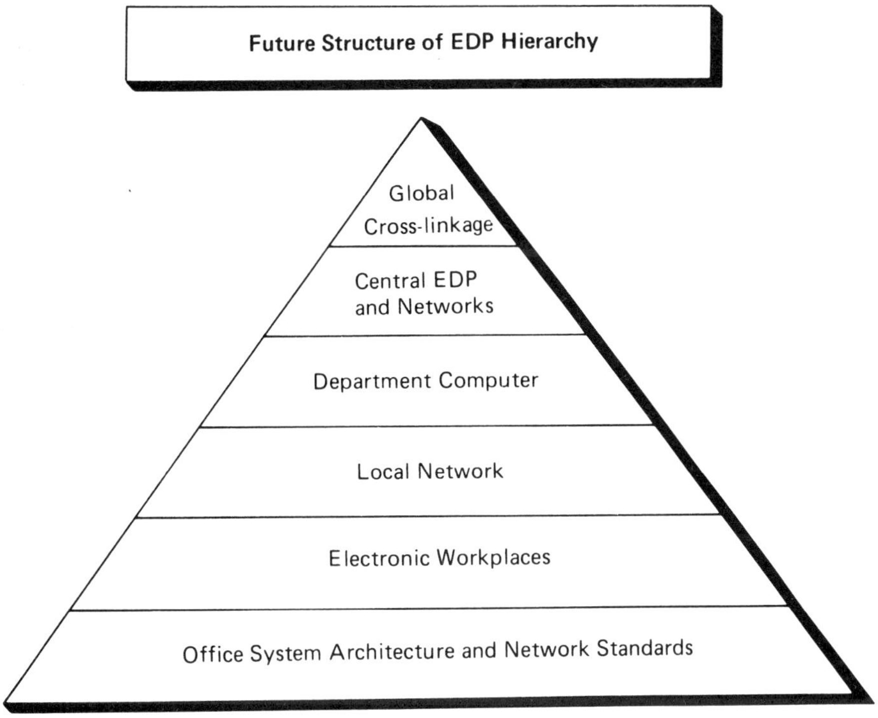

Source: Arthur D. Little D. R. 1984

Figure 10. Future structure of EDP hierarchy

continue, because of the growing need for information and for improvements in productivity in administration.

The use of computer-aided systems has clearly simplified the collection, processing and presentation of information for planning and control. Qualified employees are freed from routine work and can devote themselves more closely to the creation and further development of the methods and contents of planning. In addition, the quality of planning and the topicality of planning statements have improved.

The level of qualifications required for employees engaged in planning and control have changed. This has considerable consequences for company training. The introduction of new computer technologies and their productivity-oriented application to increase productivity is more and more determined by the need to be able to employ sufficiently qualified and specialized personnel.

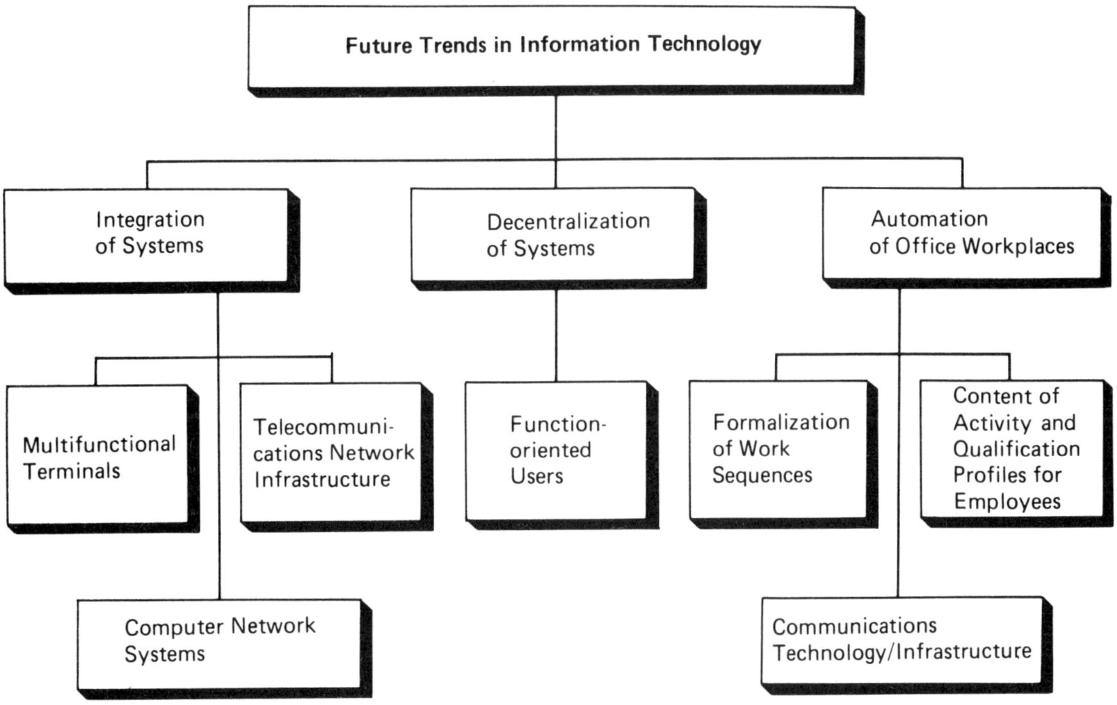

Figure 11. Future trends in information technology

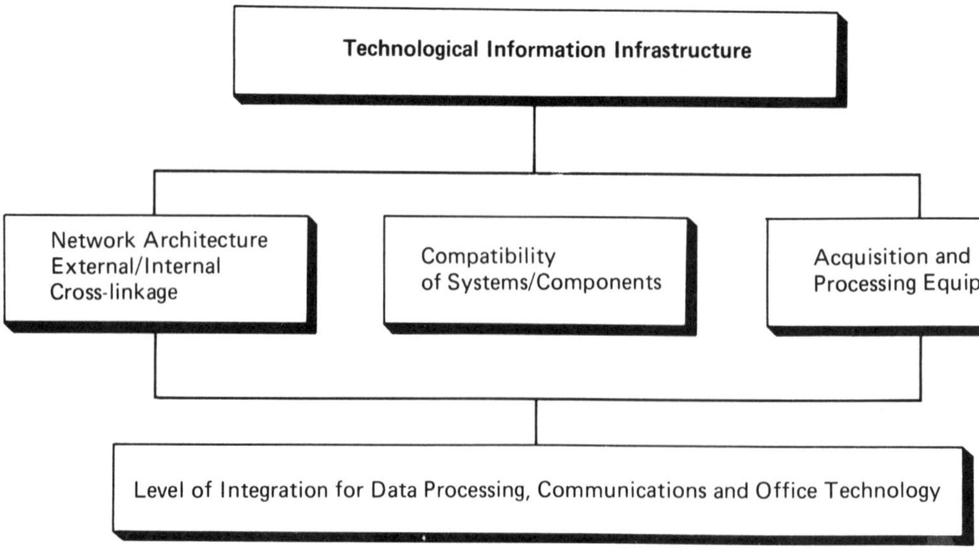

Figure 12. Technological information infrastructure

The trends in telecommunications-, office-machine- and computer-technology, and the probable changes in office-communication systems, make clear that the systems strategy in information technology must lead to integrated company-wide systems. At present, the efficient route to this objective is still in doubt: the making of main-frame resources available to individuals or the growth of integrated PC networks into a total system?

Further developments by manufacturers will require considerable improvement in application software in both cases (Figure 12). The demands on existing information systems in the planning and the control area particularly require concepts which have been proven in practice.

Summary

The use of efficient information, communication and office technologies has reached decisive importance for corporate planning. This applies to the potential use of external data bases with information, efficient techniques for transmission and receiving information, and the development of efficient hardware and software for the use of planning models.

The employment of new information technologies has dramatically expanded the opportunities for effective control in an international business. This applies in particular to the use of computer-aided systems for the collection and processing of information for control units of differing degrees of disaggregation. The progress in information technology makes it necessary to develop comprehensive training programmes for employees in planning and control. Investments in training in the area of informatics will decide in future, much more than in the past, to what extent a company succeeds in employing its existing resources to optimize productivity and to maintain its competitive performance.

Bibliography

(a) *General Literature*

R. Anselstetter, *Betriebwirtschaftliche Nutzeffekte der Datenverarbeitung*, Springer, Berlin (1984).

R. Goldberg and H. Lorin, (Eds), *The Economics of Information Processing*, Vols. I and II, Springer, New York (1982).

A.-W. Scheer, *Computer: A Challenge for Business Administration*, Springer, Berlin (1985).

A.-W. Scheer, *EDV-orientierte Betriebswirtschaftslehre, 2. Auflage*, Springer, Berlin (1985).

Hans Ulrich, *Die Unternehmung als produktives soziales System*, Paul-Haupt, Bern (1968).

N. Szyperski and E. Grochla (Eds), *Design and Implementation of Computer-based Informations Systems*, Vieweg (1979).

W. H. Machar, *Betriebswirtschaftliche Informationstheorie. Grundlagen des Informationssystems*, Gabler, Opladen (1971).

J. Berthel and D. Moews, *Information und Planung in industriellen Unternehmungen—eine empirische Studie*, Poeschel, Berlin (1970).

H. Hübner, *Informationsmanagement: Strategie-Gestaltung-Instrumente*, Duncker & Humblot, Wien (1984).

P. Mertens and J. Griese, *Industrielle Datenverarbeitung Band II, Informations- und Planungssysteme, 3. Auflage*, Gabler, Wiesbaden (1982).

R. Buehner, *Organisationsgestaltung von Informationssystemen der Unternehmung*, Gabler, Berlin (1975).

B. E. Meyer, H.-J. Schneider and G. Stübel (Eds), *Computergestützte Unternehmensplanung*, Walter de Gruyler, Berlin (1983).

S. Dworatschak (Ed.), *Management-Informations-Systeme*, Walter de Gruyler, Berlin (1971).

H. Noltemeier (Ed.), *Computergestützte Planungssysteme*, Physica, Würzburg (1976).

E. Grochla and N. Szyperski (Eds), *Modell-und computer-gestützte Unternehmensplanung*, Gabler, Wiesbaden (1973).

(b) *Special Literature*

Robert Cymbala (Booz, Allen & Hamilton), How good information can feed the Strategic Planning Process, *International Management*, 62-64 (1984).

S. Höhn, Unternehmensplanung und Konzernsteuerung—dargestellt im Rahmen der Strategie des Volkswagenwerkes, in H. Krallmann (Ed.) *Unternehmensplanung und -steuerung in den 80er Jahren*, Berlin (1982).

N. Leff, What you don't know can hurt you, *Business Week* **2781**, 12 (1983).

H.-D. Lithe and P. Maciejewski, Informationsmanagement als neue Herausforderung? Aufbau einer Informations-Infrastruktur und Organisation der Informationsflüsse, *Office Management* **4**, 328–330 (1985).

Charles R. Franz, User leadership in the systems development life cycle: A contingency model, *Journal of Management Information Systems*, **2**,(2), 5–25 (1985).

J. C. Cash, Jnr. and P. L. McLeod, Managing the introduction of information systems technology in strategically dependent companies, *Journal of Management Information Systems*, **1**(4), 5–23 (1985).

E. J. Kühn, Kommunikation und Kommunikationshilfsmaterial der Zukunft, dargestellt am Beispiel der Deutschen Shell AG, Zeitschrift für Betriebswirtschaft, **3**, 289–299 (1983).

P. Grosse, Führungsfunktionen in der Informations-verarbeitung, *IBM Nachrichten* **33** (263), 39–44 (1983).

L.C. Rhyne, The relationship of information usage characteristics to planning system sophistication: an empirical examination, *Strategic Management Journal*, **6**, 319–337 (1985).

H. J. Brightman and S.E. Harris, Is your information system mature enough for computerized planning?, *Long Range Planning*, **18**, (5) 68–73 (1985).

S. B. Yadav, Classifying an Organization to Identify Its Information Requirements: A Comprehensive Framework, *Journal of Management Information Systems*, **1**(1), 39–59 (1985).

M. E. Porter and V. E. Millar, How information gives you competitive advantage, *Harvard Business Review*, July/August, 149–160 (1985).

K. Ewusi-Mensah, Information systems for planning, *Long Range Planning*, **17**(5), 111–117 (1984).

R. Whaley, Data bank on the future business environment, *Long Range Planning* **17**(4), 83–90 (1984).

Classifying Capital Projects for Top Management Decision-Making

J. A. Piper, Department of Management Studies, University of Technology, Loughborough

This paper is an attempt to redress a perceived imbalance in the research and literature of capital project analysis. There is a plethora of work on the quantitative aspects of project analysis, yet empirical surveys show limited use of such techniques. There is limited work on the organizational processes of project selection, but there appears to be little or no work taking place on formal organizational systems for project selection.

The more quantitative literature generally takes a deductive approach using a model developed from microeconomics based on the assumption that the objective of the firm is the maximization of owners' wealth. In this paper it is argued that there is a need to take an inductive approach and place the capital investment decision in its organizational setting. This paper looks at the formal capital budgeting system within the corporate setting.

It is suggested that the specific capital investment decision takes place against the background of a set of policies and constraints, which are more or less explicit.

The selection of corporate projects is a complex issue, but to provide some structure so that the problems can be processed by the organization, a capital budgeting system is designed. Part of this system is the classification of projects according to some criteria. It would therefore appear that the purpose of this classification system is to aid capital project selection within an organizational context.

A consideration of classification systems for capital projects is undertaken, this is followed by a survey of the classification systems which have been proposed in the capital investment literature. Finally a classification system based upon specific criteria is proposed.

Classification Systems

(i) *Why Classify?*
R. N. Anthony suggests that the purpose of classification is as follows:

> To be useful, material dealing with any broad subject needs to be organized within a framework of topics and sub-topics. If the topics and sub-topics are well chosen the available material can be so arranged as to make it possible for one to reach conclusions generally applicable to each classification but not applicable to other classifications. Such conclusions or generalizations, furthermore, will have validity and significance impossible in the absence of such a framework.[1]

The author is Lecturer in Financial Management in the Department of Management Studies, University of Technology, Loughborough, Leicestershire LE11 3TU.

(ii) *What Classification System?*
On the subject of classification of capital projects, Joel Dean states:

> No definitive classification plan for investments is useful for all purposes. A capital outlay has too many facets to be described adequately by any one of them. Each facet is in effect a dimension of the outlay and a separate basis for distinguishing different types of investments.[2]

Anthony also goes on to say:

> Within a given subject area, different frameworks can be useful for different purposes. Thus in biology, the classification of plants and animals by phylum, class, order, family, genus and species is useful for some *purposes*. Comparative anatomy, which cuts across these classifications, provides a useful framework for other *purposes*.[3] (Author's italics.).

So the classification system will depend upon its purpose.

(iii) *Classify Capital Projects—for What Purpose?*
There is not one purpose, but several. For example, for accounting purposes projects may be classified by their balance sheet classification, or for control purposes by their size. In this paper consideration will be given to the purpose of project classification to aid top management decision making.

Top management are likely to be concerned to maintain and improve the EPS. When doing this they have to consider, either implicitly or explicitly, the risk strategy in relation to financing and investment in assets, and these two aspects are obviously inter-related. The complex process of developing corporate financial objectives, dividend policy, risk stance and current earnings produces a *view* as to the financial resources available for capital investment to fulfil the strategy. *View* is used here rather than *amount* to try to convey the dynamic nature of the process. Many factors will affect the amount available for capital investment, for example higher or lower profits than forecast, heavier medium term investment in working capital than expected, or very attractive investments not previously anticipated which are beyond the current view as to funds available. Thus, the traditional view of capital funds available either being a fixed amount (capital rationing), or available up to the situation where marginal cost equals marginal return (unlimited funds), are extremes of a continuum with the actual situation being somewhere between these extremes.

Within this complex climate top management have to undertake investments some of which they have actually sought as a result of the corporate policy and strategy they have developed, and some of which they have not anticipated and over which they have perhaps little control. (See Section 'A Proposal'.)

Thus it is against the background of this complex and dynamic process that the purpose of a capital project classification system has to be considered, if its purpose is to provide a framework to aid top management's decision making.

Capital Project Classification System

Joel Dean undertakes one of the most comprehensive discussions of investment classification[4], illustrating how classifications differ between companies, and presenting a classification system with 250 cells. However, he points out: 'Naturally, no management works with this array of distinctions'.[5]

He proposes a system of classification which, he states, is not for administrative convenience, but for the purpose of rate of return budgeting on the basis of the accuracy with which projections of cashflows can be made. The classification is:[6]

(1) Replacement investments, these being essentially cost saving investments.

(2) Expansion investments, the productivity being increased revenue.

(3) Product-line investments, expenditure on new products or improvement of old products.

(4) Strategic investments, these are investments whose 'benefits seep into other parts of the company,' for example improved canteen facilities. Perhaps they could be more aptly described as indirect synergistic investments.

Dean also states that:

> ... most capital expenditures ... do not fit neatly into any single category. For example a new lithographic machine may not only expand the capacity of a printing press but also improve the quality of a printer's product, add new products to his line, and reduce operating cost through lower maintenance costs.[7]

It is interesting that Kaplan considers that:[8]

> What makes a concept significant is that the classification it institutes is one into which things fall, as it were of themselves. It carves at the joints ...

The concept upon which Dean's classification is based is the characteristics of the profit estimates in terms of their potential variability. However, the concept does appear to have 'carvability'—to use Kaplan's term (i.e. the projects do not easily and clearly fall into the classifications).

Merret and Sykes' book,[9] which is considered to be an authoratative work on capital investment, contains a five category classification which they initially argue is 'for administrative purposes'[10] but they also add that the risk related categories, 'form useful categories for control purposes'.[11] The five categories are:

(a) Obligatory Investments
(b) Welfare Amenities Investments
(c) Risk-free Projects
(d) Normal Projects
(e) Speculative Projects

Although Merrett and Sykes do not make the point, (a) and (b) are basically non-profit adding,* at least in a directly observable manner, whereas (c), (d) and (e) are profit adding. Thus, the last three categories are those which would be considered in the theory of portfolio selection by relating risk to return, and selecting the portfolio of projects with the highest return for a specified level of risk or *vice versa*. There is also risk related to the non-profit adding investments in terms of cost uncertainty and a possibility that they do not achieve their objectives.

Garbutt[12] on capital investment analysis refers to a system proposed by the Treasurer of Esso Petroleum Ltd., which uses four categories with sub-categories.

(a) No-return projects;
  (i) Optional no-return;
  (ii) Obligatory no-return.
(b) Maintaining Old Business (i.e. replacement).
(c) Cost Reduction.
(d) Expansion and New Products;
  (i) New Products.
  (ii) New Designs.

Once again, these categories will overlap; Garbutt does not give the basis of this classification. Obviously, one dimension is return/no-return and (a) (i) and (ii) are based upon choice.

Van Horne[13] produces a classification based upon the source of the investment proposal within the organization. The five categories are:

(1) New products or expansion of existing products—marketing.

(2) Replacement of equipment or buildings—production.

(3) Research and development.

*Strategic in Dean's terms (*op. cit.*).

(4) Exploration.

(5) Other.

Van Horne does not actually give illustrations of the source of investment proposals for 3–5.

Bierman and Schmidt[14] devote a chapter to classifying investments and describe the following methods.

According to:

(1) the kinds of scarce resources used by the investment, e.g. cash, floor space, management time;

(2) the amount of scarce resources required;

(3) the way the project benefits by other possible investments, i.e. the extent to which investments are dependent or independent. They produce the following continuum for the interdependence of projects:

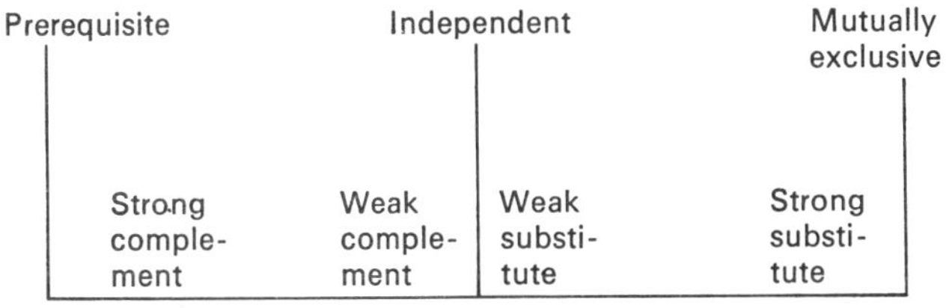

(4) the form in which the benefits are received (i.e. reduce risks, increase cashflows, or reduce accident rates);

(5) the extent to which the benefits are increased revenues or reduced costs; and

(6) the business activity to which the investment is most closely related.

Bierman and Schmidt go on to say that many other classifications could be suggested, but select item (3) above for special attention. They point out that the various combinations of complementary investments need to be considered together so that they can be considered as mutually exclusive accept or reject investments. This would appear to dispose of the classification, complementary investments.

Weaver,[15] Vice President, Corporate Planning and Appraisal, of ICI, U.S.A., states that he sees the key elements of a capital expenditure system as: 'Methods of handling individual capital projects—methods of handling compilations of all projects foreseen at a given point in time, and organization to carry through these two key roles'.

Thus, the classification system should aid as many of these elements as possible. Weaver subsequently illustrates several classification systems which ICI, U.S.A., use. Projects are classified according to objective (see top section of Figure 1), urgency (see bottom section of Figure 1), size and state of top management consideration (Figure 2). Weaver also provides a matrix for classifying projects (Figure 3) and a detailed sub-classification of replacement decisions (Figure 4).

The purpose of these classifications is not explained in detail, but the objectives can be deduced. The active/inactive* classification enables management to see the commitment to projects at a specific time. The sub-classification of replacement decisions allows specific questioning of specific projects. The classification into 'critical', 'desirable', 'necessary', is obviously to communicate the urgency of a proposal to top management.

The advantage of using size of cash outlay as a basis for classification is that it is clearly determinable within which category a project falls, and this can be used as a basis for deciding authority levels within the organization. This allows specific decentralization of the commitment of the organization with resultant flexibility, while centralizing the commitment of larger sums. The authority levels will reflect the level of decentralization within an organization.

One of the dangers of using size of cash outlay to classify proposals as a basis for establishing authority levels or the degree of analysis, is that a large number of small proposals may be undertaken which have a substantial cumulative effect. This problem can partly be resolved by also establishing total time period spend limits for each size group. Size limits are based upon the assumption that the initial commitment is the measure of overall commitment of resources, and this may not be so. In addition, size classification may perhaps be used on the basis that it also reflects risk; however the relationship between risk and size of project is complex. For example, large projects with a large property element may be easily reversible, while smaller projects involving investment in know-how or specialized assets may be totally irreversible thus having a potentially higher downside risk.

In 1967 the National Association of Accountants (U.S.A.) proposed the following classification system, based upon studies of the practice of 28 companies:

(i) location;

(ii) product line;

(iii) priority;

(iv) purpose (e.g. expansion, replacement);

(v) asset class (e.g. building or machinery);

(vi) non-asset (e.g. research and development).[16]

The report also makes the following point on the purpose of the classification system:

> (1) to provide standard descriptions which help identify the project and the kind of decision involved, and (2) to provide categories useful in summarizing the financial totals for a group of projects.[17]

A basis of classification, already touched upon by reference to Merrett and Sykes (*op. cit.*), and which needs further consideration is risk. When considering risk as a basis of classification of projects the basis of the risk must be considered. In portfolio theory risk is measured as the

*This appears to be similar to a planned/approved dichotomy.

PROPOSAL CLASSIFICATIONS

Each proposal is assigned one (and only one) of six possible classifications. The classification selected is the one which comes closest to starting the *primary* need or opportunity that the proposal is designed to fulfill.

1. *"A" New Products* - All proposals for the production or distribution of products not presently produced commercially by Atlas. A new chemical product is defined as a molecular structure or configuration different from existing products. A new mechanical product is a mechanism whose design differs distinctly from existing products. All pilot plant or laboratory products are specifically excluded from this classification. This classification includes production facilities and services used primarily for the new products (steam, power, water, compressed air, maintenance facilities, and office and laboratory space within or adjacent to process battery limits).

2. *"B" Expansion or Improvement: Production, Service, and Distribution* - All proposals pertaining to existing products, intended to increase production, service, and distribution capacity, improve product quality, or maintain or improve the Company's competitive position.
   - B.1 Production: all equipment and buildings directly involved in the manufacture of products, including inprocess storage and testing facilities.
   - B.2 Service: all utilities, roads, maintenance shops, et. when handled as a separate project. Excluded arė services primarily for labs and offices.
   - B.3 Distribution: all finished goods storage, magazines, delivery trucks, customer service facilities etc.

3. *"C" Cost Reduction* - Proposals primarily to cut costs through addition of new equipment or through modifications to existing equipment. This classification excludes projects justified primarily by the need to replace worn-out equipment (i.e., replacements).

4. *"D" Replacement* - Proposals justified primarily by the need to replace equipment that is nearly worn-out or has abnormal maintenance costs. Unlike cost reduction proposals, replacements are usually in kind, although, occasionally, a proposal calling for equipment not in kind may also qualify as a replacement if primary justification is for replacement.

5. *"E" Expansion or Improvement: Offices and Laboratories* - Proposals to expand or improve offices (including sales offices) or laboratories. Pilot plant and research equipment is included in this classification even though purchased for a specific project or product, as well as all service facilities primarily for offices and labs.

6. *"F" Corporate Policy* - Proposals for facilities which a) are required by law, b) will improve employee welfare, c) promote safety, d) will preserve or improve the corporate image, or e) result from decisions on corporate financial policy. This classification includes the replacement of a leased unit with a purchased unit.

PROPOSAL CATEGORIES

Each proposal is ranked in a category which considers its effect on profits, its degree of urgency, and whether or not it is postponable.

Critical - Proposals to protect current profits or manufacturing costs, or of a noneconomic nature, which, it is judged, must be done in the next year to avoid an emergency or significant cost penalty.

These proposals, by definition, *must* be done in the Plan year.

Desirable - Proposals, which as a whole, are highly profitable, attractive, or otherwise important to the Company.

Necesary - Proposals of the same nature as critical proposals with the exception that they are judged to be postponable one year (and occasionally two years) beyond the Plan year without signficant consequence or cost.

A portion of the Desirable and Necessary proposals, expressed as a per cent unaccomplished, is not expected to be accomplished in the Plan year.

(Source: James B. Weaver, "Organising and Maintaining a Capital Expenditure Program",

***Engineering Economist,* Vol. 20, No. 1, p. 33)**

Figure 1. Definitions of proposal classifications and categories used in capital authorizations planning

variation of outcomes, and the problem of how to diversify this risk by combinations of various projects is considered by studying the correlation between project outcomes. The statement by Carsberg and Hope summarizes the present gulf between theory and practice:

> We have assumed, on the basis of casual evidence, that the ideas of portfolio theory are not applied explicitly in the practice of business decisions.[18]

Two aspects of risk are the risk of the project or portfolio and the attitude towards that risk. The latter aspect will be determined explicitly or implicitly in the corporate policy. The risk of a project can partly be quantified, but

	MAJORS over $250,000	NORMALS
Active	• Usually first identified long range in 5YF. • Now undergoing or scheduled for active AFE development during next five quarters. • Up to date Active Plans required in addition to Proposal Sheets • Constitute a relatively firm plan. Author izations and expenditures projected by proposal in CAP quarterly reports.	• Now undergoing or scheduled for active AFE development during next five quarters. • Usually have had less complete longer range planning and development. • There is a higher probability that some proposals may not survive AFE development or may undergo significant change. • Only total levels of authorizations and expenditures are projected. Projections may be an initial proposal by proposal projection adjusted by means of a management variance.
Inactive	• Includes all major proposals in latest 5YF not currently active and not previously abandoned. • May include additional more recently identified inactive major proposals accepted into CAP.	• Accepted proposals (with a Proposal Sheet) not active for reasons of timing, priority or undue uncertainty. • Serves as a reminder and as a measure of proposal backlog.

AFE - Authorisation for Expenditure
CAP - Capital Authorisation Program (Capital Budget)
5YF - Five Year Plan

(Source: James B. Weaver, *Op.cit.*, p.17.)

Figure 2. Composition of CAP proposal inventory

is still to a major extent a matter of judgment. What is needed is a risk classification in which to put proposed profit adding investments. Sizer[19] has proposed such a framework based upon what are considered to be two of the major factors affecting the risk of a project, these are market risk and technological risk. The resulting classification is presented in Figure 5. Depending upon specific needs other risk factors could be introduced into the matrix, for example a distinction between design technology risk, production technology risk, and supply risk.

Sizer points out that:

> The categories of risk in the various boxes should be taken as examples. The board of directors and senior managers would establish the appropriate risk category for each box in the matrix.[20]

He also extends the classification to include size of projects within the matrix cells, and points out that hurdle rates must be determined by the directors dependent upon the minimum cost of capital and their attitude to risk:

> The proposed approach provides a framework within which the board of directors can discuss its attitude to risk and uncertainty and make the inevitable managerial judgments. They must decide which portfolio of projects, high and low risk, large and small, etc., is most appropriate in relation to the company's objectives, strategy and operating plans.[21]

In the preceding review of capital investment classification systems the following characteristics are used as the basis for, or part of the basis for, the various systems proposed:

(1) Accuracy of the projected estimates (Dean).

(2) Administrative factors and control (Merrett and Sykes).

(3) Choice (Merrett and Sykes, Garbutt).

(4) Risk (Merrett and Sykes, Sizer).

(5) Objective (Garbutt, Weaver, Bierman and Schmidt, NAA).

(6) Return/No Return (Garbutt).

(7) Source of Proposal (Van Horne, Bierman and Schmidt).

(8) Stage of Consideration (Weaver).

(9) Size (Weaver, Bierman and Schmidt).

(10) Interdependence (Bierman and Schmidt).

(11) Priority (Weaver, NAA).

(12) Asset type (NAA).

(13) Location (NAA).

The problem is how to select from this myriad of classifications one which meets the needs of top management decision-making within the general environment discussed in the Section on Classifications Systems.

A Proposal

Obviously, there are many potential classification systems. How are we to choose? Perhaps there is no one

These questions follow a specific order to be asked in sequence. If the answer to a question is yes, then the project classification is given. If the answer is no, proceed with the next question in the sequence.

Sequence Number	Question To Be Asked	Project Classification if Answer Affirmative
1	Does the proposal include all or part of a present Atlas Facility, where a substitution in kind might be economically justified?	Replacement D
2	Is the proposal intended chiefly to reduce present costs, without expanding capacity? (Includes both production and non-production facilities).	Cost Reduction C
3	Is the proposal concerned chiefly with the commercial manufacture of a product which cannot be commercially made by Atlas now?	New Products A
4	Is the proposal intended chiefly to expand manufacturing capacity or improve quality of present commercial products?	Expansion/ Improvement - Production B1
5	Is the proposal concerned solely with supplying utilities or other Services?	Expansion/ Improvement - Service B2
6	Is the proposal concerned with storing and handling finished goods to increase sales without increasing production capacity?	Expansion/ Imrpovement -Distribution B3
7	Does the proposal provide offices or laboratories not adjacent to productive facilities?	Expansion/ Imrpovement - Offices or Laboratories E
8	Any remaining proposals must be	Corporate Policy F

(Source: James B. Weaver, *Op.cit.*, p.34.)

Figure 3. Sequenced technique for classifying

universal system, and the system will be contingent upon the specific organization. This point will not be discussed in this paper; instead a generalized decision oriented approach will be taken.

Gerstner and Anderson,[22] discussing the developments of financial management in the seventies, make the following specific points about capital budgeting procedures:

> . . . companies are increasingly faced with capital expenditures, such as those for pollution abatement, that are non discretionary but that have marginal or no real return. This means that the hurdle rate has to be adjusted to ensure that the weighted average yield of all investment projects equals or exceeds the cost of capital.
>
> . . . quite substantial investment is necessary in projects which give no financial return at all . . . .*
>
> Attempts to respond to issues such as these have helped to swing the focus of corporate strategy from growth alone to the carefully managed and controlled deployment of assets . . .
>
> What sort of risk/return profile does our existing portfolio of businesses present to potential investors? Could we restructure to make our securities more attractive to future suppliers of capital?

Thus, besides the desire to maintain and improve the

*It should be noted that there is disagreement as to whether social and environmental investments with no return should affect the discount rate(see B. Carsberg and A. Hope, *Business Investment Decisions Under Inflation*, ICAEW, 1976, p. 56).

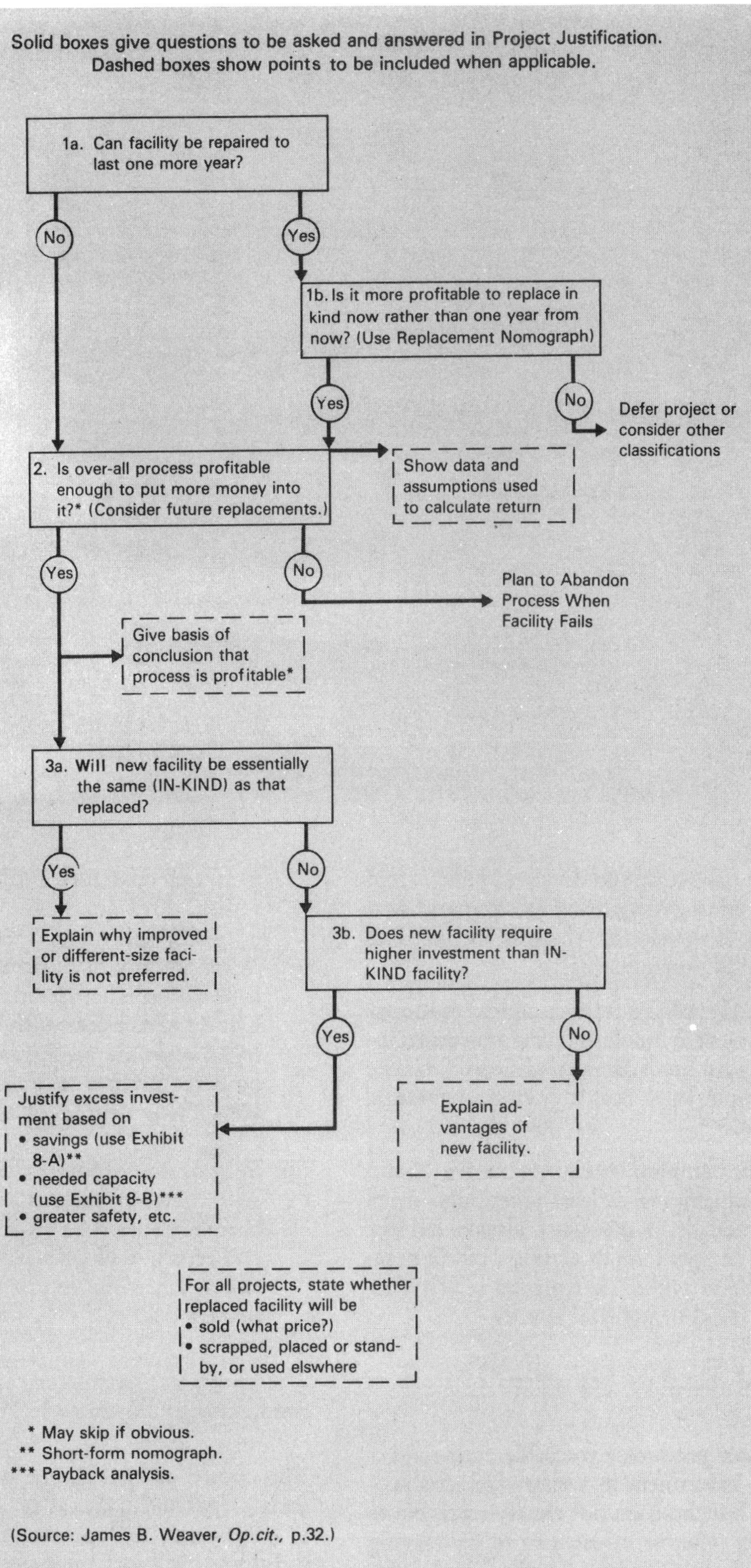

Figure 4. Guideline flowchart for preparing replacement justification

Products/ Technology	Markets	Existing: Maintain Market Share	Existing: Increase Market Share		New: Same or Similar Type of Customer	New: New Type of Customer
EXISTING	Existing Technology	Low	Medium	High	Medium	High
	Related Technology	Low	Medium	High	Medium	High
	Unrelated Technology	High	Very High	Very High	High	Very High
NEW	Existing Technology	Medium	Medium	High	Medium	High
	Related Technology	Medium	Medium	Very High	High	Very High
	Unrelated Technology	High	Very High	Too High?	Very High	Too High?

Notes: i) The categories of risk in the various boxes should be taken as examples; the executive directors would establish the appropriate risk category for each box of the matrix.

ii) More boxes may be established if considered appropriate. For example, the new markets boxes may be split to separate projects implying high initial market share and low initial market share.

Figure 5. Risk matrix for profit adding investments

EPS within a given risk stance and dividend policy from which a corporate strategy regarding existing and new products/businesses is developed, there is the need to accommodate the additional factors:

(i) In an increasingly mixed and complex economy companies are more frequently facing no-return investments of capital funds (in the traditional financial sense); for example, legal, health, environmental and social investments.*

(ii) Due to a more complex social system the choice available to companies is, at least practically, more limited. Theoretically, a company always has the choice to cease an operation or activity, but in practice it is difficult to withdraw from an activity because of legal, social or political factors.

Thus it is proposed that three key aspects of a capital project are:

(i) Does the project produce a traceable financial return? Thus an investment in welfare facilities produces benefits but these are not clearly traceable to the investment, whereas investment in cost saving machinery produces a traceable benefit. The balance between the amount of investment in return projects and no-return projects will affect the overall return.

(ii) What amount of choice does top management have in deciding whether or not to undertake a project? Choice here refers to the ability to reject a project. In an absolute sense management always has the power to reject a project, but practically there are varying degrees of choice (see below).

(iii) Within the corporate risk strategy the management will combine various projects with differing risk characteristics. The projects with no traceable financial return will primarily have cost and technical risk whereas the return investments will also have market risk.

The above characteristics can be put into the classification system illustrated in Figure 6.

The choice categories are based upon the economic, social, legal and political pressures on top management in addition to the commercial strategic pressures. The social and political pressures can either be internal or external to the organization. An example of internal pressure with no return is pressure from staff for improved canteen or car parking facilities. Obviously, in an absolute sense top management can choose to get out of the business rather than yield to these pressures, and in that sense they do have a choice. However, this is a

*Petty, Scott and Bird.[26] In a survey of 109 large American Corporations, 60 per cent ranked legal, employee safety and environmental responsibility as the most important qualitative factors that influence investment decisions.

Return \ Choice	Obligatory	Partial	Full	Risk
Return	*Example* Replacement of Boiler which has Failed.	*Example* Purchase of Additional Machinery.	*Example* Purchase of new Business or development of New Process.	Cost, Technical and Market Risk.
No-Return	*Example* Pollution Control Demanded by HM Inspector of Factories.	*Example* Improving Canteen, Facilities	*Example* Educational Endowment.	Cost and/or Technical Risk.

Figure 6. Proposed project classification system

complex problem of balance. (Note, for example, the U.K. companies that have to balance low yielding investment in the U.K. with higher yielding investment overseas.)*

Just as management always have some choice, in an absolute sense, so they never have full choice. However, in this classification system, full choice refers to a situation where there is relative freedom from social and political pressures as to whether a project is accepted or rejected (for example, the acquisition of a business unrelated to current activities). Obviously the choice in relation to a specific project could, and most likely would, differ between companies.

The classification system proposed is illustrated in Figure 7, which outlines the questions which need to be asked in order to classify a project. If the answer to question 3 ('Is the proposed investment to be part of a current activity?') is 'Yes' then it is argued that there will be pressure on top management to undertake that investment. This pressure will vary depending upon many factors (e.g. the sponsoring management's past performance and credibility, trade union pressure) and to this extent the partial choice category has many degrees between the continuum of full choice and obligatory. If one wished, a ranking system representing sub-classifications within this group could be produced. Question 3 is seen as a significant factor, but its significance will vary between firms and projects.

The return risk analysis could be undertaken within Sizer's framework (*op. cit.*). An assessment of the risk of no-return projects could be undertaken by a sensitivity analysis of the underlying assumptions of the projects' costs and the extent to which the non-financial benefits are expected to accrue.†

*Note, however, that national political risk is not covered in the classification, and so strictly the proposed classification is within a national boundary.

†Note that this classification system ignores mutually exclusive investments related to the same objective, on the basis that they would be in the same category, although they may have different risks.

What is the justification of the proposed classification over those reviewed in the section on Capital Project Classification Systems? It is argued that it concentrates the attention of top management on several key issues by providing a framework which isolates these issues: namely, the extent to which the company is having to use financial resources on obligatory investments where they have little control over the return and where some investments have no return. These investments will need to be considered when developing and revising earnings and ROI targets, and when reviewing corporate strategy.

The framework would be used in two related ways—in considering the corporate policy for capital investment and in planning the actual mix of capital investment proposals available. The obligatory, partial choice category is relatively arbitrary, as is the ICI classification of 'necessary, critical, desirable, (*op. cit.*), but the discussion by top management of which investments are obligatory, partial or choice would identify the underlying issues. An obligatory no-return investment is, in the sense of financial performance, a necessary burden. The obligatory return investments are also necessary. If these present an excessive burden or dilute financial performance to an unacceptably low level, top management must reconsider the extent to which the operations requiring these investments can be continued without hampering the financial viability of the organization. A sequential and iterative approach to using the classification is presented in Figure 8.

This figure also illustrates how the classification of a partial choice investment may be modified due to the compromise between economic, social and political pressures. Consider, for example, a U.K. based international company with U.K. based operations which are producing a poor return and which still has capital investment in the partial return category. Due to increasing obligatory no-return investments in other areas, and pressure on limited funds, the company is not able to produce a 'satisfactory return' and so reconsiders the partial investments in the U.K. operations and decides to close down the operations (i.e. revises a partial return investment into a choice investment).

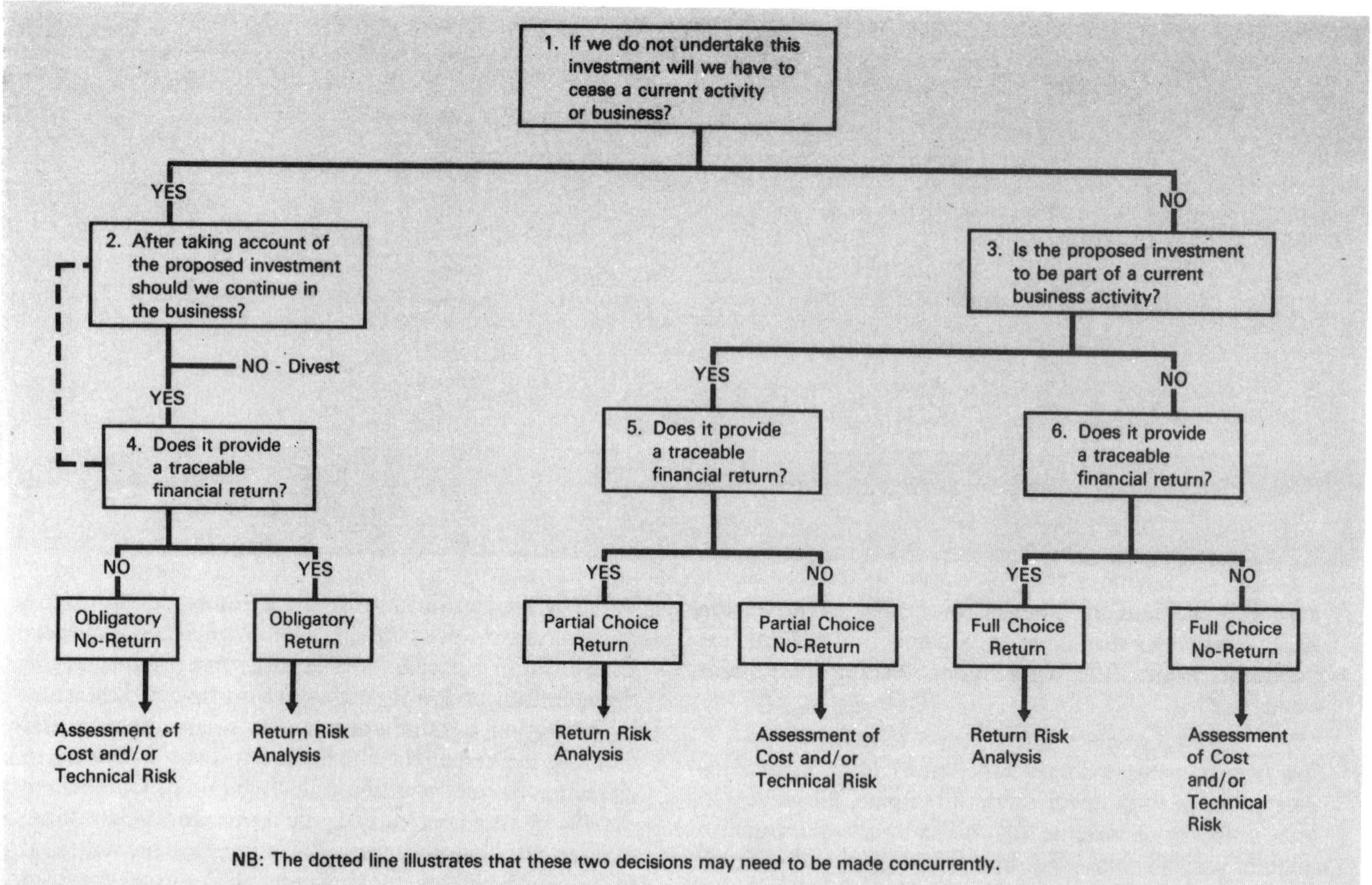

Figure 7. Tree diagram of decision oriented capital projects classification

The management will consider those projects which are not obligatory and which provide a return, and will want to try to match the gap between the desired overall return on new investment and the return on obligatory investments while at the same time balancing the various political and social pressures to invest in certain areas. In a strictly financial sense a greater return may be obtainable by investing funds in unrelated, new areas of investment, but management may have to 'buy peace' by undertaking financially less attractive investments in existing activities. Conversely, the proposed framework will illustrate to what extent management are treating full choice return investments as residual, taking what is left after obligatory and partial investments. This policy may buy short-term peace, but has no longer term implications on financial performance!

The classification also highlights the financial implications of investing financial resources in partial and full choice no-return investments. Obviously such investments will still be made, but within the context of a compromise of pressures (legal, social, financial and political) which are brought to the fore by this classification system.

The return classification can also be refined if required by using some financial criteria such as Net Present Value, Payback, Profitability Index and Internal Rate of Return.

Summary and Conclusions

Several texts on capital investment analysis appear to treat classification of capital projects as a subsidiary rather than as a central issue in the capital investment decision making process. Similarly, surveys have concentrated on financial techniques rather than project classification.

In order to handle the complex and dynamic capital investment decision process top management will require some structuring of the process; classification of capital projects can provide a useful decision-making framework. However the classification system will only be useful if it is designed to meet this purpose.

Of the myriad of characteristics of a project, those which have been selected in this paper, on the basis that they will meet the general needs of top management, are:

(i) return or no-return;
(ii) degree of top management freedom; and
(iii) the risk of the project.

There may be other factors which are considered significant and which could be added, but this would make the classification more complex. Whether or not this is done would be a matter for management choice. A system of questions has been developed to aid project classification within the system proposed (see Figure 7).

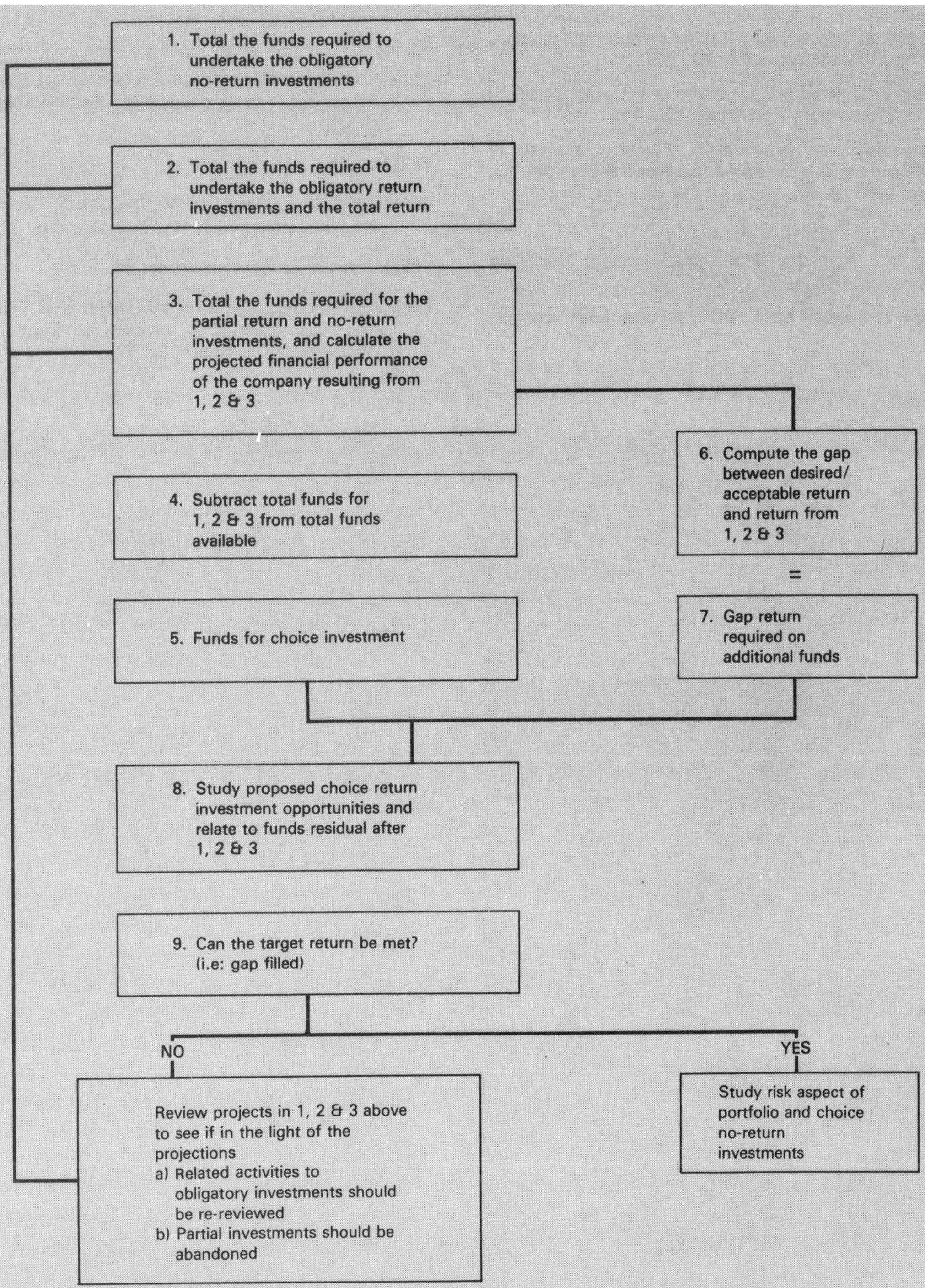

Figure 8. Decision process for investment selection (assuming capital rationing)

The issue of project classification is of major significance in structuring top management decision making on capital project selection, and further empirical study of the procedures used by organizations is necessary. Also the classification process as outlined and explained in this paper accepts that project selection involves internal politics and external financial pressures and facilitates a framework for the development of a 'satisfactory' solution by management.

References

(1) R. N. Anthony, *Planning and Control Systems: A Framework for Analysis,* Boston, Harvard University, Graduate School of Business Administration, Division of Research, p. 1 (1965).

(2) Joel Dean, *Managerial Economics*, p. 600, Prentice Hall (1951).

(3) R. N. Anthony, *op. cit.*, pp. 1–2.

(4) J. Dean, *op. cit.*, p. 601.

(5) Ibid., p. 602.

(6) Ibid., p. 603.

(7) Ibid., p. 603.

(8) A. Kaplan, *The Conduct of Inquiry* Science Research Associates, p. 50 (1964).

(9) A. J. Merrett and A. Sykes, *The Financing and Analysis of Capital Projects,* Longman. Second edition, pp. 378–380 (1973).

(10) Merrett and Sykes, *op. cit.*, p. 378.

(11) Ibid., p. 380.

(12) D. Garbutt, *A Simple Introduction to Capital Expenditure Decisions,* pp. 39–42 (1967).

(13) J. Van Horne, *Financial Management and Policy,* Prentice Hall, Fourth edition, p. 77 (1977).

(14) H. Bierman and S. Schmidt, *The Capital Budgeting Decision,* Macmillan, Fourth edition, pp. 83–98 (1975).

(15) J. B. Weaver, Organising and maintaining a capital expenditure program, *Engineering Economist,* **20,** (1).

(16) National Association of Accountants, Financial analysis to guide capital expenditure decisions, Research Report No. 43, NAA, U.S.A., 1967, p. 42.

(17) Ibid., p. 41.

(18) B. Carsberg and A. Hope, *Business Investment Decisions Under Inflation,* ICAEW, p. 22 (1976).

(19) J. Sizer, How to develop hurdle rates, an unpublished paper.

(20) Ibid.

(21) Ibid.

(22) L. V. Gerstner and M. H. Anderson, The chief financial officer as activist, *Harvard Business Review,* September–October (1976).

(23) Ibid.

(24) Unilever's submission to The Wilson Committee Reviewing the Functioning of Financial Institutions (1977).

(25) Gerstner and Anderson, op. cit.

(26) J. W. Petty, D. F. Scott and M. M. Bird, The capital expenditure decision-making process of large corporations, *The Engineering Economist,* **20** (3).

PART THREE

Executing Strategic Plans

Successfully Implementing Strategic Decisions

Larry D. Alexander, Assistant Professor of Business Strategy, Virginia Tech, Virginia, U.S.A.

Ninety-three company presidents completed a questionnaire evaluating the implementation of one strategic decision each in their respective firms. Ten strategy implementation problems were experienced during implementation by over 50 per cent of the sample group. Firms experiencing high success in implementation, according to an index of implementation success, were compared with the low-success firms to determine which problems were rated at significantly different levels. In 11 instances, the mean rating for the high-success implementation firms was significantly lower in terms of problem intensity. Follow-up interviews with 21 presidents (plus 25 governmental agency heads later on) identified five factors which help promote successful implementation.

Introduction

Although strategy implementation is viewed as an integral part of the strategic management process, little has been written or researched on it. The overwhelming majority of the literature so far has been on the long-range planning process itself or the actual content of the strategy being formulated. We have so far been giving lip service to the other side of the coin, namely strategy implementation. Consequently, it is not surprising that after a comprehensive strategy or single strategic decision has been formulated, significant difficulties are often encountered during the subsequent implementation process.

This study surveyed 93 private sector firms through a questionnaire to determine which implementation problems occurred most frequently as they tried to put strategic decisions into effect. Later on, in-depth telephone interviews with chief executive officers of 21 of these firms were conducted to comprehend these problems more fully. These interviews, combined later on with another 25 interviews with governmental agency heads in another study of implementation in the public sector by this researcher, help to identify factors which promote successful implementation.

The author is Assistant Professor of Business Strategy at Virginia Polytechnic Institute and State University, Blacksburg, VA 24061, U.S.A.

Review of the Literature

The available literature on strategy implementation was reviewed in order to identify potential strategy implementation problems. Most of the 22 potential problems were identified from such helpful works as Alexander,[1] Andrews,[2] Galbraith and Nathanson,[3] Hobbs and Heany,[4] Kotter and Schlesinger,[5] Le Breton,[6] McCarthy *et al.*,[7] Quinn,[8] Steiner and Miner,[9] and Thompson and Strickland.[10] In addition, several in-depth case studies on strategy implementation by Pressman and Wildavsky,[11] Murphy,[12] Quinn[13] and Alexander[14] also helped to identify more potential problems. Finally, a few of the 22 implementation problems were suggested by chief executive officers in earlier interviews conducted by this writer.

Companies Surveyed

The 93 firms participating in this survey were strategic business units of medium and large sized firms. Some 72 firms (77 per cent) were listed in the Fortune 500 list of leading industrials. If Fortune's second 500 list of industrials is included along with Fortune's top 50 listings for utilities, retailing and services, then 89 firms (96 per cent) responding were included on one Fortune list or another.

The firms' SBUs (strategic business units) sampled differed with respect to their size, industry and geographical location within the United States. For example, 26 (28 per cent) of the SBUs had less than 400 employees, 23 (25 per cent) had 400–999 employees, 29 (31 per cent) had 1000–4999 employees, 13 (14 per cent) had over 5000 employees, and 2 (2 per cent) were unidentified. While most of the corporations operated within a number of different businesses, this study was focused on implementing strategic decisions within individual SBUs.

The Strategic Decisions Evaluated

In the questionnaire, each responding company president (or division general manager) was asked to select one recent strategic decision that had been implemented in his SBU. He was asked to select one in which he had a great deal of personal knowledge about its subsequent implementation. Table 1 shows the types of strategic decisions that were evaluated. The main part of the questionnaire then asked the participants to evaluate the extent to which some 22 possible implementation problems actually were a problem in its subsequent implementation using a five-point Likert-type response scale. Finally, questions were asked to evaluate the overall success of the strategy implementation effort itself.

Most Frequently Occurring Problems

The 10 most commonly occurring strategy implementation problems are shown in Table 2 in descending order according to mean ratings. Two adjacent pairs of numbers on the five-point Likert response scale are combined for display purposes only as follows: minor and moderate problems (points 2 and 3), and substantial and major problems (points 4 and 5). The 10 listed items are the only ones rated as problems by over half of the sample group.

The first seven listed implementation problems occurred to at least 60 per cent of the firms. They are:

(1) implementation took more time than originally allocated by 76 per cent;

(2) major problems surface during implementation that had not been identified beforehand by 74 per cent;

(3) coordination of implementation activities (e.g. by task force, committees, superiors) was not effective enough by 66 per cent;

(4) competing activities and crises distracted

Table 1. Types of strategic decisions implemented

Type of strategic decision	No.	%
Introducing a new product or service	29	31
Opening and starting up a new plant or facility	17	18
Expanding operations to enter a new market	15	16
Discontinuing a product or withdrawing from a market	11	12
Acquiring or merging with another firm	10	11
Changing the strategy in functional departments	6	7
Other	5	5
	93	100

Table 2. Ten most frequent strategy implementation problems

Potential strategy implementation problem	Mean	Frequency of any degree of problem	=	Frequency of minor/ moderate problems	+	Frequency of substantial/ major problems
Implementation took more time than originally allocated	2·71	71 (76%)		45 (48%)		26 (28%)
Major problems surfaced during implementation that had not been identified beforehand	2·63	69 (74%)		45 (48%)		24 (26%)
Coordination of implementation activities was not effective enough	2·34	62 (66%)		45 (48%)		17 (18%)
Competing activities and crises distracted attention from implementing this decision	2·29	60 (64%)		41 (44%)		19 (20%)
Capabilities of employees involved were not sufficient	2·28	59 (63%)		40 (43%)		19 (20%)
Training and instruction given to lower level employees were not adequate	2·14	58 (62%)		47 (50%)		11 (12%)
Uncontrollable factors in the external environment had an adverse impact on implementation	2·28	56 (60%)		40 (43%)		16 (17%)
Leadership and direction provided by departmental managers were not adequate enough	2·23	55 (59%)		39 (42%)		16 (17%)
Key implementation tasks and activities were not defined in enough detail	2·09	52 (56%)		36 (39%)		16 (17%)
Information systems used to monitor implementation were not adequate	1·94	52 (56%)		43 (46%)		9 (10%)

attention from implementing this strategic decision by 64 per cent;

(5) capabilities (skills and abilities) of employees involved with the implementation were not sufficient by 63 per cent;

(6) training and instruction given to lower level employees were not adequate by 62 per cent; and

(7) uncontrollable factors in the external environment (e.g. competitive, economic, governmental) had an adverse impact on implementation by 60 per cent.

Three additional implementation problems listed in Table 2 occurred to somewhat fewer firms but still experienced by over 50 per cent of the sample firms.

Three-quarters (76 per cent) of the sampled firms found that their implementation efforts took more time than originally allocated. A number of explanations were given by CEOs in the follow-up telephone interviews. As one executive put it, 'In retrospect, we were overly optimistic in thinking how much time it would take to implement a new strategic decision. We thought that everything would work fine which it never does.' From the interviews, this problems seems to occur because top management:

(1) understates how long various implementation tasks will take to complete,

(2) downplays the likelihood of potential problems that may or may not occur, and

(3) is blind to other problems occurring altogether.

Obviously, when all three of these occur during implementation, it can greatly lengthen the time it will take to implement the decision effectively.

Solutions to the problem of taking too much time are numerous. More time should initially be allocated from the start to handle unexpected problems and, in general, the unknown. More manpower initially can be put on important strategic decisions, and particularly later on when unexpected problems emerge. In addition, rewards and penalties can also be used to bring about the desired results.

This latter suggestion is exactly how one CEO handled a strategic decision that had been dragging on and on. As he put it,

> Even though we wanted to withdraw from this particular line of fashion clothes, we kept coming up with new ideas. For every two items we'd drop from this line, we'd introduce one new one. Thus, we kept getting seduced back into this line even though I knew we had to discontinue it. After two years, I finally solved the problem by telling my staff that if you or your subordinates present me with any new sketch for this clothing line, that person will lose his job.

Major problems (and obstacles) surfaced during implementation that had not been identified beforehand were experienced by almost as many firms, specifically 74 per cent. These can be internally oriented problems brought on by the firm trying something new, insufficient advance planning, and strategy formulators not getting actively involved in implementation to name a few. Or they can be caused by externally oriented factors such as the uncertainty involved with a new product or new market, uncontrollable events in the external environment, or legal/political complications introduced by new legislation or regulations among others.

Consider what happened to one domestic oil equipment firm that was implementing its strategic decision to construct oil wells in an Arab country. All sorts of problems surfaced that had not been identified beforehand as potential problems. Certain employees could not go into that country to work on the project because of their particular race or nationality. Bringing explosives into that country to blast rock in preparation for building the oil well foundation was delayed because the host government was suspicious that they could be used against the government itself. Neither of these problems had been identified beforehand by the firm or its Arab partner, who led them to believe it really knew the ropes and how to operate in the host country. In addition, another oil firm already in that country for many years tried to put up administrative road blocks by using its contacts in various governmental agencies of the Arab country.

Clearly, some of these problems could have been identified and resolved had the firm selected a better Arab partner. In addition, some of these potential problems overlooked by its Arab partner could have been identified had the firm talked with other U.S. firms already doing business there. However, it is safe to say that some of these problems could probably never be anticipated beforehand.

The presence of competing activities and crises that distracted attention from implementing the strategic decision was yet another frequently occurring problem. Some 64 per cent of the firms experienced this implementation problem. One aerospace components firm was starting to implement one strategic decision when along came one order from an airline firm that amounted to 25 per cent of its total sales in a typical year. Obviously, considerable time and attention had to be given to this major order for about 3 months which clearly had priority over the other strategic decision. Actually, the firm decided to forget trying to implement the new strategic decision for a while and put it on hold. Given the size of the customer order, this seemed the best way to handle these competing events.

Another firm was trying to implement one strategic decision when the market for its coal-related products collapsed in 1977. Because of this unexpected crisis, pressure was put on managers at all levels to do everything possible to increase sales and profits rather than to implement this new management resource planning system. Still another firm was diverted from implementing a new overall strategy for the division and had to help a very major customer design and manufacture one of its products which was encountering major production problems. This was done to insure that this delinquent customer would get enough revenues from the sale of its products to, in turn, pay money owed to this firm. Thus, it appears that the number and type of competing activities and crises that can occur are almost limitless.

One of three things typically occurs when competing events exist. Time and attention are taken away from implementing the new strategic decision. They are taken away from other existing programs which suffer. Or often, some time and attention are taken away from the new and existing programs.

Some 60 per cent of the firms experienced uncontrollable factors in the external environment that had an adverse impact on implementation. Some of these problems are truly surprise events. Examples of these include:

(1) a hurricane tearing off a roof of a new plant which damaged equipment;

(2) the Professional Airline Traffic Controllers strike and the 25 per cent reduction in flights which reduced the demand for a firm's new jet-pull-out tractor; and

(3) a surprising upturn in an industry's sales when a firm was trying to move three plants into one new modern facility.

In this latter example, this firm competing in the abrasives industry had planned to make this move during a time of slackened demand. All economic forecasts for 1978/1979 suggested a softness in the economy; consequently, the firm thought this would be an excellent time to consolidate operations. Unfortunately, after the move got started, that year turned out to be the best year ever for the industry which caused added problems trying to satisfy high customer demand while moving operations.

While most uncontrollable problems in the external environment cannot be anticipated, contingency plans can be developed for some of them. Then, if that problem does occur, at least the firm will be in a better position to take corrective action to minimize its impact on the firm.

Two somewhat lower rated items, which are:

(1) advocates and supporters of the strategic decision left (the division or company) during implementation (experienced by only 27 per cent of the firms) and

(2) the key people who developed and made the strategic decision, did not play an active enough role in its subsequent implementation (40 per cent),

illustrate how two problems can combine to make things even worse. One company president put it this way,

> Our company was acquired by another parent firm with no background in this business. A new group vice president was installed to straighten out the mess here. He and I developed a strategy to break even in about 15 months with proper equipment, but then 6 months later, this group vice president was replaced for reasons beyond my knowledge. His replacement was not familiar with our operations, wants us now to go in about a 180 degree different direction, and only looks at bottom line results.

In another firm, a company president appointed a key subordinate to be the project manager, directly overseeing the implementation of the strategic decision. Half way through its implementation, that subordinate got so frustrated with the whole thing that he took a job elsewhere which really ground things to a halt. While the loss of a key person implementing a strategic decision can cause problems and lengthen the implementation time, the loss of the key architect of the decision can potentially stop the implementation forever.

High Versus Low Implementation Success

The sample of 93 firms was then divided into high ($n=33$), medium ($n=29$), and low ($n=31$) success depending on the relative degree of success in implementing the strategic decision. This was based on an implementation success index made up of an average of three questions rated on a five-point scale ranging from 'low extent' to 'high extent'. These questions sought to determine the extent to which the actual implementation effort:

(1) achieved the initial goals and objectives of the strategic decision;

(2) achieved the financial results (sales, income, and/or profits) that were expected; and

(3) was carried out within the various resources (money, manpower, time, etc.) initially budgeted for it.

Analysis of variance and Student *t*-tests were calculated for each of the 22 potential implementation problems to determine whether there were first significant overall differences and then specific significant differences between the high-success and low-success groups. In 21 instances, the high-success group in implementing their respective strategic decisions had lower mean scores than the low-success group for the respective problem.

Seven of the same 10 problems shown in Table 2 along with five new problems were found to be significantly different with the analysis of variance comparing high-, medium- and low-success groups. Then, in 11 instances (marked by asterisks) as shown in Figure 1, the Student *t*-test showed that the mean score for high-success implementing firms (as shown by the solid line) was significantly less than that for the low-success group of firms (as shown by the dashed line). The five implementation problems that had *t*-test significance at the 0·005 level or above are:

(1) key implementation tasks and activities were not defined in enough detail;

(2) problems requiring top management involvement were not communicated to them fast enough;

(3) changes in roles and responsibilities of key employees were not clearly defined;

(4) key formulators of the strategic decision did not play an active enough role in implementation; and

(5) major problems surfaced during implementation that had not been identified beforehand.

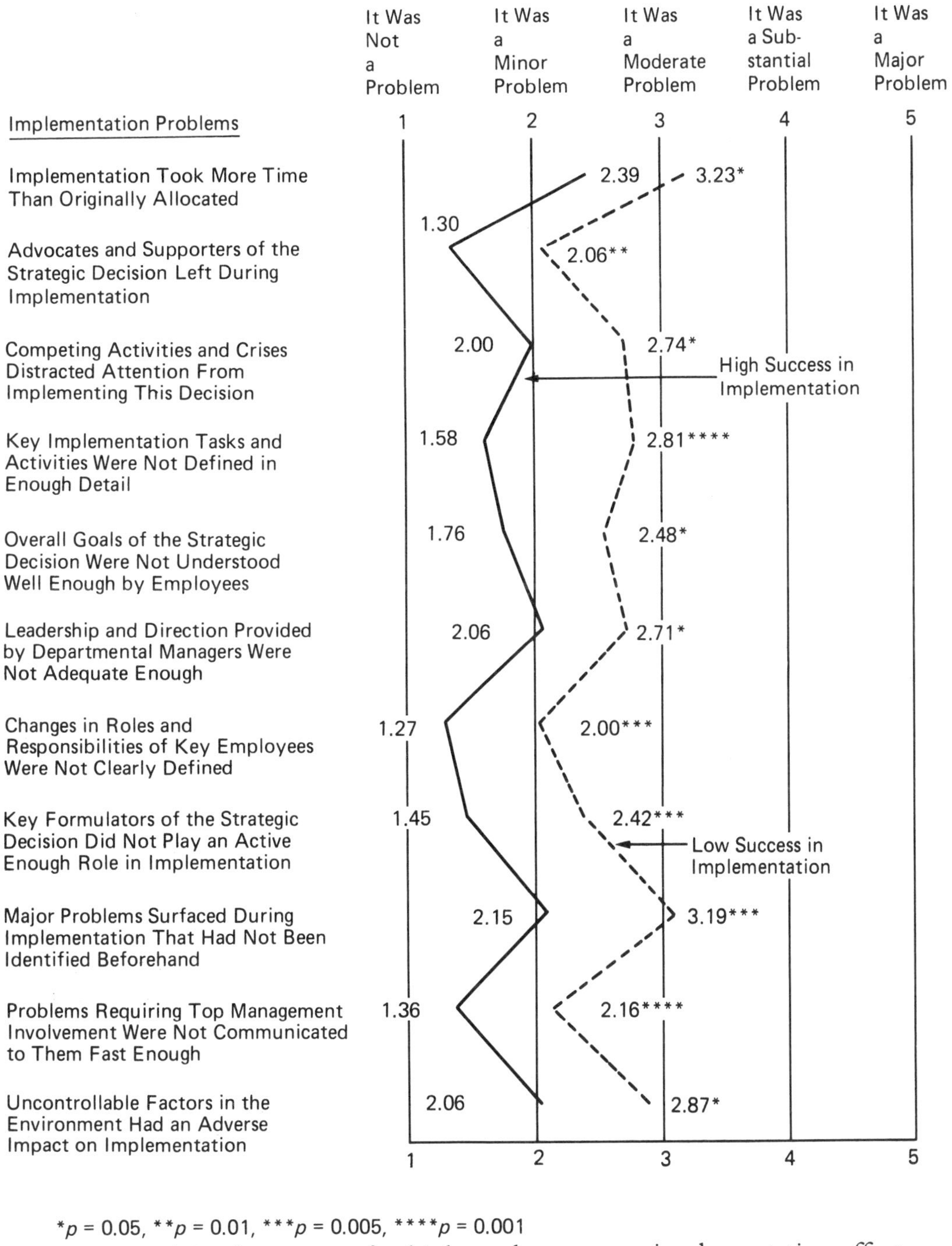

Figure 1. Mean ratings and Student *t*-tests for high- vs low-success implementation efforts

Thus, Figure 1 clearly suggests that the presence of more higher rated implementation problems has a negative effect on implementation success. Low-success firms experienced an average of 12·8 problems rated at any intensity level. In addition, 5·0 of these same 12·8 implementation items were rated as substantial or major problems by low-success firms. Conversely, high-success implementation firms experienced an average of only 9·2 problems, of which only 1·5 of them were rated at the substantial or major level.

Promoting Successful Strategy Implementation

In the followup telephone interviews with CEOs, one major purpose was to understand better various implementation problems that did hinder the implementation effort. However, another reason for these interviews was to get these executives to draw on their extensive experience and speculate on the things that help to promote successful strategy implementation. Although these generalizations are not statistically valid, they were mentioned most frequently by 21 CEOs plus 25 additional interviews with agency heads from federal and state governments in a comparison study.

Communication, Communication, Communication
This seemingly simple suggestion was mentioned more frequently by CEOs than any other single item. The reason it is repeated three times is to reflect exactly what was said by a number of these company presidents. They felt that top management must first of all clearly communicate with all employees what the new strategic decision is all about. Hopefully, it involves two-way communication that permits and solicits questions from affected employees about the formulated strategy, issues to be considered, or potential problems that might occur. In addition, communication includes clearly explaining what new responsibilities, tasks, and duties need to be performed by the affected employees. It also includes the why behind changed job activities, and more fundamentally the reasons why the new strategic decision was made in the first place. Finally, CEOs mentioned that two-way communication is needed throughout the implementation process to monitor what is actually happening, analyze how to deal with emerging problems, and in deciding what modifications might be needed in the program to make it work.

Start with a Good Concept or Idea
The need to start with a formulated strategy that involves a good idea or concept was mentioned next most often in helping promote successful implementation. In a nut shell, what this idea suggests is that no amount of time and effort spent on implementation can rescue a strategic decision that is not well formulated to begin with. More than being thoroughly planned out, the idea must be fundamentally sound. Thus, this suggests that strategy implementation can fail for one of two reasons. One is caused by a failure to do the things required during implementation to insure that a well-formulated strategy is successful. The other cause of failure is due to a poorly conceived formulated plan that no amount of implementation effort can help rescue.

Obtain Employee Commitment and Involvement
This third suggestion builds on the first two and interrelates with them. CEOs suggested that one way to accomplish this is to involve affected employees and managers right from the start in the strategy formulation process. On the contrary, when a strategic decision has been developed in a vacuum by a few people, top management should not be surprised that it is resisted during implementation by the affected employees. Top management should not be surprised if the formulated plan has major flaws in it because key employees and affected groups did not participate in its formulation. In fact, just the opposite may be true. Top management ought to be surprised if a formulated strategy, developed pretty much without key employee involvement, is implemented successfully.

Involvement and commitment should also be developed and maintained throughout the implementation process. If middle and lower level managers and key subordinates are permitted to be involved with the detailed implementation planning, their commitment typically will tend to increase. The workability of the specific action plan should also be improved simply by getting the affected employees involved—and committed—early on as well as throughout the implementation process.

Provide Sufficient Resources
CEOs mentioned at least four different kinds of resources. The obvious one is money, which, considering the sizeable scope of many strategic decisions, is a bottom line requirement. Conversely, failure to provide adequate funding may contribute to limited success or outright failure. Manpower is another key resource which can have either a positive or a negative effect on implementation. Technical expertise (or knowledge), as related to the new strategic decision, is still another resource mentioned by some CEOs. The idea suggested here is that firms need to have in-house expertise or hire a few new employees who possess it in order to implement strategic decisions involving new endeavors. A final resource mentioned is time. Sufficient time to accomplish the implementation, adequate time and attention given by top management to the new effort, and hopefully not too many other competing programs demanding the time of affected employees who will implement this one.

Develop an Implementation Plan

This final suggestion is a plea to develop many of the specifics to be done during implementation. In essence, this details who is to do what and when it is to be accomplished. A few CEOs mentioned that this plan must strike the right balance. If the implementation plan is too vague, it is of little practical use. Conversely, if the plan is too detailed, it may tend to force various functional departments to follow it precisely, even when it clearly needs to be modified.

Several CEOs also mentioned that a part of that plan should be to identify likely implementation problems. Instead of being blindly optimistic that nothing will go wrong while implementing a strategic decision, do just the opposite. Try to identify the most likely problems that might occur and then develop contingency responses for those eventualities.

Summary and Conclusions

A number of strategy implementation problems do seem to occur on a regular basis. In fact, 10 of the 22 potential problems rated occurred to at least 50 per cent of the sampled firms. While problems do occur frequently, the vast majority of firms experience them as minor or moderate problems. However, when a firm encounters several implementation problems, rated at the substantial or major level, it can have a very adverse impact on the implementation process.

Surprisingly, some of the traditional strategy implementation factors mentioned in the literature were not judged as frequently to be problems. Rated among the least frequent of the 22 implementation problems were:

- ☆ rewards and incentives utilized to get employee conformance to program were not sufficient (cited as a problem by only 18 per cent of the respondents);
- ☆ support and backing by top management in this SBU and at the corporate level were not adequate (21 per cent);
- ☆ financial resources made available were not sufficient (27 per cent);
- ☆ organizational structural changes made were not effective (33 per cent); and
- ☆ changes in roles and responsibilities of key employees were not clearly defined (38 per cent).

It may be that firms do such a good job in these areas than problems are prevented. Or it may suggest that other implementation problems identified in this study are more important than what the literature has somewhat led us to believe.

High-success firms experience implementation problems to a significantly less extent than do low-success implementation firms. In fact, some 11 problems were experienced to a significantly less extent by high-success firms when compared with low-success firms. In addition, high-success firms experienced problems rated at the substantial or major problem intensity level three times less frequently than did low-success firms. In addition, high-success firms also encountered fewer total problems during implementation.

Successful implementation in part involves preventing various implementation problems from occurring in the first place. It also involves taking quick action of resolve and address problems that do occur. Obviously, the faster corrective action is initiated during implementation, the more likely it can be resolved before it impacts adversely on the firm.

Successful implementation also involves doing the things that help promote success rather than just preventing problems from occurring. Although the five suggestions presented here are not statistically significant, they do help reinforce the importance of satisfying basic managerial tasks to help bring about success.

References

(1) L. Alexander, *Strategy Implementation Annotated Bibliography,* Harvard's HBS Case Services, Case No. 9-380-797 (1980), plus 1983 Supplement.

(2) K. Andrews, *The Concept of Corporate Strategy,* Dow Jones-Irwin, Homewood, IL (1971).

(3) J. Galbraith and D. Nathanson, *Strategy Implementation: The Role of Structure and Process,* West Publishing Co., St Paul, MN (1978).

(4) J. Hobbs and D. Heany, Coupling strategy to operating plans, *Harvard Business Review,* pp. 119–126, May–June (1977).

(5) J. Kotter and L. Schlesinger, Choosing strategies for change, *Harvard Business Review,* pp. 106–114, March–April (1979).

(6) P. Le Breton, *General Administration: Planning and Implementation,* Holt, Rinehart and Winston, New York (1965).

(7) D. McCarthy, R. Minichiello and J. Curran, *Business Policy and Strategy: Concepts and Readings,* Richard D. Irwin, Homewood, IL (1979).

(8) J. Quinn, *Strategies for Change: Logical Incrementalism,* Richard D. Irwin, Homewood, IL (1980).

(9) G. Steiner and J. Miner, *Management Policy and Strategy: Text, Readings, and Cases,* Macmillan, New York (1977).

(10) A. Thompson and A. Strickland, *Strategy Formulation and Implementation: Tasks of the General Manager,* Business Publications, Dallas (1981).

(11) J. Pressman and A. Wildavsky, *Implementation,* University of California Press, Berkeley, CA (1973).

(12) J. Murphy, Title I of ESEA: The politics of implementing federal education reform, *Harvard Educational Review,* pp. 35–63, February (1971).

(13) J. Quinn, General Motors' downsizing decision. In D. Harvey's *Business Policy and Strategic Management,* pp. 669–695. Charles E. Merrill, Columbus, OH (1982).

(14) L. Alexander, Pacific power and light: Implementation of an innovative home weatherization program. In A. Thompson and A. Strickland's *Strategic Management: Concepts and Cases,* pp. 880–905, Business Publications, Dallas (1984).

Managing Strategic Change: An Integrated Approach

Colin A. Carnall

This paper sets out to identify and discuss an integrated approach to the management of strategic changes. Managing effectiveness, dealing with organizational cultures and managing organizational politics are discussed, focusing upon how to do so in order to encourage risk-taking, creativity and learning and to build self-esteem and performance. Such an approach allows the achievement of major changes in ways which lead to employees developing a fuller understanding of the nature of the business, its problems and its future.

Introduction

Implementing organizational change effectively. This is one of the managerial challenges facing all of us. In both the private sector and the public sector, in manufacturing, banking, health care and education, this challenge is presented, often in very stark circumstances. We are concerned about value for money, the development and marketing of new products and services, flexibility, whether of design and manufacture (through computer-aided design, robots, flexible manufacturing systems), or in organizational structure and managerial style. We are increasingly concerned about product/service performance and quality. Customers and clients are ever more vocal and critical. Often they can 'vote with their feet'. If the automobile I buy tomorrow performs poorly and unreliably I am unlikely to buy that make again. In education we talk of 'parent involvement', of 'parent power'. The central focus of management is switching from internal concerns and the development of professional disciplines in isolation. For example, engineering designers, who might once have sought optimum technical solution alone, are paying real attention to design as a synthesis of technical, commercial, product and aesthetic considerations.

All organizations face challenges like these. A food-processing firm faces social changes such as new attitudes to diet, commodity market pressures, as supply problems mount, competitive pressures and the problems of bringing up to date what had been a company which had always been paternalistically managed. Banks face de-regulation, technological change and an increasingly international competition. Health and education face pressures for greater accountability, both for the use of resources, and for the quality of the services they provide. Can the professional autonomy of doctors and teachers remain unchanged? An engineering company (manufacturing packaging machinery) develops marketing and new products and leads a drive for quality as a means of re-building its position in world markets.

Analysed simply we could divide the concern over the management of major changes into two main questions. 'What changes should we implement?' and 'How may we implement them successfully?' To develop answers to these questions requires specific skills. To diagnose the need for change. To audit performance. To develop a vision of improvement. To describe or define new strategy. Achieving change also requires the skill to get things done, to achieve action. It is often disturbing and disruptive. By definition change upsets the 'status quo'. Leadership is central because to achieve effective organizational change requires us to elevate analysis over consensus. Easy options are in short supply! Implementing major organizational change demands the combination of action and analysis into a new managerial synthesis.

In this paper we propose to discuss this new managerial synthesis necessary for effective change. We propose to develop two main themes as follows:

(1) What are the managerial skills required for effective organizational change? We will examine a number of key managerial skills.

(2) Change is disruptive and disturbing. How do people experience change and how may they be

---

The author is Director of the MBA Programme at Henley—The Management College. He previously worked in the mechanical engineering industry.

helped to cope with the pressures of major changes?

All organizations deploy these managerial and coping skills to lesser or greater extents. Our purpose is to identify these two sets of skills so that managers can more effectively identify strengths and weaknesses and, thereby, further develop their capacities to achieve effective organizational change.

Managerial Skills For Effective Organizational Change

To manage change effectively involves the ability to create a new synthesis of people, resources, ideas, opportunities and demands. The Manager needs skills rather like those of an orchestral conductor. Vision is essential and creativity paramount. Yet the capacity to create systematic plans to provide for the logistics of resources, support, training and people is central to any change programme. People must be influenced, departmental boundaries crossed or even 'swallowed up'. New ideas must be accepted and new ways of working embraced. New standards of performance and quality need to be achieved. The politics of the organization are crucial. Support must be mobilized, coalitions built, opposition handled and bargains struck. The programme must be maintained, teams built and supported. People need help to cope with the stress, anxiety and uncertainties of change. Continuity and tradition must be overturned, in part, as the old is replaced by the new. Yet, continuity and tradition provides people with stability, support and meaning and should not needlessly be destroyed. The effective management of organizational change demands attention to all of these somewhat conflicting issues and challenges. So in a period of change *synthesis* is the key. In this section we shall deal with three skill areas, as follows: (i) managing transitions; (ii) dealing with organizational cultures and (iii) the politics of organizational change.

(i) *Managing Transitions*
Company A manufactures a range of engines. It is a wholly owned subsidiary of a U.S.-based multinational corporation. It supplies engines to a small number of end-user companies, each of which incorporates them into its own products. By 1980 the company was experiencing severe external and internal pressures (Figure 1).

This is a familiar enough pattern. A cycle of decline creating major challenge for management to find ways of achieving a transition to effectiveness. *The first and most important challenge was to develop an open attitude toward change.* The company had experienced little or no change in 30 years. Employees were accustomed to stability and managers possessed little or no skill in the management of change. New management at Group level, recognizing this company as declining economically, brought in a new top management team comprised of a Managing Director, Engineering Director and Finance Director. The new team moved quickly. The strategy adopted is shown schematically below (Figure 2).

External Pressures

Recession
High Interest Rate
Falling Orders

High Energy and Material Costs

New Products/Materials Technology being Adopted in Engine Design and Manufacture.

Increased Competition both from Abroad and Because Some End Users were Beginning to Switch to Build Their Own Engines

Changes at Group as a Consequence of a Change in Ownership

Internal Pressures

- Inadequate Organizational Structures
- Lack of Confidence and Fear of Change, Including the Fear of Redundancy
- Accustomed to Slow Change (or Paralysis)
- Limited Managerial Competence in Managing Change
- Lack of Experience with New Technology
- Low Productivity and Quality
- Ageing Plant with Attendant Maintenance Problems.
- Low Morale, High Absenteeism, Industrial Disputes.
- Cash Flow Problems

Figure 1. Internal and external pressures in an engine manufacturer

The first step was to test the reality the company faced and to draw people into that process of testing. Employees at all levels needed to understand the problems the company was facing. Beyond this it was essential that people be given the chance to seek out and develop solutions. Thus on the one hand, openness in negotiations and communications with employees meant that the problems were better understood. On the other hand, through involvement of employees and by bringing in new skills (particularly marketing), new ways of doing things were sought. Employees were drawn into solving problems such as quality, absenteeism, factory layout and so on. Project groups from design, marketing and the production departments became involved in seeking new products. People were given the opportunity to try out new ideas, to experiment, to seek solutions. This then started a process of attitude change. Recognizing the problems and becoming involved on processes aimed at developing solutions lead to a more open approach to the idea of change. Seen as unavoidable, employees began to recognize the possibility that constructive, albeit not painless, action was feasible. In these ways management and employees were facing the challenge identified in Figure 3 (based upon Argyris and Schon[1]).

Significant change involves learning. If reality is tested openly, and if open or constructive attitudes to change prevail, then we are most likely to achieve significant changes. Change is possible without open reality testing but only where people excluded

Testing Reality	New Attitudes and Structures	Achievements
• Threat to Closure and Redundancy		• New Technology Introduced in Manufacturing Technology and in Materials
• Encouraging Understanding of the Problems	• Developing New Attitudes to Work and to Change	
• Developing New Ideas for the Future — New Products		
• Search for New Markets and Business (Including Subcontracting)	• Training for New Technology and to Deal with Change	• Quality Control System Introduced
• Open Negotiation and Communication	• Re-organization and Contraction	• New Products
• Full Involvement of Employees and Unions	• Investment in New Technology	• Labour Flexibility

Figure 2. A strategy for change

from this testing process are not fully engaged in the changes to be implemented. If they are not involved in testing reality they can neither understand the need for change nor feel committed to the changes, let alone learn from them. One word of caution. Public or extensive testing of reality in a declining situation merely creates anxiety unless a constructive attitude to change prevails, particularly within management. Thus to argue that effective communication is enough, without giving people the opportunity and support to seek solutions to problems will merely sustain the spiral of decline. In this company the reality-testing process lead to new attitudes which themselves both facilitated, and were in turn, sustained by training programmes for new technology, improved maintenance, quality control, by the emergence of new investment and new equipment, and by reorganization (including the formation of a marketing department and the introduction of quality control systems). The spiral of decline was being reversed.

Managing this transition to effectiveness, then, demanded learning and change.

(a) Learning is produced by *exploring dilemmas or contradictions* (e.g. improved quality was essential and end-user's had to be convinced that they should continue to use company A's product *but* ageing plant, managerial problems and low morale made this difficult to achieve).

(b) Learning is based *upon personal experience and experimentation*. People will only learn if they understand the problems and are brought into the process of seeking solutions.

(c) Learning can be encouraged in a climate which *encourages risk-taking,* doing things, trying out new ideas.

(d) Learning requires the *expression of deeply held beliefs* and will *involve conflict*. Only then can ideas emerge and be properly assessed before

Testing Reality: (Problem Solving)

		Restricted (Within the Management Team)	Extensive (Involvement of Those Affected)
Attitudes to Change	Negative	Little Learning or Change	Anxiety Creating Behaviour
	Positive	Learning and Change can Occur only if *not* Dependent on Other People	Learning and Change Possible

Figure 3. Learning from changing? Implementing strategic change

being incorporated into new systems, products, strategies, etc.

(e) *Learning can be helped by recognizing the value of people and ideas.* Developing learning styles which encourage individuals rather than close off discussion and creativity.[1]

Company A had, by 1983, reduced staffing, improved the organization structure, introduced a quality control system, for the first time, achieved labour flexibility and developed new products. The leadership challenge faced successfully in this case was that of achieving change in the ways described whilst maintaining the business through very difficult times. 'Selling' the solutions to Group and 'buying' time were central to this and part of the politics of change, a matter we turn to next.

(ii) *Dealing with Organizational Cultures: a Major Financial Institution*

Company B is a large financial institution with hundreds of branches in major towns and cities in its home country. It operates internationally. In recent years it has been very successful with growth of profitability and turnover. Yet it faces major challenges. De-regulation, new technology, competition and growing complexity of the services it provides, both to private and corporate customers, are amongst the challenges it faces. The company is involved in a major programme of branch rationalization. Some branches are being closed, others remodelled to provide either private or corporate services, others are being expanded as key branches. Early on in this programme of change it became clear that the company's property management department needed attention. Its property management performance was poor and outmoded. Its capacity to plan and carry through the branch rationalization programme seemed doubtful.

Property management was the responsibility of a central department employing 250 professional staff, mainly architects and surveyors, managed by a general manager. The general manager was drawn from the senior management team on a 2-year posting. All general managers at that time had finance backgrounds. Indeed the culture of company B powerfully sustained the belief that the *only* important work was finance. All other work, whether property, computing or marketing, was secondary. Career paths for non-finance people were limited, departments being managed by people with finance backgrounds. The extent to which non-finance staff were undervalued may be seen by noting that in the property management department no one could remember anyone having any training and development since the day of their appointment. The morale of the property management department was low and the level of inter-departmental conflict (between the surveyors group and the architects group) was very high.

The company is organized into 12 regions, each managed by a Regional Director. Property management at regional level was unco-ordinated. Regional Directors took many of the decisions without being properly accountable, formally. Refurbishment decisions were under Regional Directors' control yet the costs of refurbishment were a charge on a head office account, not on the region's books. Moreover the lack of co-operation between architects and surveyors diffused any professional input into property decisions taken at regional level.

The Organizational Culture. Company B typifies the *role culture** under significant external and internal pressures. Often stereotyped as bureaucracy this culture is characterized by stability, prescription, rules and standards. Functional departments are clearly specified. This can be a very efficient culture in stable environments. Role cultures emphasize high levels of commitment by individuals either to a department, or in a professional role culture, to a particular profession. In this culture position power is a predominant form of power. But in this case the stability of the 1960s and 1970s had been replaced by the turbulence of the 1980s. Now property management expertise was essential if the branch rationalization programme was to proceed.

To detail the organizational change quickly a property management professional was brought in to take charge and develop a modern property management strategy. This was only the second time in the history of company B that a non-finance manager had been appointed to this level and the first time such an appointment had been made from outside. Under his control property management was decentralized to regional teams, managed by regional managers. Small teams, closer to the region, would be more likely to develop improved working relationships. Training and development was put in place for the professional staff. A career path was now opening up for them. All of this was moving property management toward a *task culture*. Here influence is based on expertise, the expertise needed to carry out the task. Teams of people work together to achieve objectives and tasks. This culture places demands upon people but also provides for the merging of individual and organizational objectives. It is an adaptable culture in which the needs of the task predominate rather than systems and procedures. In this case architects and surveyors now work together more closely. Regional teams are managed by architects or surveyors. For professional purposes there is a professional development role played by a deputy general manager in the, now, small head-office property management function. Arguably company B has moved toward a culture more appropriate to the challenges it faces.

*The terms role culture, task culture and power culture are taken from Charles Handy.[2]

Organizational issues which must be faced if more adaptable organizational cultures are to be achieved are as follows:

(a) *Management autonomy,* particularly with regard to reward systems. To what extent should local management have the ability to make decisions about gradings and salary dependent on market conditions and personal performance.

(b) *Interchangeability,* movement across specialist/professional boundaries by internal promotions, fixed-term secondments, or short training periods would help develop broader knowledge and experience. To what extent should promotion depend upon diversity of experience? Moves of this sort can sustain task forces or project teams. It can also reinforce individual autonomy, creativity and knowledge.

(c) *Openness or public testing* of issues and problems would also be aided by interchangeability.

(d) Recent developments in management information systems seem likely to bring about systems which managers can interrogate! This will aid *communication* partly through the *access* so provided, partly by the promise of simplification of procedures and paperwork such developments promise.

(e) Functional and professional advice can be provided to a more local level utilizing task-team approaches such as that described briefly in the case with professional development, planning and control being centrally organized. The focus should be on *business needs* rather than on professional demands.

Other organizational cultures have been identified. The *power culture* is worth a moment's thought. Frequently found in small, growing companies, including property and finance. These organizations are highly dependent on one or more strong leaders. Control is exercised from the centre and decisions are made very largely on the outcome of a balance of influence rather than on rational grounds (which the uncertainties of our changing world will rarely allow in any event). An organization with this culture can react well to change but the quality of top people is crucial. Individuals who are power-oriented, risk-taking and politically skilled will do well in this culture wherein accountability is personal and direct.

Managing in Different Cultures. One final thought on culture. We have discussed the links between organizational culture, the tasks to be performed and the rate of environmental change. But culture is a broader part of our affairs. At home and abroad we often find ourselves working with people from different occupational, local and national cultures. Effective management thus demands the capacity to deal with cross-cultural issues and influences. The important skill here is that of *empathy.* Managing change involves the need to influence people. Empathy, sensitivity to cultural differences, and the struggle to understand them and to communicate in an intelligible fashion, is essential.

The property management professional brought this skill to bear in his work with the professional staff involved in the change process described. Whilst these boundaries cannot easily be crossed, people respond to the attempt, and change programmes are all the more feasible and relevant for a leavening of cultural sensitivity. This skill will be discussed further in the section on coping with change.

(iii) *The Politics of Organizational Change*

To understand how organizations are managed, experienced and changed we need to understand the politics of organizations. In turn this involves the examination of political process, activity and skill. Why is the use of power and politics a necessary part of managing change? Partly this is because of the need for innovation.

> Innovative accomplishments stretch beyond the established definition of a 'job' to bring new learning or capacity to the organisation. They involve change, a disruption of existing activities, a redirection of organisational energies . . .[3]

Of course this is right. But the impetus to the use of power runs deeper. Any significant organizational change demands that existing ways of thinking about and talking about what we do can be overturned. Dominant views must be usurped. Experience tells us that the first attempt to articulate an alternative view, a novel concept, will fall on barren ground, very often. More likely it will meet opposition and even outright rejection. To overcome such opposition or rejection neither logic, evidence nor participation of all concerned, appears to be enough. New ideas can seem unorthodox and even risky. A manager seeking support for new ideas must be sensitive to political processes. Our discussion of the role of political skills in the management of change follows the framework set out in Figure 4.

Resources. Managers, and others, utilize a variety of resources as they engage in the politics of organization. They may have *formal authority,* or may be perceived as such, by virtue of their position. Moreover, they may have *direct control over resources.* The use of a resource control to negate change programmes is widely practised. If a change programme needs engineering resources, and if the Engineering Manager can withhold those resources, perhaps by claiming that other priorities must prevail, then change can be delayed. *Control of information, agenda and access* are all important political resources. It is commonplace to say 'Information is power'. The power to control the organization internally, power regarding the development of future policy. This point was made by Henry Kissinger when he discussed the new role

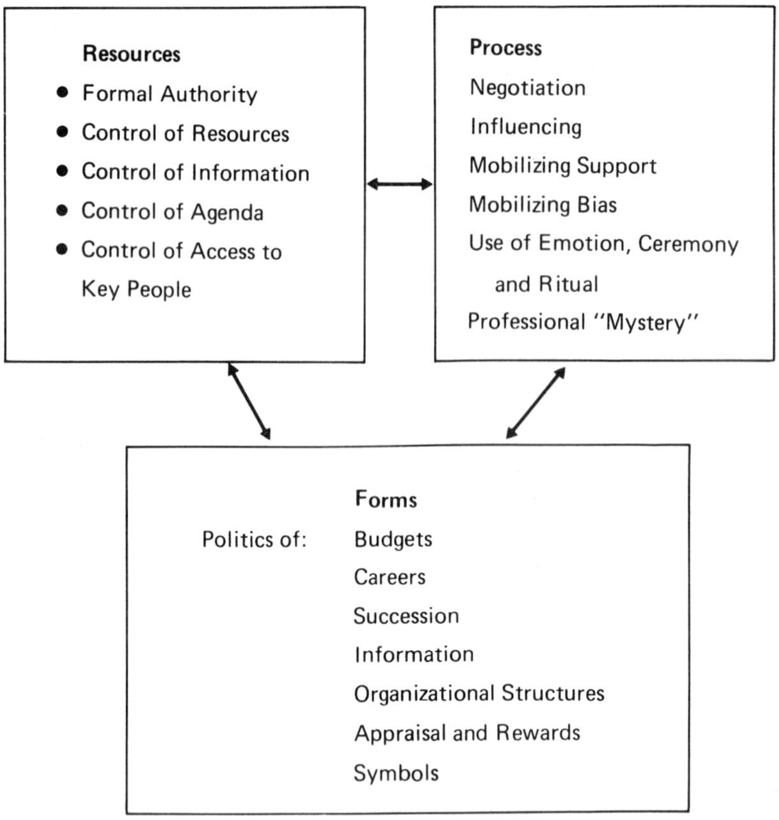

Figure 4. Politics and organization

Nixon and he had agreed for the National Security Council at the beginning of Nixon's first term.

> A President should not leave the presentation of his options to one of the Cabinet departments or agencies. Since the views of the departments are often in conflict, to place one in charge of presenting the options will be perceived by the others as giving it an unfair advantage. Moreover, the strong inclination of all departments is to narrow the scope for Presidential decision, not to expand it. They are organized to develop a preferred policy, not a range of choices. If forced to present options, the typical department will present two absurd alternatives as straw men bracketing its preferred option—which usually appears in the middle position. A totally ignorant decision-maker could easily satisfy his departments by blindly choosing Option 2 of any three choices which they submit to him. Every department, finally, dreads being overruled by the President: all have, therefore, a high incentive to obscure their differences. Options tend to disappear in an empty consensus that at the end of the day permits each agency or department maximum latitude to pursue its original preference. It takes a strong, dedicated and fair Presidential staff to ensure that the President has before him genuine and not bogus choices.[4]

Recognizing the narrowness of view which often emerges from specialist, departmental and sometimes from professional concerns, Kissinger here demonstrates the crucial importance of *controlling the presentation of options* to a President. Without doing so the President may be at the mercy of departments. Departments may preclude policy debate by the nature and range of the options presented to the President. They may also structure a policy debate by purposely obscuring differences over policy in the pursuit of consensus.

Processes and Forms of Politics. The forms politics of organizational change may take are varied. Fairly obviously, budgets, career development, succession planning information, structures, appraisal and reward systems have political dimensions. Decisions in such areas will carry a political element. We might say that this is undesirable but we should not close our minds to the possibility that the reality is different from what some would say is the ideal. To understand decisions within a budgeting context, we must consider political issues. In much the same way, to understand how changes are implemented, we need to recognize the resources, processes and forms of politics.

The politics of organizational change comprise various processes and take various forms. We identify these in Figure 4 mainly to identify the linkages between resources for power, and the processes and forms of organizational politics. These create issues and opportunities whenever changes are underway. Organizational politics is inevitable during periods of change and provides an impetus to initiative, creativity and change, if constructively managed. For many the word politics has a perjurative element to it. Managing change should be about satisfaction, concern for people, participation and the like. Everyday experience tells us that this is not enough, however. If the politics of change be accepted how may it be managed constructively? In essence this involves *managing in order to encourage risk-taking and positive attitudes to change.* Politics balanced by concern for the practical isues to be faced. Politics unconstrained leads to negative attitudes to change, low risk-taking and high levels of anxiety. The test of constructive organizational politics, then, becomes the guidelines identified above for the management of the transition to effectiveness.

Coping with Major Organizational Changes

Thus far we have considered some of the managerial skills associated with the effective management of change. We now proceed to consider the impact of change upon the people directly affected, which will often include many middle and senior managers. We are concerned here with the people who must take on new tasks, develop new skills, be transferred, regraded or re-trained. Once changes emerge people must learn to cope as individuals. We will describe a simple model of how people experience change and then consider how they can cope with the pressures created by change. Understanding this can allow senior managers to provide practical support to people undergoing change and may better enable them to avoid creating constraints on people which make their personal task of coping all the harder.

Often the problems of implementing change are discussed as 'resistance to change'. In fact the change situation is both more complex than this phrase suggests and capable of a more constructive interpretation. Managers often encourage 'resistance to change' by dealing with people as if that is the response they expect. Here we are concerned to consider the practical and positive steps which can be taken *to support people as they cope with change.*

The Coping Cycle

Change creates uncertainty, anxiety and stress. Moreover, changes which have a big impact on the work people do will affect their self-esteem. So much is well-established.[5–7] Linked to this impact on self-esteem will be a performance effect. In fact in periods of change performance is affected in three ways, as follows:

(i) The new systems, processes, methods etc., will have to be learned. This takes time and there is a *learning curve effect.*

(ii) There is also a *progress effect.* As the new system, etc. is installed and commissioned snags are ironed out and modifications introduced to achieve performance improvement. New systems do not work perfectly first time round!

(iii) Finally there is the *effect of self-esteem.* Significant organizational changes create a decline in self-esteem for many of those directly affected. This will effect performance. Whilst the links of satisfaction and self-esteem with performance are complex and not fully understood there seems to be some association of these factors.

In practice performance will decline once major changes are underway as a result of a combination of these factors. *Our view is that the main driving force to re-building performance quickly will be re-building self-esteem.* This can be helped by action on the learning curve and progress fronts. In the model we propose five stages. These are capable of more detailed analysis but for our purposes this simplified form seems workable (Figure 5). The model originates in

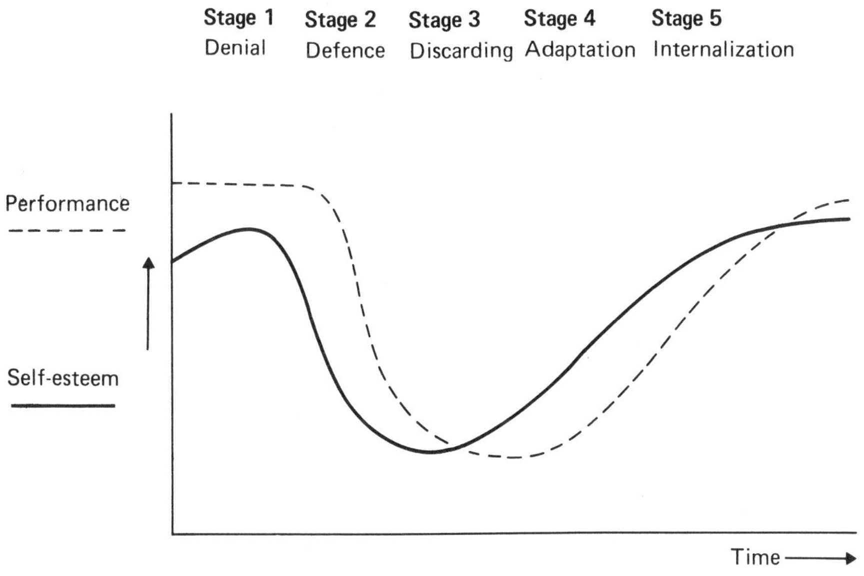

Note: Absolute levels unimportant, only relative levels are meaningful. Problems of measurement are significant but do not obscure the assessment of relative levels of performance or self-esteem.

Figure 5. The coping cycle

the literature on coping with bereavement and on work dealing with coping with personal life changes.[8]

Stage 1: Denial. 'We have always done things this way?' 'Why change, we are making a profit aren't we?' 'Don't change a winning team'. These are some of the ways denial can find expression. Faced with the possibility of change people will often find value in their present circumstances; often in work situations which they have complained of previously. This apparent paradox should not surprise us. People are impelled by contradictory motivations. Coal miners threatened with the closure of a pit will defend their pit and jobs with some vigour, yet still believe fervently that working conditions are arduous and even dangerous.

If major organizational changes come suddenly and dramatically then a kind of paralysis can often occur. People seem overwhelmed, unable to plan or even understand what is going on. Often there is a longish period of gestation as ideas are discussed and concrete changes planned. If these changes are not particularly new or dramatic then this paralysis may be felt just as intensely. However, the tendency to deny new ideas, at least at first, does seem to be a fairly general reaction. The advantages of the present situation are emphasized and attachments to the job, the work-group and the existing skills are recognized.

Thus it is that self-esteem can increase, particularly if the presence of an external threat leads to increased group coherence. If self-esteem does increase we would guess that performance would not improve, either because the discussion of impending change can absorb energy, or because often there are systems in place which may hold back performance improvement, e.g. payment systems. If the change is dramatic, novel and traumatic, say involving a sudden job change or redundancy, then this stage can involve an immediate decline in performance. Generally, however, there is a warning period and performance will not decline immediately. *One way individuals respond at this stage is to 'minimize' the impact of the change.* This allows people time to face up to a few realities.

Stage 2: Defence. However, in time reality obtrudes. The early discussion of changes leads to concrete plans and programmes of change. Now the realities of change become clearer and people must begin to face new tasks, working for a new boss, or with a different group of people, perhaps in a different department or a new location. Thus they become aware that they must come to terms with the way they work, and perhaps with changes in life more generally, if, for example, relocation, involving a house move, is required. This can lead to feelings of depression and frustration because it can be difficult to work out how to deal with these changes. This stage is often characterized by defensive behaviour. People may attempt to defend their own job, their own territory. Often this will be articulated as ritualistic behaviour. The author can remember the introduction of computer-aided learning in Business Schools many years ago. Many embraced these developments enthusiastically. Many simply rejected them; 'my subject is unsuitable'. One colleague provided an impressive show of activity on the computer, finally concluding that after much effort he had failed to make computer-aided learning work for that subject. Years later computer-aided learning in that subject is commonplace. Was this a ritual? Again this defensive behaviour seems to have the effect of *creating time and 'space' to allow people to come to terms with the changes.*

Stage 3: Discarding. There now emerges a process of discarding. The previous stages have focused powerfully upon the past. Now people begin to let go of the past and look forward to the future. We do not know how this happens. We know that support can be helpful, as can providing people with the opportunity to experiment with new systems without the pressure of formal training programmes and so on. Now it is possible for optimistic feelings to emerge. It may well be that the discarding process is impelled by an awakening sense that the present anxieties are just too much to bear, or that perhaps the future is not as forbidding as it first seemed. Now we may observe behaviour which appears to identify the individual with the changes involved. They will start to talk openly and constructively about the new system. They will ask questions about it. In a sense they will say 'Well here it is, we are committed to it, here's how I see it'. People may begin to solve problems, take the initiative and even demonstrate some leadership. Thus it is that self-esteem improves.

Discarding is initially a process of perception. People come to see that the change is both inevitable and/or necessary. It becomes apparent to them. Adaptation starts with recognition. Here we see human courage amidst difficult circumstances as the individual accepts new 'realities'. This can be exciting for individuals and groups. Taking the risks of publicly facing a new reality there is a sense in which they re-establish their own identity; the identity which may have seemed threatened by the changes being introduced. Thus it is that self-esteem begins to flow back like the returning tide.

The crisis of change creates great tensions within those involved; this much we have seen. This creates a plethora of reasons for people to feel upset and disoriented. The new job we have been assigned appears to be of lesser status, valued skills seem unnecessary, the new work appears to be frustrating. The new system or machine appears to be unusual, even frightening, although with practice it becomes commonplace. The crucial point is that this process needs time. Discarding involves experimenting and risk. Time is needed for individuals to recreate their own sense of identity and self-esteem as they 'grow' into the new situation.

Stage 4: Adaptation. Now a process of mutual adaptation emerges. Rarely do new systems, procedures, structures or machines work effectively first time. Individuals begin to test the new situation and themselves. Trying out new behaviour, working to different standards, working out ways of coping with the changes. Thus the individual learns. Other individuals also adapt. Fellow workers, supervisors and managers all learn as the new system is tried out. Finally, technical and operational problems are identified and modifications made to deal with them: thus progress is made.

Significant amounts of energy are involved here. Often the process of trial and error, of effort and set-back, and the slow building of performance, can be a source of real frustration. In these circumstances people can evince anger. This is not resistance to change. Rather it is the natural consequence of trying to make a new system work, experiencing partial, or complete, failure, which may or may not be under the control of the individuals concerned. *This anger is not evidence of attempts to oppose but rather articulates the feelings of those trying to make the new system work.* Whilst managers should ensure the right training and support is available we argue they should generally remain in the background allowing the people directly involved to make it work. By doing so that people will develop the skills, understanding and attachments needed for the system to be run effectively in the longer term.

Stage 5: Internalization. Now the people involved have created a new system, process and organization. New relationships between people and processes have been tried, modified and accepted. These now become incorporated into understandings of the new work situation. This is a cognitive process through which people make sense of what has happened. *Now the new behaviour becomes part of 'normal' behaviour.*

It seems that people experience change in these ways, initially as disturbance, perhaps even as a shock, then coming to accept its reality, testing it out and engaging in a process of mutual adaptation and finally, coming to terms with it. Self-esteem and performance varies, initially declining, and then growing again. The variation of performance flows from mutually reinforcing individual and operational causes, as we have seen. The 'engine' for rebuilding performance is the self-esteem of the people involved. Note here that we talk of relative levels (notional performance might be improved ten-fold as a consequence of new technology) the problems we have discussed may mean that in the early stages following the introduction of the new technology only 60 per cent of notional performance is achieved. Whilst this means 40 per cent of notional performance is being lost it does represent a six-fold improvement! Finally we do not suggest that people go through these stages neatly, nor that all go through them at the same time, or at the same rate. Some may not go beyond the denial of change. The important point is that people do seem to experience significant changes in these ways and that this leads on to a number of practical ways in which the problems of coping can be handled.

Coping with the process of change places demands on the individuals involved. Various issues need to be faced either by the individuals or by managers. Note however that these issues are of concern to all effected by an organizational change, including managers. We will set down a simple framework for Coping with Change: listing issues to be faced, based upon ideas from various workers in the field[1,3,5,7] and the author's own experience. These issues are identified in Figure 6. Time and space will allow no further discussion of this figure except to say that it can provide the basis of short workshops for people involved in change. Several managers known to the author arrange 2-hour workshops in groups of 10–12 people in which people are asked to discuss and then report back on the issues. They feel to be important in a period of change. This can be a powerful method facilitating a more knowledgeable and constructive approach to a major change and can lead to useful ideas. The author also remembers talking these ideas over with a senior manager in a diversified group who had introduced computerized photocomposition within a newspaper company in the early 1970s. They had

(A) Know Yourself

(1) Would I Have Chosen For This to Have Happened?
Do I Accept It?
Can I Benefit?
What is the Worst that can Happen?
Have I Experienced Similar Changes?
How Did I Cope?

(2) Can I Take Initiative?

(3) Do I Know What I Want?
What I Don't Want?

(4) Can I Cope With Stress?
Avoid Conflict
Time Management
Don't Blame Yourself

(5) Do I Take Stock of my Situation?

(B) Know Your Situation

(1) Can I Describe the Changes?
(2) Do I Know How I am Expected to Behave?
(3) Can I Try Out the New Situation in Advance?

Figure 6. Coping with changes: issues to be faced

allowed the typesetters to try out the VDUs in a test-room but not in a training environment. Providing support, they avoided any sense of formal training and were surprised to find that, allowed to learn at their own pace, the typesetters embraced the technology enthusiastically and quickly.

Re-building Self-esteem

The ground covered in this section is summarized in Figure 7, below.

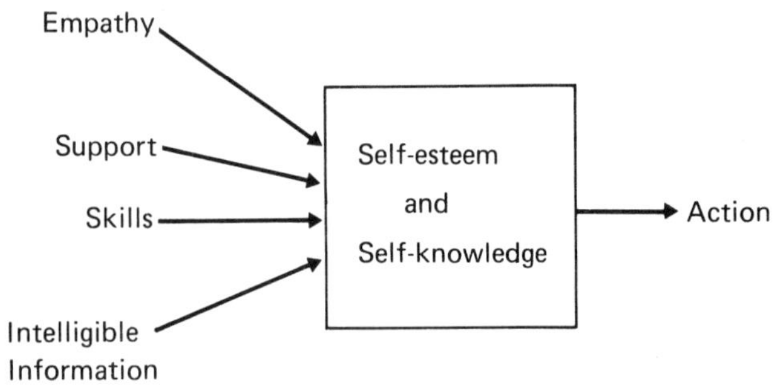

Figure 7. Re-building self-esteem

Simplifying, somewhat, we suggest that individuals have four main categories of need if they are to re-build their self-esteem amidst a programme of organizational change. They need *intelligible information*. They will probably need to develop *new skills* if only the skills of dealing with new people as colleagues or supervisors. They will need *support* to help them deal with the problems. Encouragement to try out new systems is important. Provision of short workshops planned to achieve part or all of the work discussed in the preceding section can help. Technical support to solve problems is often needed. Access to people who can help is useful. Control over the rate of personal learning should be possible. All of these things can help. First and foremost *empathy*, understanding, is a key issue. Kirkpatrick[7] rightly sees this as one of the key skills for managing change. Pierre Casse[9] defines empathy as follows:

> Empathy is the ability to see and understand how other people construct reality, or more specifically how they perceive, discover and invent the inner and outer worlds. We all use empathy. All the time. We constantly guess what people think and feel. The problem is that in most cases we guess wrongly. We assume that what is going on in somebody else's mind is somewhat identical to our own psychic processes. We tend to forget that we are different. Sometimes, drastically different. To practice empathy is to recognize and take full advantage of those differences.[9]

We see the skill of empathy as the struggle to understand. We can never fully see a situation as others see it. But we can struggle to try and individuals will respond to that struggle. They will also respond to someone, who clearly does not try. Making information intelligible to its recipient requires this skill. We need to try to see things as the recipient will in order to communicate. Often we do not try. We pass on the information we have. Usually we do so without attempting to make it intelligible, if we pass it on at all!

Conclusion

In this paper we have discussed ways and means of introducing major changes effectively. Here we wish to stress one crucial point. Effective organizations are those which introduce change quickly and in which people, employees and managers, learn about the business as this process proceeds. Achieving change without learning is possible, but sometimes not without struggle, if powerful groups oppose. Introducing change in ways which do not encourage learning is likely to entrench negative attitudes to change, in the future. Only if people and organizations change, by learning from the experience of change, can effectiveness be achieved and sustained. We have attempted to draw together a range of ideas and practical steps to help people manage change effectively.

All these ideas and steps need to be integrated for effectiveness. Only if we manage transitions effec-

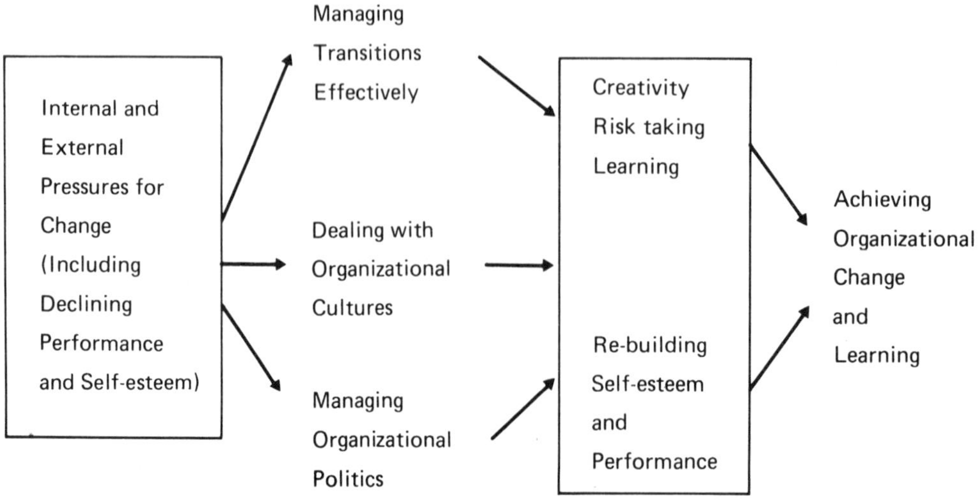

Figure 8. Managing major changes

tively can learning and change occur. This also acts as a constructive constraint on the politics of change which can so easily appear to get out of control. Moreover, managing change effectively reduces anxiety and helps those who find change stressful to cope with as individuals. This is turn leads to a more positive attitude to change. Thus it is that we come full circle. If these ideas are synthesized in a managerial approach to organizational change than there seems to be a better prospect of success and effectiveness. Difficult and demanding in practice we offer these ideas as the basis of how managers are able to see changes through. We summarize the ideas presented here in Figure 8, presented below.

The key point is that only by synthesizing the management of transitions, dealing with organizational cultures and handling organizational politics constructively, can we create the environment in which creativity, risk-taking, learning and the re-building of self-esteem and performance can be achieved. If we can sustain such a synthesis, then learning and change can follow. More important, because people have learned about the business through the process of changing, the organization will probably become more effective. By creating the conditions for extensive problem-solving and positive attitudes to change, future effectiveness is created. All of this is hard work. What we have described goes far beyond 'being nice to people'. This is the challenge we face in this changing world.

References

(1) C. Argyris and D. Schon, *Theory in Practice: Increasing Professional Effectiveness,* Jossey-Bass (1974).

(2) C. Handy, *Understanding Organisations,* 3rd Edn, Penguin (1985).

(3) R. Kanter, *The Change Masters,* George Allen & Unwin (1983).

(4) H. Kissinger, *The White House Years,* Weidenfeld & Nicolson (1979).

(5) G. Cooper, *Psychology and Management,* Macmillan (1981).

(6) M. Ket de Vries and D. Miller, *The Neurotic Organisation,* Jossey-Bass (1984).

(7) D. L. Kirkpatrick, *How to Manage Change Effectively,* Jossey-Bass (1985).

(8) J. Adams, J. Hayes and B. Hopson, *Transition—Understanding and Managing Personal Change,* Martin Robertson (1976).

(9) P. Casse, Training for the Cross-Cultural Mind, Society for Intercultural Education, Training and Research, Washington (1979).